# NIGHT'S BLACK AGENTS

For Pauline

ANTHONY HARRIS

# NIGHT'S BLACK AGENTS

## WITCHCRAFT AND MAGIC IN SEVENTEENTH-CENTURY ENGLISH DRAMA

Light thickens, and the crow
Makes wing to th' rooky wood;
Good things of day begin to droop and drowse,
Whiles night's black agents to their preys do rouse.
[*Macbeth*, III.ii.50–3]

Manchester University Press

Rowman and Littlefield

© Manchester University Press 1980

*All rights reserved*

First published 1980
by Manchester University Press
Oxford Road, Manchester M13 9PL

*USA*

Rowman and Littlefield
81 Adams Drive, Totowa, N.J. 07512


*British Library Cataloguing in Publication Data*

Harris, Anthony
  Night's black agents.
  1. Magic in literature  2. Witchcraft in
  literature  3. English drama — 17th century
  — History and criticism
  I. Title
  822'.4'0937        PR678.M/

ISBN 0-7190-0758-5 (*UK*)
ISBN 0-8476-6226-8 (*USA*)

Computerised Phototypesetting
by G.C. Typeset Ltd., Bolton, Greater Manchester

Printed in Great Britain
by the Pitman Press, Bath

# CONTENTS

07012

# ILLUSTRATIONS

# ACKNOWLEDGMENTS

I wish to record my gratitude to the trustees, librarians and members of staff of the following institutions for their assistance in the preparation of this work: the Birmingham Shakespeare Library; the Bodleian Library, Oxford; the British Library; the Chatsworth Settlement (Devonshire Collections); the City of Birmingham Polytechnic Library (especially that of the Faculty of Education and Teacher Training); the Shakespeare Birthplace Trust, Stratford-upon-Avon; the University of Birmingham Library (including the libraries of the Barber Institute of Fine Arts and, particularly, the Shakespeare Institute).

I also wish to express my thanks to the Birmingham Polytechnic Research Committee for their grant of financial assistance to help meet the costs I have incurred whilst working on this project; and also to the following individuals: Dr Stanley Wells for his guidance and encouragement in the early stages of this work; John Banks of the Manchester University Press for his enthusiastic response to the project and for his unfailingly helpful criticism as the work has developed; the late Professor T. J. B. Spencer for his ready permission to make use of the resources of the Shakespeare Institute; Dr Gareth Roberts for his generosity in allowing me to use material from his unpublished thesis, *Magic and Witchcraft in English Drama and Poetry from 1558 to 1634* (University of London, 1976); Mr John Barton for providing the photograph from which plate 17 has been taken; and finally to my wife who, in a multitude of ways, has been the greatest help of all.

The author and publishers gratefully acknowledge permission to reproduce photographs as follows: British Library (1, 8, 11, 13); John Rylands University Library of Manchester (2, 3, 4, 14); the Governors of the Royal Shakespeare Theatre, Stratford-upon-Avon (5, 10, 12, jacket); Rijksmuseum, Amsterdam (6); His Grace the Duke of Devonshire and the Trustees of the Chatsworth Settlement (7, 15); Mermaid Theatre, London (9); Birmingham Shakespeare Library (16).

# NOTE ON QUOTATIONS

Quotations from poetry and prose works of the sixteenth and seventeenth centuries are given in their original forms, apart from the customary adjustments of *i* and *j*, *u* and *v* and the substitution of the short *s*. Quotations from the plays of Shakespeare are taken from Peter Alexander's *The Complete Works* (1951) and, for consistency, quotations from other dramatic texts are also given in modernised forms, with the exception of those from *The Masque of Queenes* for the reason given on p. 68.

# CHAPTER 1

---

# MANIFOLD IMPIETIES

## THE SOCIAL SETTING

*Daniel*: **These cunning men and women which deale with spirites and charmes seeming to doe good, and draw the people into manifold impieties, with all other which have familiarity with devils, or use conjurations, ought to bee rooted out, that others might see and feare.**
[Gifford: *A Dialogue concerning Witches and Witchcraftes*]

## I

There are almost as many theories as to the nature and origins of witchcraft as there are works—scholarly and otherwise—on the subject. In examining the witchcraft beliefs and practices of the sixteenth and early seventeenth centuries in England this confusion is compounded by the fact that there was at least as much disagreement among Elizabethan and Jacobean writers on the subject as there is today. Scholars happily drew fine distinctions between witches and wise women, magicians and necromancers, but unfortunately their definitions rarely coincided and, moreover, what relevance their academic hair-splitting had for the general populace, including both witches and bewitched, is highly doubtful.

Some authorities were prepared to distinguish between the exponents of 'black' and 'white' magic, using such terms as 'witch' and 'sorcerer' for the former and 'charmer' or 'blesser' for the latter. Others, however, condemned without exception all dealings with the occult, however innocuous they might appear, and such writers saw no reason to differentiate among the various practitioners. For example, William Perkins in his *Discourse of the Damned Art of Witchcraft* (1608) declared:

> For this must alwaies be remembred, as a conclusion, that by Witches we understand not those onely which kill and torment: but all Diviners, Charmers, Juglers, all Wizzards, commonly called wise men and wise women; yea, whosoever doe any thing (knowing what they doe) which cannot be effected by nature or art; and in the same number we reckon all good Witches, which doe no hurt but good, which doe not spoile and destroy, but save and deliver. [pp. 255–6]

Reginald Scot, writing in the milder vein of his *The Discoverie of Witchcraft* (1584) recounts an anecdote concerning an individual named Pope and concludes: 'This Pope is said of some to be a witch, of others he is accompted a conjuror; but commonlie called a wise man, which is all one with a soothsaier or witch' (Book XIII, chapter xxx).[1]

Some of the problems of terminology are particularly relevant to a study of the portrayal of witchcraft and other occult practices in the drama of the period. For example, a point to be borne in mind when investigating the nature of the Weird Sisters in *Macbeth* is that to many of Shakespeare's contemporaries the word 'witch' could be applied equally to human and supernatural creatures. This is seen in Florio's *Queen Anna's New World of Words* (1611), where the Italian 'strega' is defined as 'a witch, a sorceresse. Also a hag or fairie'. The synonymous linking of witch and fairy is a further complication which is also relevant to *Macbeth*, for it removes the apparent incongruity of Hecate's command to the Weird Sisters to dance 'Like elves and fairies in a ring' (IV.i.42).

It is argued by some modern scholars that the terms 'witch' and 'fairy' were indeed identical in the Elizabethan era. Pennethorne Hughes, for example, declares in *Witchcraft* (1952) that the fairies were the surviving worshippers of the palaeolithic religion and that therefore 'the people who until the late Middle Ages were called fairies, by one name or another, were often those who, until the seventeenth century or so, were called witches' (p. 64). Lewis Spence in *British Fairy Origins* (1946), whilst carefully avoiding such a specific identification, lists numerous supposed attributes of fairies which were also applied to witches—the powers of shape-shifting and invisibility through the use of ointments, knowledge of herbal medicines, the maintenance of close links with agricultural and human fertility, for example (pp. 17–22). Katharine Briggs, whilst stressing that she is not convinced of the identical origins of witches and fairies, admits in her conclusion to *Pale Hecate's Team* (1962) that 'the strands of belief are almost inextricably entangled' (p. 222).

2

Elizabethan and Jacobean scholars, in the main, found less difficulty in distinguishing between witchcraft and sorcery. The latter was generally regarded as the art whereby the devil was summoned by charms or the drawing of magic circles, whereas witchcraft entailed the gaining of occult powers through a formal pact with the devil. Prospero can be seen as a sorcerer (or magus), using his magical arts for basically good ends, whilst Marlowe's Faustus and Alexander VI in Barnes's *The Devil's Charter* both begin their occult careers by practising sorcery but are subsequently seduced into demonic pacts and thus become witches.

Whilst the sorcerer retained control over the demons at his disposal, the witch, whether he or she realised it or not, was completely subservient to the devil. By the orthodox teaching of both the Roman Catholic and Protestant churches the witch was regarded as the victim of the devil, serving his ends but ultimately forfeiting his or her own soul. However, for most writers of the period the major interest lay in the cataloguing of the evil deeds—or 'maleficia'—real or imaginary that were ascribed to witches, with fewer expressing concern for the fates of the perpetrators of the alleged misdeeds.

This pattern is reflected in the contemporary dramas. In a few plays (*Dr Faustus* and *The Witch of Edmonton*, for example) there are sympathetic portrayals of the witch-figure but in the majority of works there is no such attempt. In such plays as *Macbeth* and Jonson's *The Masque of Queenes* the emphasis is wholly on the evil performed by the witches and of the effects on their victims with no concern shown for the inevitable destruction of the witches themselves.

A distinction can also be drawn between Renaissance and Classical witchcraft beliefs, and both forms are to be found in the dramas. *The Witch of Edmonton* is based on an actual case of 1621 and Elizabeth Sawyer engages our sympathy in part because in her we see embodied a realistic portrayal of the contemporary English witch. The Dame and her followers in *The Masque of Queenes* and Erictho in Marston's *Sophinisba* are based on Classical models and although their powers are far greater than those of the homely Mother Sawyer, they appear much more remote figures, re-enacting an archaic tradition.

Elizabeth Sawyer is the epitome of the contemporary English witch-figure—a lonely, embittered old woman, set apart from her neighbours, the victim of their superstitions and the scapegoat for their misfortunes—and her essential mundanity contrasts both with the awesomeness of the classically-based creations and the flamboyance and spurious glamour of Hecate in Middleton's *The Witch*. The latter, with its Italian setting, reflects the current Continental attitudes to witchcraft and in many essential respects these differed considerably from the most widely held English beliefs. For example, with a few very doubtful exceptions, there seems to have been little conception in England of the coven or close-knit organisation of witches that was a major feature of most Continental cases. Records of Scottish trials, on the other hand, contain several references to such groups and in fact at this time witchcraft practices in Scotland were in many respects closer to the European than the English forms. (As might be expected, the Weird Sisters in *Macbeth* reveal some traits—including possible membership of a coven—which are closer to the Scottish models than to their English counterparts.) [2]

Another basic difference between English and Continental attitudes is that, despite the occasional outbreaks of witch-hunting such as that carried out by Matthew Hopkins in the 1640s, there was nothing in England to compare with the sustained hysteria that resulted in the persecution, tortures and deaths of literally millions of so-called witches in Europe between the fourteenth and seventeenth centuries. C. H. L'Estrange Ewen, in *Witch Hunting and Witch Trials* (1929), concluded that the total number of executions for witchcraft in England between 1542 and 1736 was not more than one thousand (p. 112), a figure matched in the single year of 1524 in Como alone.

Recent research has not added appreciably to Ewen's estimate but it must be borne in mind that the uneven survival of English court records excludes any firm conclusions based on these sources. For example, the fire of Warwick in 1694 destroyed nearly all of the existing legal records for a county which has had a widespread reputation for witchcraft practices from mediaeval times to the present day.[3] On the other hand, the documents relating to the Essex Assizes have survived largely intact. Those concerned with the period between 1560 and 1680 have been analysed in detail in A. D. J. Macfarlane's *Witchcraft in Tudor and Stuart England: a Regional Study* (1970). Essex had what seems to have been a disproportionate number of witchcraft cases during the period, outnumbering the combined indictments in Hertfordshire, Kent, Surrey and Sussex, which were all fellow-members of the Home Circuit. Amongst the statistics Macfarlane deduces are that during the peak period of the 1580s witchcraft cases formed thirteen per cent of all criminal hearings, whilst the acquittal rate throughout the entire period was over fifty per cent. This contrasts markedly with the equivalent ratio on the Continent, which in France, for example, was sometimes as low as five per cent.

The Continental witchcraft persecutions appear in the main to have been instigated and maintained by the ecclesiastical authorities. This does not seem to have been the case in England, where throughout the Middle Ages there had been little pressure from Church or State to prosecute witches. Keith Thomas in *Religion and the Decline of Magic* (1971) puts forward the attractive hypothesis that before the Reformation the great bulk of the English populace had been content to protect themselves from the powers of witchcraft through a combination of Church and folk magic. With the undermining of ecclesiastical authority—and in particular the assaults on the rituals of the Roman Catholic Church—the security of this immunity was removed. Thus, from the 1560s onwards, the people turned increasingly to the courts, ecclesiastical and secular, for defence against the powers of the occult. Thomas concludes that it was for this reason that there was an upsurge of witchcraft prosecutions during the latter part of the sixteenth century and he argues that the great majority of such accusations were of a 'grass-roots' character, emanating from the general populace.

Most scholars agree that the European witch-craze developed from the persecution of the Catharsists and Albigenses in thirteenth-century France. This had heralded the establishment of the Inquisition, and the growing insecurity of the Roman Catholic Church led to attempts to crush all forms of heresy. Many of the accusations made against witches were identical to those previously brought against the heretical sects. In a series of Papal Bulls, culminating in that of 1484, sorcery and witchcraft were gradually equated with heresy. The witch-mania was really unleashed by the publication, two years later, of *Malleus Maleficarum*, a handbook for procedure against witches written by the Dominicans Kramer and Sprenger.

Although all scholars are agreed that there was a period of sustained persecution of witches in Europe, there is fundamental disagreement as to the nature of the victims of this persecution. Some writers argue forcibly that the authorities were, rightly or wrongly, attempting to eradicate a cult of witchcraft that certainly existed and was in fact firmly established. Such scholars, however, differ amongst themselves as to the nature of this cult. Montague Summers, who in translating *Malleus Maleficarum* seems to have imbibed much of the fanaticism of his mediaeval predecessors, asserted in *The History of Witchcraft and Demonology* (1926) that witchcraft was 'none other than black heresy and the worship of Satan' (p. 32), whilst the witch herself was 'the devotee of a loathly and obscene creed ... a member of a powerful secret organization inimical to Church and State ... battening upon the filth and foulest passions of the age' (introduction, p. xiv).

5

Margaret Murray, on the other hand, saw witchcraft as being much earlier in origin than any anti-Christian sect. In *The Witch-Cult in Western Europe* (1921) she declared that 'underlying the Christian religion was a cult practised by many classes of the community . . . it can be traced back to pre-Christian times, and appears to be the ancient religion of Western Europe . . . it was a definite religion with beliefs, ritual and organization as highly developed as that of any other cult in the world' (p. 12). Miss Murray claimed that amongst the secret adherents of this pagan cult were such figures as William Rufus and Joan of Arc, both of whom were sacrificial victims of their own primitive religions. Between 1929 and 1968 the articles on Witchcraft in successive editions of the *Encyclopaedia Britannica* were written by her and summarised her theory as though it were a matter of established fact. Many scholars, whilst rejecting her more extreme ideas, accepted her basic premise that mediaeval witchcraft had primeval origins. The emphasis on fertility, both human and agricultural, in witchcraft rites was quoted as one such surviving element, whilst another was the prominence of animals—real and simulated—in the reported ceremonies of witches.[4]

However, recent scholarship has assailed Miss Murray's thesis from a variety of viewpoints. Hugh Trevor-Roper in two articles on *Witches and Witchcraft* in *Encounter* (May, June 1967) places the witch-craze in its historical context, demonstrating its social and political origins and likening it to the persecution of the Jews through the centuries. He also demonstrates how the Reformation gave fresh impetus to the anti-witchcraft movement, with Protestants and Roman Catholics vying with each other to display their religious zeal in eradicating this non-existent cult. The hypothesis also comes under heavy attack from Norman Cohn in *Europe's Inner Demons* (1975). He offers a largely psychological explanation for the mediaeval witch hysteria and convincingly demonstrates that Miss Murray's views were propounded in a most unscholarly manner, with unproven theories expressed as undisputed fact and with highly selective quotations from the original sources (pp. 107–15). Although Miss Murray was herself an anthropologist, her theories and those of her successors have also been strongly attacked from this quarter. Scholars have found very similar notions to those attributed to mediaeval witches embedded in the beliefs of primitive societies in various parts of the world today. They are agreed that these exist in imagination only for nobody has discovered a real society of witches in any of these communities. Relating studies of contemporary witchcraft to what is known of its mediaeval counterpart, such scholars reject the thesis of a cult of witches, secret or otherwise. As Lucy Mair expresses it in *Witchcraft* (1969), 'In fact Miss Murray invented a religion for the purposes of her argument' (p. 229).

Although the weight of modern scholarship, therefore, disposes one to regard the mediaeval witch-craze as being founded on a tragic delusion, in examining the drama of the early seventeenth century one must attempt to reconstruct the prevailing views of the period. Whilst a very few scholars denounced the cruel and absurd persecutions that many innocent people suffered, the majority of the learned fully accepted the existence of witchcraft and saw in it a clear manifestation of the powers of anti-Christ, requiring the sternest measures to eradicate it. This is the overwhelming viewpoint of the surviving written evidence and it is a reasonable assumption that this attitude was accepted by the populace at large.

It is interesting to conjecture how far such opinions were carried over into the theatres and how the audiences responded to the portrayal of witchcraft and other supernatural activities on stage. A glimpse of one such reaction is provided by the anecdote of an incident during a performance of *Doctor Faustus* in Exeter. Faustus, in summoning Mephistophilis, appeared to invoke an actual devil which joined in the action, to the horror of audience and players alike. 'The players ... contrarye to their custome spending the night in reading and in prayer got them out of the town the next morning.'[5]

Beyond this apocryphal tale there is no firm evidence of the effect of the enactment of the occult on the plays' audiences. However, the Elizabethan and Jacobean playhouses were microcosms of their wider societies and it therefore seems likely that the majority of spectators would have seen in the theatrical portrayal of witchcraft an enactment of actuality and would have regarded it with the varying degrees of hostility that characterised the prevailing consensus of opinion on the subject. Indeed, as we shall see, inferences regarding the contemporary attitudes can reasonably be drawn from the treatment of witchcraft in the plays themselves. The playwrights were professionals, in the main, aiming to satisfy popular tastes and reflecting rather than leading current opinion. With few exceptions, the dramatic treatment of witchcraft, on the evidence of the surviving plays, follows a definite pattern, and this may well mirror the developing attitudes to the subject throughout the sixteenth and seventeenth centuries.

## II

These shifting viewpoints can be traced in part through an examination of the anti-witchcraft statutes of the period. There had been considerable witchcraft activity in England during the Anglo-Saxon period, if not earlier. Documentary evidence attests to the widespread practice of nearly all the forms of 'black' and 'white' magic that survived into the post-mediaeval period, including the harming and curing of people and animals through charms and spells, the raising of storms and the destruction of crops.[6] However, although several edicts were passed, such as that under King Alfred, which was clearly based on the Law of Moses—'Those women who are wont to receive enchanters and magicians and wizards or witches—thou shalt not suffer them to live'—it was not until 1542, in the reign of Henry VIII, that the first law against 'conjurations and witchcraftes and sorcerie and enchantments' became one of the Statutes of the Realm.

It is significant that this Act was introduced under the secular rather than the ecclesiastical jurisdiction, for this strengthens the impression that the English Church, even before the Reformation, took a far more lenient attitude towards witchcraft and magic than did its European counterpart. Even in cases where guilt was established the punishment was generally penance or the pillory. By the mid sixteenth century the Church was apparently content to leave major witchcraft trials to the secular courts, merely dealing with minor cases or helping to determine the validity of claims of demonic possession.

Henry VIII's Statute was mainly concerned with the employment of sorcery and magical arts in treasure-hunting, although the use of enchantments 'to waste, consume or destroie anie person in his bodie, members or goodes, or to provoke anie person to unlawful love' were also made felonies, punishable by death. However, the pattern of tolerance was maintained in practice for there is only one recorded instance of the full penalty being exacted under the Act before its repeal in 1547.

The next Act 'against conjurations and witchcraftes' became law under Elizabeth I in 1563. There was a change of emphasis in that, whilst the basic elements of the previous Act, including treasure-seeking, were retained, greater stress was placed on other aspects of witchcraft. The invocation and conjuration of evil spirits became felonies and the practices were divided into: bewitching to death; injuring persons or cattle; seeking treasure or lost things; *trying* to provoke unlawful love or to kill, maim or injure a person. A second Act under Elizabeth, passed in 1580/1, introduced a political element in that the use of witchcraft to determine the length of the Queen's reign or the nature of the succession became capital offences.

Nevertheless, the generally lenient treatment of witchcraft, both in the Statute Book and in the application of the laws, was still evident. Under the 1563 Act it was only the use of witchcraft to inflict death that was subject to the extreme penalty. Other offences were punishable by a combination of prison and pillory for one year, the offence becoming a capital crime only if it was repeated.

The courts' leniency in practice is seen in the sentences that followed one of the most notorious witchcraft trials of the Elizabethan period, held at St Osyth, Essex, in 1582. During the hearings the magistrate and self-appointed prosecutor-in-chief, Brian Darcy, adopted many of the procedures hitherto found only in Continental witch-trials: false promises of leniency in return for confessions and the accusations of others; the use of young children to inculpate the accused; and, worst of all, the presumption of guilt, the onus being on the prisoners to prove their innocence in an increasingly hysterical atmosphere in which the slightest suspicion or rumour was taken as undoubted proof. In all, thirteen women were convicted, whilst six were either discharged or acquitted. However, despite the manifest injustice of much of the proceedings, most of the sentences were light. Only two of those convicted were executed and they had admitted causing six deaths by witchcraft. The others were found guilty of such charges as inflicting wasting diseases and destroying cattle, crops and farm buildings and thus, under the terms of the 1563 Act, escaped the full penalty.

This would not have been the case had they been convicted under the Statute of James I, introduced in 1604 and remaining in force until 1736. Under this Act the penalties were stiffened in that more offences, including the infliction of bodily harm, became punishable by death. In addition, certain witchcraft practices were specified in greater detail. The owning of familiar spirits was made a felony, whereas hitherto this had not been a crime in itself but merely one means of establishing guilt. Much of the evidence at St Osyth had been concerned with the alleged keeping of familiars but such accusations had been made as additional proofs of guilt rather than as culpable offences in themselves.

The new Statute led to an increase in the practice of searching a suspect's body for the 'mark' or 'teat' whereby the witch supposedly suckled her familiar. At the Lancaster trial of 1612 Anne Chattox admitted allowing a spirit to have 'a place of her right side neere to her ribbes for him to sucke upon'.[7] She was also charged that she 'at a Buriall at the new Church in Pendle, did take three scalpes [skulls] of people, which had been buried, and then cast out of a grave ... and tooke eight teeth out of the said

Scalpes'. This was contrary to another item in the 1604 Statute which declared it a felony to 'take up anie dead man, woman or child out of his, her, or their grave, or anie other place where the bodie resteth, or the skin, bone or anie other part of anie dead person, to be emploied or used in anie maner of witchcraft, sorcerie, charm, or enchantment'.

James had had his own belief in the powers of witchcraft strengthened by his personal involvement in the case of the North Berwick witches who, led by a schoolmaster named Dr John Fian, were accused of plotting against the life of James himself. Two of the charges at their trial involved the alleged discovery of the devil's marks on several of the prisoners and the supposed use of parts of a corpse in the furtherance of their spells. One of the first to suffer under the new Act was Joan Harrison, who was executed at Hertford in 1606. A chest discovered in her house contained 'all the bones due to the Anatomy of man and woman, and under them haire of all colours that is customarily worne'.[8] There are, however, few other recorded cases of grave rifling, although the Jacobean dramatists made full use of this ghoulish practice in their portrayals of the more sensational aspects of witchcraft.

During the first part of James's reign, until 1616, there were at least thirty-five recorded executions for witchcraft, fifteen of these following the trials at Lancaster and Northampton in 1612. However, the popular conception of James's credulous acceptance of witch-lore and superstition requires some modification. In fact, his analytical mind demanded clear proof of guilt and, as he had declared in his *Daemonologie* (1597), 'Judges ought indeede to beware whome they condemne: For it is as great a crime (as Salamon sayeth) to condemne the innocent, as to let the guiltie escape free'.[9] On several occasions James intervened in witchcraft cases, either to stop the trial or to pardon the condemned. The most famous instance was his unmasking in Leicester in 1616 of the boy imposter, Smythe, who had already seen nine persons sent to the gallows following his false charges of demonic possession. James's intervention saved the lives of a further six accused, although one died in prison before he could be freed. James's increasing scepticism is probably reflected in the fact that from 1616 until the end of his reign in 1625 there are only five recorded executions for witchcraft in England.[10]

Although the Statutes represent the official view, their clauses and even more their enactment give some indication of the current general attitudes. The Acts could only be enforced in response to accusations and the trial records that have survived probably give a clearer picture of the opinions of the general populace, on occasions giving a fascinating insight into the attitudes of both accusers and accused. Some of the most interesting accounts of trials are contained not in the official records but in the pamphlets that were produced to coincide with the hearings.

The majority of these publications are anonymous and the standards of writing and printing vary greatly.[11] Some have clearly been hastily produced by enterprising printers to capitalise on the latest sensational trials, whilst others are extremely detailed accounts, where the writer was an eye-witness of the investigations or had access to the court records. In some instances the author was the presiding magistrate or otherwise officially connected with the case and was writing to justify or publicise the court proceedings. Other publications are the work of persons closely involved with a particular episode, anxious to present their case to a wider audience than that available in the courts. The extremely circumstantial account of *The Most Strange and Admirable Discoverie of the Three Witches of Warboys* (1593), involving the alleged possession of the five daughters of Robert Throckmorton, is one such work. Another is Edward Fairfax's *A Discourse of Witchcraft* (1621) in which, following the acquittal of the persons accused of bewitching his two daughters, he attempted to clear the children and himself of any suspicion of fraud or malice by writing his version of the case.

The account of the pre-trial hearings at St Osyth in 1582 has already been referred to. W.W., *A true and just Recorde, of the Information, Examination and Confession of all the Witches, taken at S. Oses in the Countie of Essex* (1582) was almost certainly the work of the presiding Justice of the Peace, Brian Darcy. One of the most sinister elements of this unwholesome affair was the accumulation of an apparently damning case on the flimsiest of evidence. Under Darcy's McCarthy-like interrogatory technique, a subtle blend of gentle persuasion and brutal threats, both accusers and accused saw proof of witchcraft in the most innocent of happenings. Ursula Kemp, following her own confession which was prompted by Darcy's false promise of leniency, told of a visit to her neighbour and fellow-prisoner, Elizabeth Bennett:

> She went unto Mother Bennets house for a messe of milke, the which shee had promised her: But at her comming this examinate saith shee knocked at her dore, and no bodie made her any answere, whereupon shee went to her chamber windowe and looked in therat, saying, ho, ho, mother Bennet are you at home? And casting her eyes aside shee saw a spirit lift up a clothe lying over a pot, looking much lik a Ferret. And it beeing asked of this examinate why the spirite did looke upon her, shee said it was hungrie.

The witness has clearly accepted without question the examiner's unspoken contention that the innocuous ferret must in fact have been a familiar spirit. Mention has already been made of the use of very young children's testimony in this case. Thomas Rabbett, the eight-year old bastard son of Ursula Kemp, gave damning evidence against her. This device was taken to what in other circumstances would have been farcical extremes with the solemn presentation of the witch-finding percipience of 'an infant not a year old' who, while being carried by its mother past Ursula Kemp's house,

> cryed to the mother, wo, wo, and poynted with the finger to the wyndowe wardes: And likewise the chyld used the like as shee passed homewards by the said window, at which she confessed her conscience moved her, so as shee went shortly after and talked with the said Ursley, whereupon shee used suche speeches as moved her to complaine.

Ursula's response could hardly have been unexpected, but the credulity and superstition that were the mainsprings of so many accusations, where natural disasters—so widespread in rural England at this time—were ascribed to witchcraft, are clearly evident in the testimonies of witness after witness in the St Osyth case. The most unlikely of coincidental events, sometimes from many years previously, were dredged up and offered as proof of the demonic powers of the accused. There was, for example, the testimony of Thomas Rice, who stated:

> that about xiiii. dayes past, Joan Robinson came unto the house of this examinate, and desired to borrowe a Hayer [hedge-cutter], the which his wife denied her, saying, that she was to use it her selfe, whereat shee departed, and presently after there arose a great winde, which was like to have blowen downe their house. And the next day after one of his Kine could not calve without helpe, it being drawen from her, died, and the Cowe was in danger and did hardly escape ... And sayeth also, that he thinketh the same to be done by the said Joan by some witchcraft.

This pattern of vengeance, partly through the creation of a storm, following a supposed rebuff, is of course reflected in the revenge by the Weird Sisters on the sailor's wife in *Macbeth* (I.iii).

One of the most vivid pamphlets of the Jacobean period is Thomas Potts's description of *The Wonderfull Discoverie of Witches in the Countie of Lancaster* (1613). Potts was clerk of the court during this famous case, involving a vendetta between two families in the Forest of Pendle, which resulted in the 'discoverie' of thirty-five alleged witches, of whom ten were hanged. (The case provided elements of the plots of Heywood and Broome's *The Late Lancashire Witches* (1634) and Shadwell's *Lancashire Witches, and Tegue O'Divelly the Irish Priest* (1681), both of which are examined below, in Chapter Eleven.) At the trial the testimony of one family destroyed the other and then the survivors turned suicidally upon themselves, with children testifying against parents and vice versa.

One of the many moments of high drama occurred when young Janet Device was called to give evidence.

> The said Jennet Device, being a yong Maide about the age of nine yeares, and commanded to stand up to give evidence against her Mother, Prisoner at the Barre: Her Mother, according to her accustomed manner, outragiously cursing, cryed out against the child in such fearefull manner, as all the Court did not a little wonder at her, and so amazed the child, as with weeping teares shee cryed out unto my Lord the Judge, and told him, she was not able to speake in the presence of her Mother . . . No intreatie, promise of favour, or other respect, could put her to silence, thinking by this her outragious cursing and threatning of the child, to inforce her to denie that which she had formerly confessed against her Mother, before M. Nowel: Forswearing and denying her owne voluntarie confession, which you have heard, given in evidence against her at large, and for want of further evidence to escape that, which the Justice of the Law had provided as a condigne punishment for the innocent bloud shee had spilt, and her wicked and devilish course of life.
>
> In the end, when no meanes would serve, his Lordship commanded the Prisoner to be taken away, and the Maide to bee set upon the Table in the presence of the whole Court, who delivered her evidence in that Honorable assembly, to the Gentlemen of the Jurie of life and death.

This same Janet Device found herself playing a different role some twenty-one years later when she was one of those condemned for witchcraft, though apparently not executed, at the Lancaster trials of 1633.

The obvious bias of Potts's account is seen in subtler guise in his description of the evidence of Janet's brother James, one of the accused. He described a meeting at his mother's house at which had been discussed, among other matters, the freeing of members of the family held in Lancaster Castle, 'Killing the Gaoler at Lancaster; and before the next Assizes to blow up the Castle there; to that end the aforesaid Prisoners might by that meanes make an escape and get away'. He concluded his evidence by describing the conspirators' departure:

> And this Examinate further sayth, that all the said Witches went out
> of the said House *in their owne shapes and likenesses*: and they all, by
> that they were forth of the doores, were gotten on horse-backe *like
> unto foales*, some of one colour, some of another, and Prestons wife
> was the last; and when shee got on horse-backe *they all presently
> vanished out of this Examinates sight*. [my italics]

The prosaic account of these unexceptional events is given a damning
impression by Potts's implications that although the accused left 'in their
owne shapes and likenesses' they could have performed some feat of shape-
shifting if they had so desired; that although their horses were 'like unto
foales' they were in reality devilish spirits in this form, being used to
transport them; and that their departure took the form of instantaneous
vanishing.

As has been seen, confessions of witchcraft were sometimes extracted
under the pressure of skilful cross-examination, but on other occasions
cruder means were employed. Doctor Fian, the ostensible leader of the
North Berwick witches, accused of conspiring against the life of King
James, suffered hideous torture at James's personal command. Certain
clauses of the 1604 anti-witchcraft Act reflected James's view that witches
could be detected by 'the finding of their marke, and the trying the
insensiblenes therof and their fleeting [floating] on the water'.[12] Some
horrifying outbreaks of licensed cruelty ensued, where pre-trial confessions
of witchcraft were extracted through the exertion of physical torture. In
1613 Mary Sutton from Milton, near Bedford, was suspected of being the
cause of various mysterious fatal maladies that had afflicted both cattle and
humans in the vicinity. She was seized on the orders of one Master Enger
and taken to a dammed-up mill-pool.

> When being throwne in the first time she sunke some two foote into
> the water with a fall, but rose againe and floated upon the water like a
> planke. Then he commanded her to be taken out, and had women
> readie that searched her and found under her left thigh a kind of Teat
> which after the Bastard sone confest her Spirits in severale shapes as
> Cats, Moales, etc. used to sucke her.
> Then was she the second time bound crosse her thumbes and toes,
> according to the former direction, and then she sunke not at all, but
> sitting upon the water, turned round about like a wheele, or as that
> which commonly we call a whirlepoole. Notwithstanding Master
> Engers men standing on each side of the damme with a roape tossing
> her up and downe to make her sinke, but could not.[13]

Although the unfortunate woman at first 'as boldlie as if she had been
inocent asked them if they could doe anie more to her', it is hardly

surprising that finally her spirit failed her and she not only admitted all the accusations but also inculpated her mother, confessions that led to both their executions. The indirect influence of James is also evident in the investigations into the alleged activities of the five 'Witches of Northamptonshire' who were executed in 1612. The swimming test on this occasion was ordered by the Justice of the Peace and the author of the pamphlet describing the case justifies this by a lengthy quotation from James's *Daemonologie*.

Such outbreaks of organised cruelty and officially sanctioned witch-hunting on a fairly large scale are fortunately exceptional. Nevertheless, on the limited evidence available, there does seem to have been an upsurge of witchcraft persecutions during the early part of James's reign. The scholarly writings of this period also reflect the monarch's published views, giving an overall impression of intolerance which compares unfavourably with the humane attitudes expressed in some of the learned works on witchcraft printed during the Elizabethan era.

At least two of the latter were inspired in part by the clear injustice of the St Osyth proceedings. George Gifford, a priest who lived in Essex from 1582 until his death in 1620, published *A Dialogue Concerning Witches and Witchcraftes* in 1583. Written, as the title suggests, in dialogue form, Gifford's views are expressed by Daniel, a sceptical scholar, whilst Samuel typifies the credulous countryman. Through the latter he satirises the ready acceptance of the existence of familiars which was such a feature of the St Osyth proceedings:

> In good sooth, I may tell it to you as to my friend, when I goe but into my closes [enclosures], I am afraide, for I see nowe and then a Hare; which my conscience giveth me is a witch, or some witches spirite, shee stareth so uppon me. And sometime I see an ugly weasele runne through my yard, and there is a foule great catte sometimes in my Barne, which I have no liking unto.

Reginald Scot's *The Discoverie of Witchcraft*, published in 1584, was in many ways the most significant of all the Elizabethan writings on the subject. He makes several direct references to the St Osyth hearings and does not disguise his feelings about them, and about Darcy's conduct in particular.[14] The work is imbued with a profound anger at the folly and superstition of many of the activities associated with the persecution of witches and expresses deep concern for the victims of such attacks. Scot's approach reflects the rationalism expounded by Johannes Wier in *De Praestigus et Incantionibus ac Veneficiis* (1563) and he declares thus his purposes in writing the book:

And bicause it may appeare unto the world what trecherous and faithless dealing, what extreame and intollerable tyranie, what grosse and fond absurdities, what unnaturall and uncivil discourtesie, what cancred and spiteful malice, what outragious and barbarous crueltie, what lewd and false packing, what cunning and craftie intercepting, what bald and peevish interpretations, what abhominable and devilish inventions, and what flat and plain knaverie is practised against these old women; I will set downe the whole order of the inquisition, to the everlasting, inexcusable, and apparent shame of all witchmongers.

[book I, chapter ix]

Although Scot does not deny the existence of occult powers, his sturdy common sense convinced him that the great majority of so-called witches were, at worst, victims of their own maliciousness or folly. After listing the incredible crimes with which they were frequently charged—from 'incestuous adulterie with spirits' to the cannibalistic devouring of their own children—he roundly declares: 'If more ridiculous or abhominable crimes could have been invented, these poore women (whose cheefe fault is that they are scolds) should have been charged with them' (book II, chapter x). He concludes that: 'If it were true that witches confesse, or that all writers write, or that witchmongers report, or that fooles beleeve, we should never have butter in the chearne, nor cow in the close, nor corne in the field, nor faire weather abroad, nor health within doores' (book III, chapter xiv).

The work seems to have had considerable impact on Scot's contemporaries, although not always in the way in which the author intended. Ironically, the book is such a treasure-house of magic lore (with charms, spells and conjuring rituals set out, complete with diagrams) and contains such a host of authentic witchcraft tales and racy anecdotes that its main influence seems to have been to act as a source-book for other writers—including Shakespeare, Jonson and Middleton—most of whom culled the witchlore and ignored the accompanying ironic comments and refutations.

James I, on his accession to the English throne in 1603, ordered all copies of Scot's work to be destroyed. He had written his *Daemonologie*, published in Edinburgh in 1597 and reprinted by an enterprising London publisher in 1604, partly as a response to Scot's book. Like Gifford's work, it is written in the form of a dialogue, with Epistomen voicing James's opinions. The work draws heavily on Biblical and Classical sources, in contrast to Scot's blend of ancient and contemporary lore. It was also very much influenced by current Continental writings, reflecting the Scottish affinities with European beliefs. For instance, his description of typical witches is much more applicable to the European model than to her English counterpart: 'They are ... some of them rich and worldly-wise, some of them fatte or corpulent in their bodies, and most part of them altogether given over to the pleasures of the flesh' (book II). In contrast, Scot's description is typical of the accounts of most other English writers—and seems far more akin to reality: 'One sort of such as are said to bee witches, are women which be commonly old, lame, bleare-eied, pale, fowle, and full of wrinkles. ... They are leane and deformed, shewing melancholie in their faces, to the horror of all that see them' (book I, chapter iii).

As was noted previously, James urged caution in condemning those accused of witchcraft and he also argued against the punishment of children involved in occult activities, 'for they are not that capable of reason as to practise such things' (book III). Nevertheless, he urged strong measures against the convicted:

> The prince or magistrate for further tryals cause, may continue the punishing of them such a certaine space as he thinkes convenient; But in the end to spare the life, and not to strike when God bids strike, and so severely punish in so odious a fault and treason against God, it is

1    Three witches and their familiar spirits: Joan Flower and her daughters, Margaret and Philippa, who were executed at Lincoln on 11 March 1618 [1619]. The woodcut is taken from the pamphlet, *The Wonderful Discoverie of the Witchcrafts of Margaret and Philip[pa] Flower* (1619).

not only unlawful but comparable to the sin of witchcraft itselfe.

[book III]

James's stern injunctions are seen in practice in the pamphlet account of the North Berwick conspiracy, *Newes From Scotland* (1591). The King took a leading part in the examination of several of the accused and also seems to have instigated the tortures inflicted on Fian following his abortive escape from captivity and subsequent denial of his previous confession:

> Whereupon the kinges majestie perceiving his stubbourne wilfulnesse, conceived and imagined that in the time of his absence hee had entered into new conference and league with the devill his master, and that hee had beene agayne newly marked, for the which hee was narrowly searched, but it could not in any wise bee founde, yet for more tryall of him to make him confesse, hee was commanded to have a most straunge torment, which was done in this manner following.
>
> His nailes upon all his fingers were riven and pulled off with an instrument called in Scottish a Turkas, which in England wee call a payre of pincers, and under everie nayle there was thrust in two needels over even up to the heads: At all which torments notwithstanding the Doctor never shronke anie whit, neither would he then confesse it the sooner for all the tortures inflicted upon him.
>
> Then was hee with all convenient speed, by commandement, convaied againe to the torment of the bootes, wherein hee continued a long time, and did abide so many blowes in them, that his legges were crushte and beaten together as small as might bee, and the bones and flesh so brused that the bloud and marrowe spouted forth in great abundance, whereby they were made unserviceable for ever.

Whatever doubts might later have grown within James's own mind, it is hardly surprising, in view of such well publicised evidence of his attitude towards those accused of witchcraft, that the predominant tone of the ostensibly learned and rational works on the subject should be uniformly hostile after his succession to the English throne. Typical of such writings is Perkins's *A Discourse of the Damned Art of Witchcraft*, which was written in 1602 at the end of Elizabeth's reign but, significantly, not published until 1608. Perkins approved, in certain circumstances, of the use of torture, including 'the rack or some other violent meanes to urge confession ... when the partie is obstinate'. As was noted previously, he (like James) drew no distinction between the practitioners of 'black' or 'white' magic, and (again like James) he declared that they should all be subject to the same penalty.

Both Scot and Gifford had admitted the possibility of genuine witchcraft existing in rare cases and agreed that those who practised it should be 'rooted out' and punished. However, they also argued that the great majority of those who were regarded as witches were the victims of either false accusations or self-delusion and should be treated with appropriate leniency. Perkins, on the other hand, declared that all those who practised magic, whether their supposed powers were genuine or not, should:

> come under this sentence of Moses, because they deny God, and are confederates with Satan. By the lawes of England, the thiefe is executed for stealing and we think it just and profitable: but it were a thousand times better for the land, if all Witches, but specially the blessing Witch might suffer death. [p. 256]

## Notes to Chapter 1

1  Reginald Scot, *The Discoverie of Witchcraft*, edited by Brinsley Nicholson (1886, reprinted 1973).

2  Lilian Winstanley in *Macbeth, King Lear and Contemporary History* (1922), pp. 103–15 and H. N. Paul in *The Royal Play of Macbeth* (1950), pp. 255–64, indicate numerous affinities between the Weird Sisters and Scottish witches, which Shakespeare may or may not have taken into account.

3  J. H. Bloom in *Folk Lore, Old Customs and Superstitions in Shakespeare's Land* (1929) cites numerous cases of alleged witchcraft occurring in south Warwickshire in the early part of this century and states that the area was a 'strong-hold' for 'black' witches in particular (p. 92). Two contemporary plays with witchcraft themes—David Rudkin's *Afore Night Come* (1962) and John Bowen's television drama *Robin Redbreast* (1970) are set in the south Warwickshire/Worcestershire area.

4  See, for example, Pennethorne Hughes, *Witchcraft* (1952), pp. 99–100.

5  This anecdote exists in at least three different versions—see E. K. Chambers, *The Elizabethan Stage*, vol. 3 (1923), p. 424. The story seems to have been originally circulated by the Puritans as part of their anti-stage propaganda. (See also Winifred Smith, 'Anti-Catholic propaganda in Elizabethan London', *Modern Philology*, XXVIII (1930–1), pp. 208–12.)

6  See G. L. Kittredge, *Witchcraft in Old and New England* (1929), pp. 27–34.

7  *The Wonderfull Discoverie of Witches in the Countie of Lancaster ... by Thomas Potts, Esq.*, ed. G. B. Harrison, Bodley Head Quartos (1929).

8  *The most cruell and bloody murther committed by an Inkeepers Wife, called Annis Dell, and her Sonne George Dell ...* (1606).

9  James I, *Daemonologie*, book III.

10  For a full defence of James's reputation see Kittredge, pp. 276–328 and Paul, pp. 75–130.

11  Many of the pamphlets, together with all the printed books of the period, are contained in the University Microfilm Library (Ann Arbor, Michigan). Some of the most notable have been reproduced in modernised form in Barbara Rosen's anthology, *Witchcraft* (1969).

12  *Daemonologie*, book III.

13  *Witches Apprehended, Examined and Executed, for notable villainies by them committed both by Land and Water ...* (1613).

14  See, for example, the opening of the appendix, 'A Discourse upon Divels and Spirits', chapter 33.

# CHAPTER 2

# LIBERTIES OF SIN

## THE LITERARY BACKGROUND

> *Antipholus:* **They say this town is full of cozenage;...**
> **Dark-working sorcerers that change the mind,**
> **Soul-killing witches that deform the body...**
> **And many such-like liberties of sin.**
>
> *[The Comedy of Errors*, I. ii]

### I

Magic and witchcraft are constantly recurring elements in such early English poetry as the mediaeval ballads and the poems of the Arthurian cycle. In the fourteenth-century *Sir Gawain and the Green Knight*, for example, the Lady temptress, with her magic girdle, is an enchantress in the Morgan le Fay tradition, whilst the demonic, shape-shifting Green Knight himself is also a stock figure of fairy-lore.

However, in comparison with the enormous prose output on the subject of witchcraft in the Elizabethan and Jacobean eras, the subject received surprisingly little attention from the poets of the period. Spenser's *The Fairie Queene* (1590–8) provides us with one of the very few portrayals of a witch of any length or quality. In book III, canto seven, the 'faire Florimell', needlessly fleeing from Arthur, encounters a witch who is described in terms typical of the English tradition, both in her appearance and way of life:

There in a gloomy hollow glen she found
A little cottage, built of stickes and reedes
In homely wize, and wald with sods around,
In which a witch did dwell, in loathly weedes,
And wilful want, all carelesse of her needes;
So choosing solitary to abide,
Far from all neighbours, that her devilish deedes
And hellish arts from people she might hide,
And hurt far off unknowne, whom ever she envide.

[Stanza vi][1]

The hag has a son who is very much in the 'homme sauvage' tradition of European literature. He is akin to Caliban in *The Tempest*, and just as Miranda arouses Caliban's desires so Florimell's beauty inflames 'his brutish mind / No love, but brutish lust, that was so beastly tind [kindled]' (stanza xv). When Florimell flees from his advances, his desire turns to frenzy and his mother tries to restore him, with a blend of maternal care and folk medicine, 'with herbs, with charms, with counsell and with tears' (stanza xxi).

When these fail, she summons a 'hideous beast ... monstrous mishapt ... that feeds on women's flesh, as others feede on gras' (stanza xxii), which unsuccessfully pursues Florimell. To console her son the witch, with the help of spirits, creates an image of Florimell, dresses it in the maiden's garments, and animates it with a devil. The son only briefly enjoys his Pygmalion-like beloved, for the foolish Braggadacchio—mistaking the figure for the real Florimell—captures it and makes it his mistress. As Spenser reminds us, by taking this demon-lover, the knight (as surely as Faustus following his intercourse with the spirit of Helen) may 'thinke himself in heaven, that was in hell' (canto VIII, stanza xix).

Spenser portrays another witch-like figure in Acrasia, who enthralls Mordant in the Bower of Bliss (book II). This episode is drawn from the Classical image of the enchantress Circe[2] and it is possible that she was also in part, the inspiration for the portrayal of Duessa in book I.[3]

Classical witchcraft traditions are also reflected in other poems of the period. A song by Thomas Campion included in his *The Third and Fourth Book of Ayres* contains borrowings from Theocritus, *Idylls*, II, and Virgil, *Eclogues*, VIII.

Thrice tosse these Oaken ashes in the ayre,
Thrice sit thou mute in this inchanted chayre;
Then thrice three times tye up this true loves knot,
And murmur soft, shee will, or she will not.

Goe burn these poysnous weedes in yon blew fire,
These Screech owles fethers, and this prickling bryer,
This Cypresse gathered at a dead mans grave:
That all thy feares and cares an end may have.

Then come, you Fayries, dance with me a round,
Melt her hard hart with your melodious sound.
In vaine are all the charmes I can devise:
She hath an Arte to breake them with her eyes.[4]

The tossing of ashes, taken from Virgil, is also included by Ben Jonson in his portrayal of witchcraft rituals in *The Masque of Queenes* (ll. 265–7). Amongst his spell-making ingredients are the feathers of a 'scrich owle'—a detail both writers have taken from Ovid's account of Medea's rites in *Metamorphoses*, VII. Campion's theme of the inability of witchcraft to generate true love is a recurring element of much of the poetry and drama of the period and the final ironic line of the song refers to another commonly held belief, namely the power to bewitch or 'fascinate' by staring into the eyes of the victim or beloved. Cornelius Agrippa defined the art thus: 'Fascination is a binding, which comes from the spirit of the Witch, through the eyes of him that is bewitched, entering to his heart' (*Three Books of Occult Philosophy*, I. i, Paris, 1567, English translation by 'J.F.', 1651).

It is around this traditional belief that John Donne develops a typical metaphysical love conceit in *Witchcraft by a Picture*:

I fixe mine eye on thine, and there
    Pitty my picture burning in thine eye,
My picture drown'd in a transparent teare,
    When I looke lower I espie;
    Hadst thou the wicked skill
By pictures made and mard, to kill,
How many wayes mightst thou performe thy will?

But now I have drunke thy sweet salt teares,
    And though thou poure more I'll depart;
My picture vanish'd, vanish feares,
    That I can be endamag'd by that art:
    Though thou retaine of mee
One picture more, yet that will bee,
Being in thine owne heart, from all malice free.[5]

Donne combines two distinct ideas here: the concept of fascination, together with the use of sympathetic magic by making and then destroying an image of a prospective victim. The spell is broken by the speaker's destruction of the two reflected images of himself—in the tear and in his mistress's eye itself—but by fixing 'mine eye on thine' he has in fact implanted his love within her heart. The fact that this love is 'from all malice free' confirms that witchcraft has not, in reality, been at work here, just as the lady's ability to cry indicates that she is no witch.

Attempts to engender love through witchcraft are a constant motif in the orally transmitted ballads of this and earlier times. Typical of these is the tale of *Alison Gross*, 'The ugliest witch in the north countrie'. When her intended lover rebuffs her:

> She's turned her richt and round about,
>     And thrice she blew on a grass-green horn;
> And she sware by the moon and the stars aboon,
>     That she'd gar me rue the day I was born.
>
> Then out she's ta'en a silver wand,
>     And she's turned her three times round and round;
> She's mutter'd sic words, that my strength it fail'd,
>     And I fell down senseless on the ground.

The repetition of thrice, the invocation of the moon and stars, the use of a green horn and a silver wand are all recurring aspects of such ballads, which are the clearest poetic expressions of the folk-lore traditions on which so many of the popular attitudes to witchcraft were founded. Here the victim is transformed into an 'ugly worm' (a common fate, with obvious sexual implications) and is finally rescued by the Fairy Queen:

> She took me up in her milk-white hand,
>     And she straiked me three times o'er her knee;
> She changed me again to my ain proper shape,
>     And I nae mair maun toddle about the tree.[6]

In addition to these traditional tales, bound by neither time nor place, ballads were composed and printed in broadsheets to record current sensational events. It is in these equivalents of the rapidly printed prose pamphlets that we find the most extensive treatment of witchcraft and the supernatural in verse form. A favourite topic was the birth of monstrous children, sometimes clearly identifiable as Siamese twins.[7] Such horrifying progeny were popularly seen as the fruits of sin, especially of a witch's intercourse with the devil in the form of an incubus. The misshapen offspring themselves were also frequently regarded as being morally warped—their outward deformity reflecting their inner depravity. Caliban's vitiated condition is indicated by his monstrous appearance and Richard III's corruption is underlined by his mother's description of him as:

> Thou elvish-mark'd, abortive, rooting hog,
> Thou that wast seal'd in thy nativity
> The slave of nature and the son of hell.

[Richard III, I.iii. 228–30]

In the ballads no sympathy is expressed for the unfortunate parents or their offspring—most of whom died soon after birth—and similarly the verse accounts of witchcraft trials are solely concerned with the more sensational aspects of 'maleficia' associated with the case, with no attempts made to arouse pity for the accused. Some of the prose pamphlets were prefaced by doggerel verses in the ballad tradition. The account of the 1566 Chelmsford trial has such an introduction,[8] whilst a later case at Chelmsford, that of 1589, is described in a separately printed ballad. This latter is typical of the vast majority of such works, consisting as it does of a series of stock phrases and refrains cobbled together and adapted to suit this particular case. The ballad compares very badly with the detailed pamphlet account of the affair,[9] the only references to the actual trial being the number of the accused, the alleged attacks on cattle and the use of children to testify against their parents:

*A Newe Ballad of the Life and Deaths of three Witches Arrayned and Executed at Chelmes-forde, 5 July 1589*

> List Christians all unto my Song
> Twill move your Hearts to Grace,
> That dreadful Witchcraft hath been done
> Of late about this place.
> But three that cryed the Devills name
> With those that did them follow,
> Now to Justice are brought home
> To swing upon our Gallow.
>
> Theres scarce a month within these Yeares
> But Witchcraft fowle is done,
> And manie are the weeping teares
> These Satans Fiendes have rung.
> Though they sought Mercie ere the rope
> Soon as the Judgments read
> Who gainsays the Devills Hope
> Is all when they are dead.
>
> A vile long life they have run on
> Regarding not their end,
> Their minds still bent to crueltie

Not minding to amends.
Men and cattle they Bewitched,
No peace thay gave to Rest,
But yet in time their partes were switched
By marks upon their Breasts.

As to the Storie now to tell
The truth I will Declare,
It was the Witches Children small
That they did not be ware.
For God into their Infants Hearts
Did pour the Light of Reason,
And all against their Mothers spoke
Of Witchcraft and of Treason.

Evil were the tales of their demands
Sprung from the Depths of Hell,
And terrible the work of their Commaunds
As did the Children tell.
Now has the Judge the Sentence read
And ended in our town
The rule of Imps and Spells and Dread
For manie miles aroun.

So listen Christians to my Song,
The Hangmans swung his rope
And on these Gallows hath been done
An end to Satans Hope.
Give the News from Chelmes-forde Town
To all the World be spread,
A crew of evil Witches have gone down,
Hanged by the neck, all three are dead.

The ballad's tone of callous indifference, not to say positive enthusiasm, at the executions is hardly surprising in an age when it was more likely that one would be hanged for sheep-stealing than witchcraft. The accused had confessed that they had brought about the deaths of numerous adults and children and therefore suffered the death penalty under the terms of the 1563 Act. It is unlikely, therefore, that their fates would have aroused much compassion among the local populace and the ballad probably provides a fair reflection of the prevailing attitudes to such episodes.

## II

The relatively limited concern with witchcraft apparent in Elizabethan poetry is paralleled in the plays of the period; there are scattered references

25

to the subject in many plays but in very few is it a leading theme. This was due in part to the fact that there was no tradition for the dramatic portrayal of witchcraft before this time. The principal supernatural phenomena to be depicted on stage had been the devils who had figured in many of the mediaeval miracle and morality plays, especially those concerned with such themes as the Last Judgment and the Harrowing of Hell.

Several later plays retained vestiges of these elements. In Marlowe's *Doctor Faustus* (*c.* 1588–92), for example, the representation of the Seven Deadly Sins and the juxtaposition of the symbolic Good and Bad Angels are remnants of the earlier tradition, as is the climax, in which Faustus is carried off to Hell, in much the same way as were the sinners of the mediaeval plays. (See Chapters Eight and Ten). In these works the demonic figures were as frequently sources of humour as of awe, the playwrights using the age-old weapon of ridicule to combat a potentially terrifying force, and these crudely farcical elements are also evident in *Doctor Faustus*, particularly in the 1616 version, which is probably the nearest text we have to Marlowe's original work.[10]

The play is also one of many to depict the miraculous activities of magicians and conjurors, but it is unique in that it is the only Elizabethan work to portray an individual's progression from magician to witch.[11] Faustus takes this fatal step when he makes, at his own suggestion, the demonic pact that binds him to the service of the devil in return for twenty-four years of apparently unlimited earthly power. The taking of the diabolic oath is depicted on stage but his ensuing debasement is merely related. He vows to worship Belzebub: 'To him I'll build an altar and a church. / And offer lukewarm blood of new-born babes' (v. 13–14).[12] He later promises:

> Never to name God or to pray to him,
> To burn his scriptures, slay his ministers,
> And make my spirits pull his churches down. [vi. 99–101]

There are obvious practical difficulties of staging here and whether Faustus actually carries out the more sensational of his vows is not made clear, but the fact that he makes them and in so doing renounces God is sufficient to show that he has indeed become a witch.

In addition, the play contains many elements of traditional witch-lore: Faustus's powers of shape-shifting, of invisibility and of supernatural flight, for example. The signing of the devil's pact with his own blood and his subsequent inability to utter the name of Christ without physical torment—'Ah, rend not my heart for naming of my Christ'—also comply with current beliefs. More modest versions of the pact are found in the confessions of several witches of the sixteenth and seventeenth centuries. Elizabeth Style, tried in Somerset in 1664, admitted having dealings with the devil who 'promised her Mony and that she should live gallantly, and have the pleasure of the Worlde for Twelve Yeares if she would with her Blood sign his Paper, which was to give her soul to him.'[13] The play is, in part, an exemplar of the inevitable fate of those who practise witchcraft. Whilst much of the interest in the central sections of the work revolves around Faustus's acts of 'maleficia', in the final scenes he achieves tragic stature, his 'hellish fall' arousing the Aristotelian emotions of both fear and pity.

The remaining dramatic portrayals of witches in the Elizabethan period are far more innocuous. John Lyly created two very different examples in Dipsas in *Endimion* (1588) and Mother Bombie, in the play of that name (*c.* 1589). The former is based partly on the classical tradition, with her use of 'herbs, stones, spells, incantation, enchantment, exorcisms, fire, metals, planets or any practice' to perform her arts. She echoes Ovid's Medea (*Metamorphoses*, VII) in her claim that she can 'darken the Sun by my skill, and remove the Moon out of her course'. Hecate in Middleton's *The Witch* makes similar boasts and they also share the same limited powers over the human will. As Dipsas admits:

> Therein I differ from the Gods, that I am not able to rule hearts; for were it in my power to place affection by appointment, I would make such evil appetites, such inordinate lusts, such cursed desires, all the world should be filled with superstitious heats, and extreme love ... This I can—breed slackness in love, though never root it out.
>
> [I. iv][14]

However, unlike Hecate, Dipsas is treated throughout most of *Endimion* as a comical character, certainly not one to be feared. This impression is reinforced in Act V, scene ii, when Cynthia pronounces final judgment on her and reveals the emptiness of her boasts:

> Thou hast threatened to turn my course awry, and alter by thy damnable Art the government I now possess by the eternal Gods. But know thou, Dipsas, and let all the Enchanters know, that Cynthia being placed for light on earth, is also protected by the powers of heaven. Breathe out thou may'st words, gather thou may'st herbs, find out thou may'st stones most agreeable to thine Art, yet of no force to appal my heart, in which courage is so rooted, and constant persuasion of the mercy of the Gods so grounded, that all thy witchcraft I esteem as weak, as the world doth thy case wretched.

Cynthia is an allegorical representation of Queen Elizabeth, who had been the apparent object of a witchcraft plot in 1578, when three wax images transfixed by hogs' bristles had been found, the central figure having 'Elizabeth' inscribed on it.[15] It will be recalled that the Statute of 1580/1 had been designed to counter the use of witchcraft as an instrument in treasonable activities. In equating Cynthia with Elizabeth, Lyly is indicating the Queen's divinely given immunity from the assaults of witchcraft. Unlike many classical witches, and despite her boastful claims, Dipsas is unable to alter the moon's path or its position of supremacy in the heavens and, similarly, diabolically inspired attacks on Elizabeth will inevitably fail.

Mother Bombie is an even more harmless figure than Dipsas—in fact, she is not a witch in the true sense for she seems to have inherited her occult powers, which are mainly in the form of fortune-telling, rather than gained them through charms or supernatural pacts. She denies Silena's charge that she is a witch with the words: 'They lie, I am a cunning woman' (II.iii). She is, in other words, a wise woman, of a harmless kind. This is confirmed by her words and behaviour throughout the play and particularly by the final summary of her activities in V.iii:

> *Silena:* Mother Bombie told me 'my father knew me not, falsely bred,
>     truly begot'—a bats on Mother Bombie!
> *Dromio:* Mother Bombie told us we should be found cosners,
>     and in the end be cosned by cosners, well fare, Mother Bombie!
> *Riscio:* I heard Mother Bombie say that thou shalt die a beggar,
>     beware of Mother Bombie!
> *Prisius*: Why, have you all been with Mother Bombie?
> *Lucio:* All, and as far as I can see [she] foretold all.
> *Memphio:* Indeed she is cunning and wise, never doing harm but still
>     practising good.

In *Twelfth Night* (*c.* 1600) Feste, in his baiting of Malvolio, ironically offers to take his water to the wise woman. This is presumably to cure his alleged madness or at least to trace the origins of his supposed possession, which was generally thought to be inflicted by witchcraft. However, Shakespeare does not develop this theme, which would be an unnecessary complication in the working out of the plot.

Similarly, he ignores the witchcraft potential in his treatment of the possession of Antipholus in *The Comedy of Errors* (*c.* 1592). This work, based as it is on Classical sources, does of course contain several supernatural elements and combines ancient and contemporary witchcraft beliefs. Antipholus's early description of Ephesus is in the older vein, whilst at the same time having clear affinities with Elizabethan London:

They say this town is full of cozenage;
As, nimble jugglers that deceive the eye,
Dark-working sorcerers that change the mind,
Soul-killing witches that deform the body,
Disguised cheaters, prating mountebanks,
And many such-like liberties of sin.

[I.ii. 97–102]

In Act II Christian concepts are introduced, as well as a blend of witchcraft and fairy lore, in Dromio's words:

O, for my beads! I cross me for a sinner.
This is the fairy land: O! spite of spites.
We talk with goblins, owls, and elvish sprites:
If we obey them not, this will ensue,
They'll suck our breath, or pinch us black and blue.

[II.ii. 187–91] [16]

Dromio later warns his master to beware of the wiles of a courtesan, comparing entanglement with her to the diabolical pact:

Some devils ask but the parings of one's nail,
A rush, a hair, a drop of blood, a pin,
A nut, a cherry-stone;
But she, more covetous, would have a chain.
Master be wise: an if you give it her,
The devil will shake her chain and fright us with it.

[IV.iii. 66–71]

There are scattered references to witchcraft in several other of Shakespeare's early plays. In *The Merry Wives of Windsor* (c. 1600), for example, Falstaff disguises himself as a wise woman and is denounced as a witch by Sir Hugh Evans: 'By yea and no, I think th 'oman is a witch indeed. I like not when a 'oman has a great peard' (IV.ii. 202–3). The Herne the Hunter episode in Act V, with Falstaff disguised as the demon spirit, complete with horned head-dress, is more related to fairy lore, but if there is any substance in the Murrayite theory of the primaeval origins of witchcraft and its links with primitive animal rites, both this scene and Bottom's magical donning of the ass's head in *A Midsummer-Night's Dream* might owe something to these ancient folk memories. [17]

The contrast between the supposed excesses of Continental witchcraft and the generally milder English equivalent is implied in the appropriately humorous exchange in *All's Well That Ends Well* (1602):

*Clown:* Why, sir, if I cannot serve you, I can serve as great a prince as
  you are.

29

*Lafeu:* Who's that? A Frenchman?
*Clown:* Faith, sir, 'a has an English name; but his fisnomy is
    more hotter in France than there.
*Lafeu:* What prince is that?
*Clown:* The Black Prince, sir; alias, the Prince of Darkness; alias the
    devil.

[IV.v. 32–9]

In more serious vein, it is in Shakespeare's portrayal of an alleged Continental witch—Joan la Pucelle in *Henry VI, Part One* (1592)—that we find the fullest treatment of witchcraft in his Elizabethan plays. There is little indication in the early scenes that Joan is a witch; in fact her patriotism and courage are given due emphasis, whilst, on the English side, it is her supposed harlotry rather than her indulgence in occult practices that is stressed. In this respect, her beauty is frequently alluded to, aligning her with the Continental view of the witch-figure.

The witchcraft aspect is not fully seen until Act V, firstly when Joan summons her familiar spirits to help her in her final enterprise. Although some of the more sensational aspects of witch-lore are featured in this scene, the treatment is not wholly unsympathetic, with the patriotism still prominent:

*Joan:* Where I was wont to feed you with my blood,
    I'll lop a member off and give it you,
    In earnest of a further benefit,
    So you do condescend to help me now.
                          *The spirits hang their heads*
    No hope to have redress? My body shall
    Pay recompense, if you will grant my suit.
                          *They shake their heads*
    Cannot my body nor blood-sacrifice
    Persuade you to your wonted furtherance?
    Then take my soul; my body, soul and all,
    Before that England give the French the foil.
                              *They depart*
                            [V.iii. 14–23]

However, the tone changes radically in the final scene, which descends to melodrama and crude chauvinism, with Joan brutally repulsing her aged father and attempting to gain immunity by falsely claiming pregnancy through the Dauphin or any numbers of French lords.

*Henry VI, Part Two* (*c.* 1591) features the conspiracy episode in which the Duchess of Gloucester uses occult means in her treasonable plot. Holinshed describes Margery Jourdain, one of those involved, as 'the Witch of Eie' and records the use of sympathetic magic:

> The matter laid against them was, for that they (at the request of the said duchesse) had devised an image of wax, representing the king, which by their sorcerie by little and little consumed; intending thereby in conclusion to waste and destroie the king's person.[18]

Shakespeare, however, ignores the witchcraft factor—despite the similarities with the supposed plot against Elizabeth in 1578. Instead, he provides a scene (I.iv) which is closer to Stow's account of the incident, where Roger Bolingbroke confesses that: 'he wrought the said Negromancie at the stirring and procurement of the said Dame Elainor, to knowe what should befall of hir, and to what estate she should come'.[19]

The necromancy offers greater opportunity for spectacle, rivalling that contained in the contemporary plays *Doctor Faustus* and *Friar Bacon and Friar Bungay*. It also has embryonic affinities with the more elaborate Apparitions sequence in *Macbeth* (IV.i). Both the Duchess and Macbeth desire information relating to the fates of kings and seek this knowledge from occult sources. The Weird Sisters are habitually associated with darkness—in this scene Macbeth addresses them as 'secret, black and midnight hags' (l. 47)—and the conjuring episode in the earlier play takes place during:

> Deep night, dark night, the silent of the night,
> The time of night when Troy was set on fire;
> The time when screech-owls cry and bandogs howl,
> And spirits walk and ghosts break up their graves. [16–19]

After the Spirit has been conjured, amongst thunder and lightning, it replies to three questions put to it by Bolingbroke on behalf of the Duchess, who cannot address it directly. Similarly, Macbeth is warned by the First Witch to 'Hear his speech, but say thou nought' (l. 70). The three Apparitions respond to Macbeth's unspoken questions in terms which are as cryptic as those uttered by the oracular Spirit in the earlier scene.

The foregoing brief but representative survey suggests that if indeed the Elizabethan players were 'the abstract and brief chronicles of the time'—and there is no reason to suppose that they were not—the subject of witchcraft was regarded lightly in the main. The dramatic approach was generally comic rather than tragic and opportunities for a fuller or more serious treatment were sometimes ignored. It is perhaps dangerous to draw conclusions from such slender evidence, but the very fact that there is such slight treatment of the theme seems to confirm that, despite the apparent increase in witchcraft prosecutions from 1560 onwards, the subject did not loom overlarge in the preoccupations of most Elizabethans. However, just as the tone in the Jacobean prose writings became uniformly more hostile, so the dramas of the later period were considerably more sombre in their portrayals of the practice of witchcraft.

### Notes to Chapter 2

*1*     *The Poetical Works of Edmund Spenser*, edited by J. C. Smith and E. De Selincourt (Oxford, 1912).

*2*     See M. Y. Hughes, 'Spenser's Acrasia and the Circe of the Renaissance', *Journal of the History of Ideas*, 4 (1923), pp. 381–99.

*3*     Gareth Roberts argues this in *Magic and Witchcraft in English Drama and Poetry from 1558 to 1634* (unpublished thesis, University of London, 1976). See also Dr Roberts's article 'Three notes on uses of Circe by Spenser, Marlowe and Milton', *Notes and Queries* (new series), vol. 25 No. 5 (October 1978).

*4*     *The Works of Thomas Campion*, edited by Walter R. Davis (Garden City, N.Y., 1967).

*5*     *The Poems of John Donne*, edited by Herbert Grierson (Oxford, 1933).

*6*     *The Oxford Book of Ballads*, edited by James Kinsley (Oxford, 1969).

*7*     Shakespeare satirises such extravagances in the sales-patter of Autolycus in *The Winter's Tale* (IV.iv. 260–85).

*8*     *The examination and confession of certain Wytches at Chensforde in the Countie of Essex ... 1566.* (Extracts from the pamphlet, in modernised form, are included in Rosen, *Witchcraft*, pp. 72–82.)

*9*     *The Apprehension and confession of three notorious Witches. Arreigned and by Justice condemned and executed at Chelmes-forde, in the countye of Essex, the 5. day of Julye, last past. 1589.* (See Rosen, *Witchcraft*, pp. 182–9.)

*10*     See W. W. Greg, *Marlowe's 'Doctor Faustus' 1604–1616: Parallel Texts* (Oxford, 1950), pp. vii–viii.

*11*     Alexander VI in Barnes's *The Devil's Charter* (1607) follows a similar path—see Chapter Eight.

*12*     *Doctor Faustus*, edited by John D. Jump, The Revels Plays (1962).

*13*     Quoted in Christina Hole, *Witchcraft in England* (1947), p. 126.

*14*     Quotations from *Endimion* and *Mother Bombie* are taken from *The Complete Works of John Lyly*, vol. 3, edited by R. Warwick Bond (1902).

*15*     See Kittredge, pp. 87–8.

*16*     These lines are clearly faulty in the folio texts and are the subject of much scholarly dispute—the New Arden edition, edited by R. A. Foakes (1962) contains a discussion of the matter (p. 37).

*17*     The Herne the Hunter scene, with its assemblage of characters disguised as fairies and other supernatural creatures, encapsulates a wealth of contemporary folk-lore and superstition. The gulling of Falstaff by the false Fairy Queen figure is similar to many such incidents of the period, and the 'trial-fire' sequence, whereby his lustful nature is 'proved' is a comical echo of the current trials by ordeal.

*18*     *Shakespeare's Holinshed*, edited by W. G. Boswell-Stone (1896), p. 253.

*19*     John Stow, *The Annals of England*, p. 622. Kittredge recounts this fascinating case, pp. 81–4.

# CHAPTER 3

# MIDNIGHT HAGS

## THE WEIRD SISTERS IN *MACBETH*

*Macbeth:* **How now, you secret, black, and midnight hags!**
　　　　**What is't you do?**
*All:* 　　　　　　　　**A deed without a name.**
　　　　　　　　　　　　　　　　*[Macbeth*, IV.i.47–8]

One of the first plays to provide an extended portrayal of the darker aspects of witchcraft and magic was *Macbeth*, which was probably first performed in 1605 or 1606. However, the precise nature of the principal exponents of the supernatural in the play—the Weird Sisters—remains a matter of much scholarly dispute. The term 'weird' in itself poses difficulties, for its meaning for a Jacobean audience was very different from its principal current usage. The word is derived from the Old English 'wyrd' and Old Scandinavian 'wurd', both nouns meaning 'fate, lot or destiny'. It was not until the nineteenth century that the sense of 'unaccountably mysterious, uncanny, odd' appeared and C. T. Onions, in the *Oxford Dictionary of English Etymology*, states that 'the later currency and adjectival use is derived from its occurrence in the story of Macbeth'.

'Weird' is the customary Shakespearean editorial form but in the First Folio it appears as 'weyard' except on three occasions when 'weyward' is used (I.iii.32, I.v.8 and II.i.20').[1] Both forms probably reflect the

33

contemporary double syllabic pronunciation, which completes the rhythm of such lines as: 'The Weird Sisters, hand in hand, / Posters of the sea and land' (I.iii.32–3). Shakespeare presumably took the term 'weird' from his main source, Holinshed, who in his *Chronicles of Scotland* describes the first encounter with Macbeth thus: 'It fortuned as Makbeth and Banquho journied towards Fores ... there met them three women in strange and wild apparell, resembling creatures of the elder world'. Although 'elder' implies ancient or of supernatural origin, Holinshed is here clearly identifying the creatures as human. However, he then confuses the issue by adding that: 'Afterwards the common opinion was, that these women were either the weird sisters, that is (as ye would say) the goddesses of destinie, or else some nymphs or feiries, indued with knowledge of prophesie by their necromanticall science, bicause everie thing came to pass as they had spoken.'[2]

Thus Holinshed offers three alternative identifications: the creatures were *either* mortals *or* goddesses of destiny *or* fairies endowed with necromantic powers. As we have seen, nymphs and fairies could be either mortal or supernatural figures, but the reference to 'necromanticall science' implies the human practice of divination through demonology. Holinshed keeps his options open still further by his qualifying phrase 'as ye would say' and his reference to 'the common opinion', which could not necessarily be relied upon.

He is more precise in his account of the subsequent events. The later prophecies to Macbeth are made by 'certeine wizzards in whose words he put great confidence' who warn him to beware of Macduff, whilst 'a certeine witch, whom hee had in great trust, had told that he should never be slaine with man born of anie woman, nor vanquished till the wood of Bernane came to the castell of Dunsinane'. Shakespeare of course assigns these separate prophecies to the earlier 'weird sisters' but the apparently deliberate ambiguity of Holinshed's account of the nature of these creatures is retained, and indeed compounded by their being merged with the 'wizzards' and 'witch' of the later incidents.

If Shakespeare went to any other of the possible sources of *Macbeth* he would not have found any clarification of this matter. Buchanan's *Rerum Scoticarum Historia* states: 'On a certain night ... three women appeared to him [Macbeth] of more then human stature'—the latter being one of the hallmarks of certain types of fairy. *The Chronicle of Andrew of Wyntoun*—one of Holinshed's own sources—records:

He saw thre women by gangand,

And thai thre women than thocht he
Thre werd sisters like to be.[3]

Much of the debate concerning the nature of the Sisters has centred, rightly or wrongly, on the fatalistic associations of the term 'Weird'. One variation of the conception of the Sisters as latter-day versions of the Classical goddesses of destiny is their alignment with their Scandinavian equivalents—the Norns. This idea was first mooted by Fleay in the nineteenth century and was reiterated by Kittredge in his edition of *Macbeth* (1939). However, any case built exclusively around the word 'weird' is extremely suspect, for Shakespeare, in his use of the term, seems merely to be following Holinshed who, as we have seen, is carefully noncommittal in his own account of the women's true natures. Although Kittredge sees the tragedy as 'inevitably fatalistic', he admits that Shakespeare 'never gives us the impression that a man is not responsible for his own acts'. To view the Weird Sisters simply as Jacobean equivalents of the Parcae is to ignore many of the ambiguities in their presentation.

Nevertheless, it is undeniable that the Sisters do reveal traits which link them with figures of ancient mythology. To what extent they control Macbeth's future as opposed to merely foretelling it is a matter of much debate, but even if their powers are limited to those of prophecy, this gift can equate them with the oracles of the Classical era. Macbeth's cry: 'Stay, you imperfèct speakers' (I.iii.69) is possibly a reflection of the ancient view of the partial nature of oracular utterances, and the Sisters' prophecies made to Macbeth through the Apparitions in IV.i are as ambiguous as any pronounced by the Delphic prophetess.[4]

Once having tempted Macbeth and incited him to set out on his fatal path, the Weird Sisters seal his fate by tormenting him in a manner reminiscent of the ancient Furies. It is quite feasible that such phenomena as the dreams that rack Macbeth nightly and the ghost of the murdered Banquo are created by the Sisters as part of their overall design to drive Macbeth to a state of despair. A Christian dimension is also present here, for such a condition of nihilism as Macbeth reaches and expresses in his vision of life as 'a tale / Told by an idiot, full of sound and fury, / Signifying nothing' (V.v.26–8) marks the final stage of the way to damnation, a stage previously reached by Marlowe's Faustus.

Such intermingling of Classical and contemporary elements, particularly in the portrayal of supernatural figures, is a common phenomenon in Renaissance literature. Dante's Hell is inhabited by such diverse creatures as Medusa, the Harpies and the Furies, and his Geryon has its antecedents in both Virgil and the Book of Revelation. As well as the blurring of ancient and modern concepts there is also a frequent merging of forms within figures supposedly based on a particular period. For all his erudition, Jonson creates witches in *The Masque of Queenes* that are a blend of Furies and Gorgons, and they carry spindles, which are normally part of the accoutrements of the Parcae. Ariel in *The Tempest* adopts the form of a Harpy but behaves in a Fury-like manner when he assails the consciences of the 'three men of sin' in III.iii.

The Senecan influence in *Macbeth* has long been recognised.[5] Lady Macbeth has elements in common with both Medea and Clytemnestra and the contents of the Weird Sisters' cauldron also seem to have been derived in part from Studley's version of *Medea*. The cauldron sequence also borrows from Lucan and from Ovid's *Metamorphoses*, VII, and it is therefore not surprising if the Sisters exhibit a combination of characteristics— human and supernatural, Classical and contemporary. In this they conform to the pattern of many such creations and it is dangerous to attempt to limit their natures to any single form.

The difficulties inherent in such an approach are evident in W. C. Curry's *Shakespeare's Philosophical Patterns* (1937). He makes out a very strong case for the Sisters being 'not ordinary witches but demons or devils in the form of witches' (p. 60). However, on occasions either his argument breaks down or he is forced to ignore or make light of contrary evidence. He argues, for instance, that one aspect of their demonic natures is their ability 'to melt into thin air and vanish like a dream ... they simply fade into nothing' (p. 79). Demons were thought to possess this gift but it was not exclusively theirs—witches and fairies also had this power. Curry also suggests in this connection that the Sisters' 'movements from place to place are not continuous necessarily' (p. 79) but this conflicts, as he admits, with the First Witch's plan to sail to Aleppo in a sieve.

Curry's comment on Banquo's words, addressed to the Sisters, is also significant. Banquo asks them to foretell his future: 'If you can look into the seeds of time, / And say which grain will grow and which will not' (I.iii.58–9). According to Curry:

> Demons know the future development of events conjecturally though not absolutely ... If time is the measure of movement of corporeal things and if corporeal things move and develop according to the impulses latent in that treasury of forces called 'rationes seminales', then these seeds of matter may literally be called the seeds of time and demons have the power of predicting which grain will grow and which will not. [p. 48]

This may well be so, but Curry chooses to ignore the more mundane fact that human witches were also thought to have prophetic powers. Particularly apposite here is the belief that witches could affect actual rather than metaphorical harvests and predict their quality. Spalding in *Elizabethan Demonology* (1880) cites the case of Johnnet Wischert who was:

> indicted for passing to the green-growing corn in May, twenty-two years since, or thereby, sitting thereupon tymous in the morning before the sun-rising; and being there found and demanded what she was doing, thou answered, I shall tell thee; I have been piling the blades of the corn. I find it will be a dear year; the blade of the corn grows withersones and when it grows songatis about, it will be a good, cheap year. [p. 101]

(Withersones—a variation of 'withershins/ widdershins'—signifies a course contrary to the apparent path of the sun. It was considered to be an unlucky omen, whilst the converse—songatis—was regarded as a sign of good fortune.)

Even more significantly, Curry ignores the ironic force of the recurrence of this image later in the play. In III.i Macbeth recalls the Sisters' greeting to Banquo:

> then, prophet-like,
> They hail'd him father to a line of kings.
> Upon my head they plac'd a fruitless crown,
> And put a barren sceptre in my gripe. [58–61]

He mourns the loss of his soul: 'Given to the common enemy of man, / To make them kings—the seeds of Banquo kings!' (ll. 68–9). During his second encounter with the Sisters (IV.i) Macbeth requires them to obey his commands 'Though bladed corn be lodg'd' (l. 55). This is a reference to the belief cited by Scot that witches were thought to be able to 'transferre corne in the blade from one place to another' (*Discoverie*, book I, chapter iv). The powerful images of upheaval and universal destruction that follow culminate in Macbeth's vision of 'the treasure / Of nature's germens tumble all together, / Even till destruction sicken' (ll. 58–60).

Curry shows that 'Nature's germens' are the hidden seeds of life, originating in the mind of God. They cannot be destroyed, but by their being tumbled together in confusion, following the triumph of the forces of Hell, they would become barren or produce only monstrosities.[6] As Dover Wilson states in the New Cambridge *Macbeth*: 'In other words, Macbeth speaks of a time when the devil will not only have made an end of God's world, but will have rendered its re-creation for ever impossible' (p. lxiii). The fact that this conception of the ultimate triumph of Satan is expressed

37

in imagery reminiscent of that used by Banquo during the first meeting with the Sisters reinforces our view of the degree to which Macbeth has succumbed to demonic forces in the intervening period.

Curry also argues that such phenomena as the air-drawn dagger and the ghost of Banquo are manifestations of the same demons that adopt the forms of witches. Such elements are of course capable of other explanations, including the psychological. On the other hand, if one considers solely the scenes in which the Weird Sisters appear there can be no doubt that they conform to some of the most widely held of contemporary beliefs concerning witches. The Jacobean theatregoer, whether he was a firm believer or a sceptic in his attitude to real-life witches and their alleged powers, would have recognised in the Weird Sisters a portrayal of some of the most traditional beliefs concerning witches—in their actions, their motives and their probable appearance.

The fact that they are, as Banquo informs us, 'so withered and so wild in their attire' with 'choppy fingers . . . skinny lips . . . beards' (I.iii.44–6) is in line with the traditional witch-figure as she is described by such writers as Scot and Harsnett.[7] The placing of Banquo's description is important, coming as it does in the passage where Shakespeare is clearly following Holinshed's account. The creatures described by Banquo are in marked contrast to the three stately figures in Elizabethan dress portrayed in the woodcut illustration of the incident in the 1577 edition of Holinshed.[8] In fact, throughout the first two scenes in which the Weird Sisters appear (I.i and I.iii) Shakespeare seems to be at great pains to emphasise the witch-like qualities of his creations. The sailor's wife berates the First Sister with the proverbial phrase 'Aroynt thee, witch!' (I.iii.6)[9] and the whole of this anecdote is redolent with traditional witch-lore.

The motive of vengeance following a supposed petty slight (the refusal of the chestnuts) is typical of the trivial incidents recorded in many of the witch trials of the period, where the alleged revenge was out of all proportion to the original insult and often involved the infliction of death on the victim or the destruction of his possessions. The Second Witch's action of 'killing swine' is also in accord with this belief, for pigs were amongst the most common objects of such supposed attacks. The raising of storms was traditionally held to be within the power of witches, although Scot in *The Discoverie of Witchcraft* attempts to refute this belief: 'Nor anie other indued with meane sense, but will denie that the elements are obedient to witches, and at their commandment; or that they may at their pleasure send rain, haile, tempests, thunder, lightning' (book III, chapter xiii). Scot is here clearly attacking a popular superstition and thus the thunder and

**2** A woodcut from Holinshed's *The Chronicles of Scotland* (1577 edition) depicting the meeting of Macbeth and Banquo with the Weird Sisters. The illustration reflects Holinshed's setting of the encounter in 'woodes and fieldes' but the elegant appearance of the Sisters conflicts with the text's account of their 'strange and wild apparell'.

lightning which accompany the Sisters' every appearance can be seen as their own creation, as is certainly the case with the storm that assails the 'tempest-tost' sailor. Also part of common lore are the offers by the Second and Third Witches to provide winds to help raise the storm.

The whole of the opening sequence of I.iii, up to the entrance of Macbeth and Banquo, can be seen as a portrayal of a witches' sabbat, with the reduction of the traditional thirteen participants to the dramatically more wieldy three, in itself a number with many occult associations. Following the traditional pattern of such assemblies, the Sisters begin by recounting their magical exploits performed since their previous meeting.[10] They then proceed, through chanting and ritualistic dancing, to concoct a spell aimed at the destruction of their next victim—Macbeth. The cauldron sequence in IV.i can be regarded as a more elaborate version of this same spell-making process, while I.i, which clearly opens 'in media res', can be viewed as the final stage of a sabbat where the participants, having selected Macbeth as their adversary, are arranging the time and place for their encounter with him.

Thus each of their three scenes can be regarded as dramatised variations of the witches' sabbat, as it was traditionally conceived.[11] In these portrayals Shakespeare might well have had in mind a specific series of such meetings—those depicted in the pamphlet *Newes From Scotland* which, it will be recalled, described the supposed activities of the North Berwick witches and in particular their attempts on the life of King James. It has long been recognised that Shakespeare probably drew on this event for the episode of the 'tempest-tost' sailor. During the winter of 1589–90 James was returning home to Scotland with his bride, Anne of Denmark. His fleet was beset by a series of violent storms, which drove James's ship far off course without actually sinking it. The North Berwick witches were charged with raising the storms and one of the accused, Agnes Sampson (or Tompson), admitted that a cat, which they had first christened, was taken out to sea and drowned, being conveyed 'by all these witches sayling in their riddles or cives [sieves]'.[12] The First Witch in *Macbeth* is of course going to sail in a sieve in her pursuit of the sailor. Attached to the unfortunate cat were the 'cheefest parts of a dead man, and severale jonts of his bodie'. This spell-making device was expressly forbidden under James I's 1604 anti-witchcraft edict, but the First Witch gleefully displays her newly acquired 'pilot's thumb', which will presumably be added to her collection of diabolic properties.

There are further parallels between the North Berwick case and Shakespeare's portrayal. The witches in the former concluded their assembly and 'tooke handes on the land and daunced this reiel or short daunce ... until they entred into the kerk of north Barrick'. (At their trial they performed their dance 'before the Kings Majestie, who, in respect of the strangenes of these matters tooke great delight to bee present at their examinations'). If James did see *Macbeth* in performance, which seems likely,[13] he could have renewed his delight by witnessing the dance whereby the charm is 'wound up' prior to Macbeth's entry in I.iii.

Agnes Sampson also admitted that in a further attempt on the King's life she 'tooke a blacke Toade, and did hang the same up by the heeles three daies, and collected and gathered the same venome as it dropped and fell from it in an oister shell, and kept the same venome close covered until she could obtaine any parte or peece of foule linnen cloth, that had appertained to the Kings Majestie ... if she had obtained any one peece of linnen cloth which the King had worne and fouled, she had bewitched him to death, and put him to such extraordinary paines, as if he had beene lying upon sharp thornes and endes of Needles'. This is reminiscent of the first object placed in the cauldron in IV.1:

Toad that under cold stone
Days and nights has thirty-one
Swelt'red venom sleeping got
Boil thou first i' th' charmed pot.                    [6–9]

When this attempt failed, Agnes Sampson made a wax image of the King, over which were pronounced the words, 'This is King James the sext, ordonet to be consumed at the instance of a noble man, Francis Erle of Bodowel [Bothwell].'[14] If this device had been successful, James's body would have wasted away or dwindled, peaked and pined in the same

**3**  The North Berwick witches plead with their judges. The seated figure is probably King James I, who 'tooke great delight to bee present at their examinations'. The woodcut forms the frontispiece of the pamphlet, *Newes From Scotland* (1591).

41

manner as that of the storm-tossed mariner.[15]

James's imperviousness to these varied and concerted assaults was attributed to the strength of his Christian faith. The pamphlet concludes:

> It is well knowen that the King is the child and servant of God, and they [the accused] but servants of the devill, hee is the Lords annointed, and they but vesselles of Gods wrath: he is a true Christian, and trusteth in God, they worse than Infidels, for they onely trust in the devill, who daily serve them, till he have brought them to utter destruction.

Shakespeare's portrayal of a treacherous attack on the divinely appointed Duncan by a disloyal kinsman who is aligned with the forces of witchcraft is paralleled in the Scottish case, where the instigator of the conspiracy was almost certainly the nobleman named by Agnes Sampson—Francis, Earl of Bothwell. He was James's cousin and heir to

**4**   A woodcut from *Newes From Scotland* depicting the alleged activities of the North Berwick witches and their ostensible leader, John Fian. The cameos may have been the inspiration for several of the witchcraft elements in *Macbeth*.

the Scottish throne should James die without progeny. Barbara Napier, another of the accused, confessed that the reason for their attacks on James was 'that another might have ruled in his Majesties place'.[16] Bothwell was tried but insufficient evidence could be brought against him and he was acquitted, although those investigating the case, including James himself, strongly suspected his involvement. If James saw *Macbeth*, he would surely have been struck by the similarities between the dramatised conspiracy and that which had in reality endangered his own life.

Another possible link between *Macbeth* and *Newes From Scotland* is provided by the woodcut illustration that forms a frontispiece to the pamphlet and appears again in the body of the text. The engraving depicts a variety of scenes related to the witches' confessions. These include a vivid portrayal of a 'tempest-tost' vessel, barely surviving a severe battering from winds and waves. The cameo alongside this shows a line of four female figures, the first of whom is about to add an ingredient (presumably the toad's venom) to a concoction simmering in a cauldron suspended above a blazing log fire. This could have provided the initial stimulus for the spell-making sequence in IV.i. Another scene shows the devil addressing a group of women from a crude pulpit. A seated male figure is recording the scene and this is Fian, who confessed that he acted as 'clarke' at their assemblies 'and that he wrote for them such matters as the Divell still pleased to commaund him'. The depiction of a diabolic figure apparently emerging from a circular vessel might have inspired the sequence of demonic apparitions which presumably rise from the cauldron in IV.i. Beside this is portrayed a well-dressed male figure in a recumbent pose, leaning on one elbow. This probably represents one of the alleged victims of Barbara Napier, who was indicted 'for bewitching to death Archibalde, last Earle of Angus, who languished to death by witchcraft'. The person in the woodcut is thus wasting away in a similar manner to the 'master o' th' Tiger'.

There are many other aspects of the Weird Sisters that align them with contemporary witchcraft beliefs. Amongst these are the possession of animal familiars and the ability to fly through fogs and storms of their own making, as indicated in I.i; their sudden disappearance in I.iii; and the incantation sequence, with the gruesome spell-making items in IV.i. Thus it seems clear that many current concepts of witchcraft, as it was thought to be practised by mortals, are present in Shakespeare's portrayal of the Weird Sisters. Nevertheless, it is undeniable that they possess qualities or at the very least project an aura which transcends the merely human. Perhaps the blend of mortal and supernatural elements was suggested by the indecisiveness of Holinshed's account but the ambiguity inherent in their

43

natures, far from being a defect, is a positive virtue in dramatic terms.

The air of mystery surrounding the Sisters is an integral part of the illusion which is a central theme of a work where 'nothing is but what is not'. In considering the Weird Sisters it is perhaps wise to bear in mind Keats's concept of 'negative capability' whereby 'man is capable of being in uncertainties, mysteries, doubts, without any irritable reaching after fact and reason'. The dramatic effectiveness of the indeterminate nature of the Sisters can be seen by a comparison with such straightforward, mortal witches as Maudlin in Jonson's *The Sad Shepherd* or the central figure in *The Witch of Edmonton*. They would not have prompted the questions voiced by Banquo and shared by the audience:

> Live you, or are you aught
> That man may question? . . .
>    I' th' name of truth,
> Are ye fantastical, or that indeed
> Which outwardly ye show?             [I.iii. 42–54]

Nor would they have caused Macbeth to ponder the true import of their 'supernatural soliciting', in a manner similar to Hamlet's demand of his father's ghost, 'Be thou a spirit of health or goblin damn'd?' (I.iv.40). It is significant that the Sisters are at their least potent, dramatically, in III.v and the interpolated passages in IV.i, when they are represented as mortals, indulging in trivial songs and dances but lacking the enigmatic aura which elsewhere surrounds their words and actions. Just as in *A Midsummer-Night's Dream* Shakespeare revolutionised the centuries-old view of fairies and transformed the demonic spirit Robin Goodfellow into a 'knavish sprite', so in the Weird Sisters he produced a unique creation, founded on but transcending ancient and contemporary beliefs of witchcraft and the supernatural.

### Notes to Chapter 3

*1*   H. N. Paul in *The Royal Play of Macbeth* (p. 225) argues that 'weyward' has no fatalistic connotations and that it is used rather in the sense of wayward or wilful. However, this does not take account of Shakespeare's indebtedness to Holinshed or to the fact that on the one occasion that the word is clearly used in this sense, in Hecate's description of Macbeth in III.v.11, it is spelt in the First Folio as 'wayward'.

*2*   Quoted in Geoffrey Bullough, *Narrative and Dramatic Sources of Shakespeare*, vol. 7 (1973), pp. 494–5.

*3*   Quoted in Bullough, p. 476.

*4*   The parallels are compounded by the fact that Renaissance scholars believed that the oracles of Delphi and elsewhere were animated by demonic spirits akin to the Apparitions that address Macbeth in IV.i. (See R. H. West, *The Invisible World* (1939), pp. 31–2).

5    See Bullough, pp. 451–5 and Kenneth Muir, *The Sources of Shakespeare*, (1977), pp. 212–14.

6    *Shakespeare's Philosophical Patterns*, pp. 31ff.

7    Scot, *Discoverie*, book I, chapter iii; and Samuel Harsnett, *A Declaration of Egregious Popishe Impostures*, p. 136. Coleridge felt that the Sisters bore 'a sufficient resemblance to the creatures of vulgar prejudice to act immediately on the audience'.

8    They also, as Banquo describes them, have little in common with the three stately and decorous quasi-sibyllae who greeted King James on his visit to Oxford in 1605—an episode which some scholars see as a possible source for this scene. (See Paul, pp. 17–22, and Bullough, pp. 470–2.)

9    The phrase is echoed in *King Lear*, III.iv.129, and is described thus in *Ray's North-Country Words* (1691): 'Rynte, by your leave, stand handsomly; as 'Rynt you, witch,' quoth Bessie Locket to her mother; Proverb: Cheshire.'

10   James I in *Daemonologie* states that witches meet in covens to give 'account of their horrible and detestable proceedings past'.

11   In this discussion no account is taken of the Hecate scene (III.v) or the short sequences in IV.i (ll. 39–43 and 125–32) which are generally regarded as additions to the original text. Consideration of their part in the stage history of *Macbeth* will be found in Chapter Ten.

12   *Newes From Scotland*, ed. G. B. Harrison (1929).

13   Paul argues that the first performance of *Macbeth* was at Hampton Court on 7 August 1606 and that it was written specially to coincide with the visit of James's brother-in-law, Christian IV of Denmark. Whether or not this was the case, it is probable that the play was written with royal patronage in mind.

14   Quoted in Murray, *The Witch-Cult in Western Europe*, p. 53.

15   Holinshed in *Chronicles of Scotland* describes how King Duff, one of Duncan's predecessors, was subjected to a witchcraft conspiracy that involved 'rosting upon a woodden broch [spit] an image of wax at the fier, resembling in each feature the kings person' (Bullough, p. 481). James I in *Daemonologie* describes the demonic technique of 'wasting': 'To some others ... hee teacheth, how to make Pictures of waxe or clay: That by rosting thereof, the persones that they beare the name of, may be continuallie melted or dryed awaie by continuall sicknesse'.

16   Murray, *Witch-Cult*, p. 56. Miss Murray records how, following the failure of the conspiracy, Bothwell went into exile and died in poverty in Naples (pp. 55–9).

# CHAPTER 4

# MURD'RING MINISTERS

## THE DEMONOLOGY OF *MACBETH*

> *Lady Macbeth:* **Come to my woman's breasts,**
> **And take my milk for gall, you murd'ring ministers,**
> **Wherever in your sightless substances**
> **You wait on nature's mischief.**
>
> [*Macbeth*, I.v.44–7]

## I

In developing his argument that the Weird Sisters are demonic spirits in human form, W. C. Curry in *Shakespeare's Philosophical Patterns* argues that Shakespeare chose to represent the demons as witches rather than devils because the latter's portrayals on the contemporary stage had degenerated into mere comic portrayals suggesting little of 'the terror and sublimity of a metaphysical world of evil'. Whilst this is largely true, he then makes the far less tenable assertion that in their dramatic representations 'witches had acquired no such comic associations. They were essentially tragic beings who, for the sake of certain abnormal powers, had sold themselves to the devil' (pp. 60–1). Although this might have been true of witches in general, the witch as she was portrayed on the Elizabethan stage was, as was noted in Chapter Two, rarely a tragic figure.

Lyly's Mother Bombie, for example, is a harmless eccentric, a subject for jest rather than fear. Falstaff's disguising himself as Mother Prat in *The Merry Wives of Windsor* is also an occasion for knock-about comedy rather than the 'terror and sublimity' required by Curry. This farcical tradition was maintained in the early Jacobean period with the portrayal of such an innocuous figure as Heywood's Wise Woman of Hogsdon (*c.* 1604) who is a blend of midwife and fortune-teller rather than a practitioner of malign deeds. In fact, it was later in the Jacobean period that the more sombre aspects of witchcraft came into prominence in the theatrical portrayals, with *Macbeth* heralding this development rather than being part of an established tradition.

In the modern theatre it is often difficult to achieve the desired effect in the presentation of the Weird Sisters, with the ludicrous replacing the awe that their appearance and actions should inspire. A. P. Rossiter in *Angel With Horns* (1961) suggests that the desired effect might best be achieved today by the characters wearing African tribal masks. Orson Welles, in his 'voodoo' production of the play in 1936, portrayed the Sisters as witch-doctors, an experiment that failed to impress the critics. On the other hand, in the Zulu version of the Macbeth story, *Umabatha*, by the South African playwright Welcome Msombi, which was staged at the Aldwych Theatre, London, in 1972, the Sisters are transformed with striking effect into tribal sorceresses.

Despite the problems of staging the witchcraft scenes effectively—problems that are more apparent today than in Shakespeare's time—the Weird Sisters are effective and meaningful characters in their own right. Their portrayal as flesh and blood creatures, exhibiting the qualities of human witches (whatever their true natures), reacting on each other and on other persons, marks a significant dramaturgical advance. The representation in *Doctor Faustus* of the diabolic spirit Mephistophilis in human form, subject to human passions, is to some extent comparable but the Sisters take on a wider role, fulfilling the same functions as such phenomena as the dreams, omens and ghosts of earlier Shakespearean drama.

The ambiguity of their utterances is similar to the prophetic dreams of Calpurnia and Clarence. This is seen particularly in the illusory prophecies of the Apparitions which the Sisters conjure up for Macbeth; misinterpretation is as fatal for him as it was for Clarence or Caesar. In this respect dramatic action replaces cumbersome narrative for, whilst dreams have to be recounted after the event, we actually see and hear the Apparitions as they deliver their fateful messages. Similarly, the rituals of the augurers in *Julius Caesar* and the responses of the oracle of Apollo in *The Winter's Tale* are merely reported at second hand whereas the rites and prophecies of the Sisters are performed and spoken on stage.

47

Moreover, whilst the supernatural phenomena of the earlier plays generally make only a single appearance—if they are represented on stage at all—the Weird Sisters appear on three occasions, excluding the Hecate scene, and the audience is continually reminded of their existence, even when they are absent from the stage. Macbeth's letter to his wife in I.v. recounts his meeting with them and reinforces the impression that 'they have more in them than mortal knowledge' (ll.3–4). The scene opens with Lady Macbeth already reading the letter and there is no need to define the 'They' of the opening words. On the night of Duncan's murder Banquo informs Macbeth that he 'dreamt last night of the three Weird Sisters' (II.i.20) and Macbeth's reply, 'I think not of them', deceives neither Banquo nor the audience. Macbeth's immediate reaction to the appearance of Banquo's ghost is to seek out the Weird Sisters 'to know / By the worst means the worst' (III.iv.134–5) and almost his final words are to curse the 'juggling fiends' who have contributed so much to his destruction.

The Sisters also take over some of the roles previously played by the—dramatically speaking—one-dimensional ghosts. In particular, their first encounter with Macbeth is reminiscent of Hamlet's first meeting with the ghost of his father. The reactions are similar in that neither is at first sure whether the 'supernatural soliciting' is for his good or ill fortune and in both cases the meetings help to crystallise thoughts and feelings already harboured by the protagonists. Shakespeare of course continues to make use in *Macbeth* of the conventional ghost device to suggest guilt or impending nemesis and Banquo's ghost in this respect is similar to those that haunt Brutus and Richard III. There is, however, one important difference in that the ghost, together with all the other supernatural phenomena in *Macbeth*, including such portents as the 'air-drawn dagger' and the unnatural disturbances on the night of Duncan's murder, can be closely related to the Weird Sisters and their diabolic powers, whilst similar elements in *Julius Caesar*, for example, do not have this unifying quality.

Shakespeare's dramaturgic use of ghosts also shows an advance at about this time in his portrayal of the spirit of Hamlet's father, where the ghost appears on two crucial occasions and its presence is apparent throughout the whole play, from the opening scene onwards. Similarly, despite the comparative brevity of their actual appearances, the influence of the Weird Sisters is all-pervasive. Their short opening scene establishes the aura of evil and deception which is to dominate the whole play and their brief interchange before Macbeth's arrival in I.iii introduces themes which are to be reflected and developed in the principal plot. They recount exploits of killing and vengeance, with the sufferings of the ill-fated sailor anticipating those of Macbeth and his wife. They, like the sailor, will be bereft of sleep and Macbeth's soul, like the seaman's bark, is to be 'tempest-tost' and finally 'wracked' under their malign influence.

## II

Although it is difficult to determine the precise extent of the power of the Weird Sisters over Macbeth's destiny, he is closely linked with them from the outset. The opening scene makes clear that the Sisters' next meeting will be for the express purpose of encountering Macbeth. In I.ii the 'bleeding Captain' reveals that Banquo has played almost as prominent a part as Macbeth in the battle in which the Sisters display such interest and Duncan's two 'captains' are returning together from the conflict, but it is clear that the Sisters' main business is with Macbeth.

Just as the ghost in Hamlet will speak only to his son, so the Sisters refuse to answer Banquo's questions, merely putting their fingers to their lips. They do not speak until Macbeth addresses them and even then, significantly in view of their enigmatic natures, they ignore his question, 'What are you?', and proceed with their fateful salutations. Another link between Macbeth and the Sisters is the frequently noted echo of their chant at the end of I.i in his first words: 'So foul and fair a day I have not seen' (I.iii.38). A further connection, not generally recognised, is suggested in Ross's description of Macbeth in I.ii as 'Bellona's Bridegroom'. As well as the obvious comparison with Mars, a secondary implication may lie in the fact that Bellona was equated by the Saxons with the 'walcyries', who were in turn regarded as murderous, flying witches, the terms being interchangeable.[1]

Thus Macbeth, in various ways, is linked with the Weird Sisters from the beginning of the play, although this does not necessarily indicate that they exercise full control over his destiny. Their strictly limited powers over the fate of the sailor, whereby 'Though his bark cannot be lost / Yet it shall be tempest-tost' (I.iii.24–5), suggest that in a similar manner their control over Macbeth is circumscribed. They can expose him to temptations but, ultimately, if his soul (the 'bark') is lost it will be by his own doing.

Throughout the play Macbeth is seen as a man prepared to act rather than passively await his destiny. In the account of the battle in I.ii he is described as 'disdaining fortune', and in contemplating the murder of Duncan he rejects the alternative means for the fulfilment of the Sisters' prophecy, to which he briefly pays lip-service: 'If chance will have me King, why, Chance may crown me, / Without my stir' (I.iii 143–4). As the play progresses his defiance of fate increases. In the cavern scene (IV.i) he attempts to 'take a bond of Fate', whereby he will make his own 'assurance double sure' by compelling destiny to fulfil its promises made to him. To this end, he decides to kill Macduff despite the Apparitions' apparently reassuring utterances. But when Birnam Wood does come to Dunsinane Macbeth renews his battle with the Fates with the defiant cry: 'Blow, wind, come, wrack; / At least we'll die with harness on our back' (V.v.51–2) —words strongly reminiscent of the sufferings of the ill-fated and literally storm-tossed mariner of I.iii.

Despite the apparent victory of Fate, Macbeth's downfall seems to be due to inherent weaknesses rather to any outside influences, whether human or supernatural. As many critics have pointed out, the Sisters' first greetings to Macbeth are completely non-committal. It is he who reacts to their prophecy that he shall be 'king hereafter' by immediately contemplating the murder (or murders) necessary to bring this about. As Bradley states in *Shakespearean Tragedy* (1904): 'The prophecies of the Witches are presented simply as dangerous circumstances with which Macbeth has to deal' (p. 343). The fact that Macbeth reacts as he does to the 'supernatural soliciting' (and, as Bradley points out, the Sisters do not solicit but merely announce facts) suggests that they have done well in singling him out for their attentions. If Curry is right and they are demons in human form—'the instruments of darkness', as Banquo calls them—they are behaving here in a comparable manner to Mephistophilis in *Doctor Faustus* and the Black Dog in *The Witch of Edmonton*, and they might also be equated with the 'Spirits / That tend on mortal thoughts' whom Lady Macbeth invokes in I.v. They have seen in Macbeth a being whose potential for evil marks him out as a likely victim who needs but the barest encouragement to set his soul at risk. In uttering their greetings the Sisters are sowing the 'seeds of time' and, in a reversal of the Parable of the Sower, they know that in Macbeth's case the seed will fall on fertile ground; the 'grain will grow' within him and bring about his damnation.

Whatever might be thought of Banquo's later behaviour, his reaction to the prophecies that he receives from the Sisters is in marked contrast to his companion's. It is true that they do not predict such immediate advancement as is contained in their words to Macbeth but, as Hunter notes in the New Penguin *Macbeth* (1967), 'Banquo recognises the evil and sees it as something threatening, but outside himself' (p. 12). Although many critics, including Bradley and Muir, have suspected Banquo of, at the very least, tacit acceptance of Macbeth's murder of Duncan, it is difficult to believe that Shakespeare would have portrayed James I's reputed ancestor in such a manner. He certainly does not adopt Holinshed's depiction of Banquo as Macbeth's accomplice and the most that can be said is that Banquo appears to keep to himself the suspicions that he must have had and which he in fact voices in the soliloquy at the beginning of Act III. He has presumably attended the coronation ceremony but this would appear prudent, especially when one sees the reaction provoked by Macduff's ill-advised gesture in remaining absent.

It is possible to see in Banquo's apparent acquiescence an extreme instance of the precept of Divine Right, which condemned rebellion even against tyrants. In *Richard II* York behaves in this fashion, betraying his son Aumerle's revolt to the newly crowned Henry IV. However, against this, James I himself had declared that allegiance to the king should extend 'to their lawfull heires and posterity' and by this token Banquo should have confronted the usurper and championed Malcolm.[2]

If Banquo's character appears ambivalent, this is in line with the other 'good' persons in the play—Malcolm and Macduff for example—whose words and actions are far from unflawed. Nevertheless, Macbeth certainly acknowledges the contrast between himself and Banquo's 'royalty of nature'. The latter's affirmation after the discovery of Duncan's murder, uttered mainly for Macbeth's benefit—'In the great hand of God I stand'—is particularly apt, for Macbeth on one level is identifiable with Antichrist in the basic Good/Evil conflict of the play. Banquo's avowal is to some extent reminiscent of the admission by Fian and his North Berwick witches that James I was ultimately immune from their diabolic machinations because 'Il est un home [*sic*] de Dieu'.[3]

Nevertheless, Banquo is not entirely untouched by his contact with the Sisters and something of their evil possibly contaminates his mind. He dreams of them and prays: 'Merciful powers / Restrain in me the cursed thoughts that nature / Gives way to in repose!' (II.i.7–9). These 'cursed thoughts' may be suspicions of Macbeth or, more likely in view of his evocation of the 'merciful powers', temptations on his own behalf. As Curry points out in *Shakespeare's Philosophical Patterns*, he is importuning here 'precisely that order of angels which God, in his providence, has deputed to be concerned especially with the restraint and coercion of demons' (p. 81). It is ironic that Macbeth later plans the murder of Banquo partly to free himself from 'the affliction of these terrible dreams / That shake us nightly' (III.ii.,18–19). Banquo's appeal to Christian spirits is in stark contrast to Macbeth's image in II.i of witchcraft presenting 'Pale Hecate's offerings' (l. 52), and even more to Lady Macbeth's awesome prayer to the demonic spirits in I.v.37–51.

She is invoking here demons either similar to or identical with those which seek to possess Macbeth's mind, the essential difference being that Macbeth is accosted by such spirits—or their agents—who see in him a potential victim, whilst Lady Macbeth, actively and apparently in full awareness of the consequences, summons them herself. In this speech she commits herself, body and soul, to the blackest rites of witchcraft. Her desire that the devilish spirits should unsex her is generally seen as part of her effort to expel all feminine weakness from her mind, but even more than this might be involved here. Diabolical spirits, by their very natures, were sexless. They could take on external appearances of men or women but, as Cornelius Agrippa declared in *Three Books of Occult Philosophy*, 'there is none of the Demons ... is to be supposed male or female, seeing this difference of sex belongs to compounds, but the bodies of Demons are simple' (pp. 403–4).

Is Lady Macbeth in fact, in her all-consuming desire to let nothing stand between herself and her ambitions, so determined to overcome the weaknesses of her own 'milk of human kindness' that she is here attempting to transform herself into such a spirit? Macbeth knowingly puts his soul at risk in order to achieve his aim and at this stage of the play Lady Macbeth's drive for power is even greater than her husband's. Malcolm's final verdict on her as a 'fiend-like queen' might be even more appropriate than he realises.

Moreover, the fact that in this diabolical invocation Lady Macbeth knowingly and willingly seeks the aid of evil spirits would be sufficient for such authorities as Bodin and Perkins to condemn her as a witch.[4] The speech is to some extent comparable with that of Joan la Pucelle in *Henry VI, Part One* (v.iii), when she summons her attendant spirits and, in order to achieve her desires, vows to sacrifice her 'body, soul and all'. Throughout the play, and particularly in this section, Lady Macbeth shows clear affinities with another witch-figure from literature—Seneca's Medea. Inga-Stina Ewbank, in *Shakespeare Survey, 19*, pp. 82–94, makes out a convincing case for the parallels between Lady Macbeth's speech and Medea's invocation to Hecate, and her desire to be unsexed before the murder of her own children.

It is certainly true that Lady Macbeth's commitment to evil is powerful enough to sustain her in the role she has set herself—to accomplish Duncan's murder—but as the play progresses the humanity she has sought to repress reasserts itself. Her entreaty is granted in strictly limited terms, for she prays merely that she will not be swayed from her 'fell purpose' and that there will be no intervention of natural feelings 'between th' effect and it', that is, Duncan's death. Unlike her husband, she seems incapable of looking beyond the actual deed to its inevitable consequences, one of which is that her 'access and passage to remorse' will be reopened, liberating emotions which will culminate in her sleep-walking and suicide.

These events form the climax of her disillusionment and despair, and possibly of her guilt at what she has done—to her husband if not to others. But it is also possible to see in the sleep-walking episode (V.i.) evidence that she is possessed by the demon Nightmare. This malign spirit was traditionally thought to oppress men in their sleep and it has affinities with Queen Mab, whose nocturnal activities are described by Mercutio in *Romeo and Juliet*, I.iv. The spirit had close associations with witchcraft. It is included in Scot's famous list of terrifying demons in *The Discoverie of Witchcraft* (book VII, chapter xv), and in Middleton's *The Witch* Hecate's son Firestone goes on nocturnal expeditions with the Nightmare. As with his treatment of the Weird Sisters, Shakespeare seems to be deliberately inexplicit in his treatment of Lady Macbeth's sleep-walking but the Doctor's conclusion that 'More needs she the divine than the physician' (V.i.72) clearly implies the need for the exorcism of evil spirits.

However, her behaviour is not wholly consistent with one actively possessed, even in the latter part of the play. This is particularly evident in the Banquet Scene (III.iv) where her self-control reasserts itself, if only through a tremendous effort of will which leaves her exhausted and where, as Muir suggests in the New Arden *Macbeth*, 'Satan would seem to be divided against himself, on the one hand driving Macbeth to exhibit his guilt, and on the other enabling Lady Macbeth to shield him' (p. lxxi). Nevertheless, she would appear to be particularly vulnerable to 'thick-coming fancies' at night. During her sleep-walking we learn that she 'has light by her continually', and a particularly effective dimension of irony is added if it is felt that she is indeed being tormented by the diabolic Nightmare—the nocturnal order of the very demons which she has herself summoned to her body and which Macbeth calls to his aid in the form of 'night's black agents'. In her invocation she refers specifically to such spirits:

> Come, thick night,
> And pall thee in the dunnest smoke of Hell,
> That my keen knife see not the wound it makes,
> Nor heaven peep through the blanket of the dark,
> To cry 'Hold, hold!'                                   [I.v.47–51]

The blanket of night, far from offering this security of darkness, has become a source of smothering dreams which cannot be shaken off.

53

Macbeth's sleeplessness is of course one element in his own mental disintegration and when he speaks of the 'affliction of these terrible dreams / That shake us nightly' (III.ii.18–19) it is arguable that he too is being racked by the devilish Nightmare, which has been raised by the Weird Sisters as one of their means of driving him to destruction. They seem to have this power, for the First Witch has earlier vowed that as part of her vegeance on the sailor 'Sleep shall neither night nor day / Hang upon his penthouse lid' (I.iii.19–20). As was suggested previously, Banquo's 'cursed thoughts that nature / Gives way to in repose' might well be of the type induced specifically by the Nightmare spirit, and the demon might also have been present at the very moment of Duncan's murder, for Donalbain and his companion in the second chamber both seem to sense its evil influence: 'There's one did laugh in's sleep, and one cried 'Murder!' / That they did wake each other' (II.ii.22–3). It is significant that before returning to sleep they say their prayers and ask God's blessing, as if to exorcise devilish spirits from their minds, and equally significant that Macbeth is unable to join in their prayer, even though he 'had most need of blessing'. Just as it was believed that a person possessed by evil spirits could not utter the name of God or recite the Lord's Prayer, so Macbeth finds that even the single word 'Amen' sticks in his throat.

His inability to sleep is heralded by the voice he hears immediately after this proclaiming:

> 'Sleep no more;
> Macbeth does murder sleep . . .
> Glamis hath murder'd sleep; and therefore Cawdor
> Shall sleep no more—Macbeth shall sleep no more.'       [II.ii.35–43]

The triple nomenclature is reminiscent of the Weird Sisters' greetings to Macbeth in I.iii and according to contemporary belief they would have been quite capable of creating such an effect as this disembodied voice as a prelude to the mental torments they will subsequently inflict on Macbeth. On the other hand, the voice can be regarded as no more than a hallucination springing from Macbeth's over-wrought mental state, and his ensuing sleeplessness can be seen as the inevitable psychosomatic reaction to such an experience. It is not made clear whether Lady Macbeth hears the voice or not. She asks Macbeth on his return from Duncan's room, 'Did you not speak?' which implies that she has heard a voice in addition to the owl's scream and the cricket's cry. However, this might have been Donalbain's cry of 'Murder' rather than any metaphysical utterance.

Such optional explanations—with rational or supernatural bases—can also be applied to the other apparently unnatural phenomena which Macbeth experiences. For some critics, such as Coleridge and Bradley, and also apparently for Lady Macbeth herself, the visions of the 'air-drawn dagger' and the ghost of Banquo are purely subjective and are evidence of Macbeth's vivid imagination, over-wrought mind or guilty conscience. This viewpoint is also reflected in the arguments of scholars adopting a neo-Freudian approach to Macbeth's mental state. Thus, for Marjorie Garber, in *Dream in Shakespeare: from Metaphor to Metamorphosis* (1974), the dagger is 'a self-made omen, a sign unambiguously produced by the mind of the man who interprets it' (p. 110).

On the other hand, for such critics as Curry, there is no doubt that all the phenomena have diabolic origins and are evidence of Macbeth's increasing possession by malign forces. For example, Curry declares that the dagger 'is an hallucination caused immediately, indeed, by disturbed bodily humours and spirits, but ultimately by demonic powers, who have so controlled and manipulated these bodily forces to produce the effect they desire' (p. 84). It is certainly true that the phenomena grow in intensity as the play progresses and as Macbeth becomes increasingly enmeshed in the Witches' toils. He remains calm, at least during his soliloquy, throughout the first such experience, attempting to interpret and rationalise the spectacle of the dagger. He reacts far less calmly to the voice crying 'Sleep no more' and responds with physical violence to the third vision—that of Banquo's ghost. The apparitions culminate in those raised by the Sisters in the cavern (IV.i) and here they reach a climax of awesome intensity which is followed by Macbeth's most heinous crime—the murder of Macduff's family. The two earlier phenomena of the dagger and the ghost had stimulated Macbeth to the murder of Duncan and the resolve to seek out the Sisters—actions which had also hastened his progress towards self-destruction.

There can be no doubt that the Sisters create the final group of Apparitions. They raise them from their cauldron and describe them as 'our masters', that is, diabolic spirits of a higher order than themselves in the demonic hierarchy. They also summon the ghost of Banquo in this scene and it appears 'blood-boltered' in the same manner as on its previous manifestation. If the Sisters are capable of raising these spirits, there is no reason why they cannot have been responsible for the other phenomena. Certainly, according to contemporary demonology, all of the 'sights' were capable of this interpretation. James I, for example, wrote in his *Daemonologie* that witches 'can make spirits, either to follow and trouble persons, or haunt certaine houses' (book II). The fact that Banquo's ghost

55

appears only to Macbeth is in accord with James's own explanation of this popular belief, a tradition which Shakespeare also employs in *Hamlet*, III.iv. James declared:

> For if the Devil may forme what kinde of impressions he pleases in the ayre ... why may he not far easier thicken and obscure so that the aire that is next about them by contracting it strait together, that the beames of any other man's eyes cannot perce thorow the same to see them.                                    [book II]

However, as has been indicated previously, all of these phenomena (and such additional apparently unnatural occurrences as the sights and sounds observed during the night of Duncan's murder) are equally capable of rational interpretation. It is perhaps as ill-advised to seek for one single explanation here as it is in attempting to define the Weird Sisters, for the apparently deliberate ambiguity of the portrayal of the latter is in fact reinforced by the undefined nature of the prodigies with which they are associated.

## III

To whatever degree of diabolic possession Macbeth ultimately succumbs, his acceptance of the powers of witchcraft is a far slower process than that of Lady Macbeth who, as we have seen, invokes and submits herself to complete demonic possession on her first appearance in the play. Whilst she attempts to eradicate from herself all humane feelings, Macbeth on at least two occasions of extreme crisis affirms his continuing humanity. When his wife taunts him with cowardice for deciding against Duncan's murder he retorts: 'I dare do all that may become a man; / Who dares do more is none' (I.vii.46–7). He responds to her frantic attempts to rally him when he is confronted by Banquo's ghost and is 'quite unmann'd in folly' in similar vein, declaring, 'What man dare, I dare' (III.iv.99). He proclaims that he is a man, retaining human emotions, 'Ay, and a bold one that dare look on that / Which might appal the devil' (III.iv.59–60). Despite this assertion, the ghost's appearance leads him to seek a second meeting with the Weird Sisters, and a comparison of his behaviour during his two encounters with them gives a clear picture of his spiritual degeneration through the course of the play.

The Weird Sisters themselves imply a distinct change in Macbeth by their words immediately before the two meetings. Prior to the first, his approach is heralded by the Third Witch, in strictly factual, non-committal terms: 'A drum, a drum! / Macbeth doth come' (I.iii.30–1). In Act IV his arrival is greeted by the far more sinister: 'By the pricking of my thumbs, / Something wicked this way comes' (IV.i.44–5). Macbeth has become an anonymous 'thing' surrounded by an aura of evil, an effect which is in line with his wider loss of personal identity in the latter stages of the play, when he is increasingly referred to merely as 'the tyrant'.

The second meeting is throughout a far more overtly evil occasion than the first. Before the earlier encounter the Weird Sisters indulge in an intricate spell-making dance built around the magical number three and concluding with the cry that 'the charm's wound up'. At this stage of the play it is not absolutely clear whether this charm is for Macbeth's good or ill, but there is no such doubt about the cauldron sequence which precedes Macbeth's arrival in Act IV. The Sisters are concocting 'a charm of powerful trouble' and creating a spell so evil in its implications that it must remain 'a deed without a name'. The three noncommittal if in part prophetic greetings of the first meeting are paralleled by the three demonic Apparitions, uttering their illusory messages in the second encounter.

Similarly, Macbeth, in his words and actions, exhibits significant changes in his attitude to the Sisters in the two scenes. At the first meeting he is with Banquo and the Sisters have arranged the encounter. On the second occasion he seeks them out, alone. The Sisters know of his coming and are prepared but he, likewise, is ready for this meeting and has come with questions to which he demands answers. On the heath his first words, 'Speak if you can', show that he is unsure of the nature of the creatures that have accosted him and his uncertainty is underlined by the questions he puts to them:

> What are you? . . .
> Say from whence
> You owe this strange intelligence, or why
> Upon this blasted heath you stop our way
> With such prophetic greeting?

[I.iii.47–77]

By the time of the second meeting he has no doubts as to their diabolic natures, as his initial greeting shows: 'How now, you secret, black, and midnight hags!' (IV.i.47). Although he is still not certain of the precise nature of their occult powers—'I conjure you by that which you profess— / Howe'er you come to know it' (IV.i.50–1)—he has had ample evidence of their prophetic powers since their first meeting and of the fact that they have 'more in them than mortal knowledge' (I.v.3). 'Conjure' here has the sense of 'command' or 'adjure' but Macbeth's use of the term at this moment suggests his awareness of the demonic qualities of the creatures

57

5      'I conjure you by that which you profess—
        Howe'er you come to know it—answer me.'
      Ian McKellen as Macbeth, with Susan Dury, Judith Harte and Marie Kean
      as the Weird Sisters, in Trevor Nunn's studio production of *Macbeth* for the
      Royal Shakespeare Company in 1976.

with whom he is dealing. Ironically, his speech is a prelude to the conjuration of the diabolic Apparitions, who are summoned to respond to Macbeth's questions. Moreover, he is under no illusion that the Sisters intend anything but harm to him. After the first encounter he ponders, 'This supernatural soliciting / Cannot be ill; cannot be good' (I.ii.130–1), but he now has no such doubts.

Despite this, he is determined to learn 'by the worst means the worst'. Marjorie Garber, in *Dream in Shakespeare*, sees his visit to the witches' cavern as 'the tragic concomitant of the journey to the wood in the comedies' (p. 115). It is true that Macbeth, like the characters in the lighter plays, both learns and reveals much of himself and his true nature during this scene, and this serves to confirm the impression which has already been created whereby he can be equated with Antichrist. The pride and 'vaulting ambition' which drive him to kill the 'gracious' and divinely appointed Duncan are reminiscent of Lucifer's revolt in Heaven, whilst the Porter scene (II.iii) has clear affinities with the mediaeval *Harrowing of Hell* plays, the role of Satan being transferred to Macbeth.[5]

Macbeth's consultation of the Sisters has analogies with Saul's visit to the Witch of Endor, as it is described in 1 Samuel 28. Saul, like Macbeth, is a ruler who has fallen from grace and his visit to the witch was seen by many of Shakespeare's contemporaries as an act of folly leading to inevitable damnation. James I in *Basilicon Doron* declared: 'Consult therefore with no Necromancier nor false Prophet upon the successe of your warres; remembering on king Saules miserable end: but keepe your hand clene of all suth-sayers, according to the command in the Lawe of God dilated by Jeremie' (p. 99).

The historical Witch of Endor seems to have been some sort of oracular figure, acting as a medium to transmit spiritual messages, but by the Renaissance period she was firmly equated with conventional witchcraft. A painting of the scene by the Netherlands artist Jacob von Amsterdam,

6  A detail from *King Saul with the Witch of Endor* by Jacob von Amsterdam, painted in 1526. The work portrays the witch as a sorceress, complete with many of the trappings of the Classical witch-figure.

dated 1526, depicts her as a blend of witch and sorceress in the Classical tradition. She is portrayed as a hag attended by an aged crone and a pan-like creature, together with a familiar spirit in the form of an owl. A cauldron simmers by her side and she is drawing a magic circle with her enchantress's wand. Although there are no comparable English paintings from this period, it is clear that she was viewed in a similar manner; the Authorised Version of the Bible, printed in 1611, has a running-title for the episode stating that 'Saul consulteth a witch'.

The Weird Sisters' summoning of the Apparitions is similar to the calling up of the spirit of Samuel. The Apparitions are demonic spirits and many scholars, including James I, believed that the spirit of Samuel was the devil himself. James argued that the devil, when summoned by necromancy, 'will oblishe himselfe, to enter in a dead bodie, and there out to give such answers of the event of battels, of maters concerning the estate of commonwelths, and such like other great questions' (*Daemonologie*, Book I). It is for knowledge of such momentous matters that Macbeth seeks out the Weird Sisters.

The ambiguity of the Apparitions' advice to Macbeth is similar to the deceptive nature of the counsel given to Saul. Scot, in *The Discoverie of Witchcraft*, expresses profound scepticism of her supposedly prophetic powers. He compares her with Mother Bungie, the well-known contemporary fortune-teller, and with the so-called 'Pythoness of Westwell', whose trickery had recently been exposed and who had confessed that her apparently spiritual utterances had been produced by means of 'right Ventriloquie' (*Discoverie*, book VII, chapter xiii). He roundly condemns her as 'a verie cousener ... a cousening queane, that taketh upon hir to doo all things, and can doo nothing but beguile men' (book VIII, chapter ii). He also states that 'it is the divels condition, to allure the people unto wickednes, and not in this sort to admonish, warne, and rebuke them for evill' (book VII, chapter xiii). This is precisely the function of the Apparitions, whose role it is to draw Macbeth 'on to his confusion'. Scot also compares the Witch of Endor to 'juglers (which be inferior conjurors)' (book VII, chapter xii) and Macbeth realises too late that he, like Saul, has been the victim of 'juggling fiends'.

The immediately ensuing scenes maintain the equation of Macbeth with anti-Christian forces. The killing of Lady Macduff and her children is reminiscent of Herod's destruction of the Innocents, another recurring theme of the Mystery Play Cycles.[6] The scene at the English court (IV.iii) reinforces this impression still further. Ross's account of the condition of Scotland under Macbeth suggests that the Hell facetiously invoked by the drunken Porter has become a reality. He describes the country as a land 'where sighs, and groans, and shrieks, that rent the air, / Are made, not mark'd; where violent sorrow seems / A modern ecstasy' (ll. 168–70). This state of misrule is implicitly contrasted with the condition of England under the saintly King Edward. The exchange between Malcolm and the Doctor concerning the 'most miraculous work in this good king' (l. 147) in curing the king's evil contains a welter of references to the monarch's 'sanctity' and 'healing benediction', his 'heavenly gift of prophecy' and it concludes with the affirmation that 'sundry blessings hang about his throne / That speak him full of grace' (ll. 158–9). The king's divinely endowed prophetic powers contrast with the diabolic utterances of the Apparitions upon which Macbeth is at this moment relying and the whole episode underlines the falseness of his position.

It was popularly believed that the monarch's ability to heal by touch was an innate spiritual force, possessed only by a legitimate ruler. Cures attributed to Elizabeth I were cited as proof that the Papal Bull of Excommunication had been ineffectual and James I, despite his personal distrust of what he considered a superstitious rite, was persuaded to continue with the tradition to consolidate his royal position. Macbeth's usurping role is therefore stressed still further by the implied contrast drawn between himself and King Edward, an impression which is strengthened even more by the recurring imagery of the final stages of the play, where Malcolm and the English army are portrayed as healing forces, intent on purging Macbeth's disease-ridden kingdom.

In committing his initial crime of killing Duncan, who, like Edward, is equated with Christian forces, Macbeth is fully prepared to 'jump the life to come'. From henceforth he has no doubts that he has forfeited his soul and it is for this reason that the unspoken questions which the three Apparitions answer are all concerned with this life, with whether Macbeth will indeed 'still have judgment here'. His opening address to the Weird Sisters in IV.i (ll. 50–61) reveals the horrifying depths to which he has been reduced since the early stages of the play. In his obsessive craving for peace of mind, free from the terrible dreams that afflict him and to be secure from his mortal enemies, Macbeth has previously prayed, 'let the frame of things disjoint, both the worlds suffer' (III.ii.16). The frame is the universe, enveloping both the celestial and terrestrial worlds, and Macbeth, for temporary relief from his torment, is willing to see the universe destroyed. This is only eclipsed by the even more blasphemous vision with which Macbeth concludes his address to the Weird Sisters in the cavern. He recounts, in a series of vivid images, the destructive powers of witchcraft. For example,

61

his words, 'Though you untie the winds and let them fight / Against the churches' (IV.i.52–3) are in accord with the many accounts of the Devil's conflict with God taking the form of physical attacks on churches, either through storms or by means of the supposed actions of demons, in human or animal form.[7] He concludes with the demand:

> though the treasure
> Of nature's germens tumble all together,
> Even till destruction sicken—answer me
> To what I ask you. [IV.i.58–61]

As was noted above, Macbeth is here conjuring up a vision of the final triumph of Satan, a vision which is in stark contrast to the apocalyptic image, reminiscent of the Last Judgment, that he describes before the murder of Duncan, when the King's virtues:

> Will plead like angels, trumpet-tongu'd, against
> The deep damnation of his taking-off;
> And pity, like a naked new-born babe,
> Striding the blast, or heaven's cherubin hors'd
> Upon the sightless couriers of the air,
> Shall blow the horrid deed in every eye,
> That tears shall drown the wind.                    [I.vii.19–25]

By the time of the cavern scene Macbeth is 'in blood / Stepp'd in so far' that the image of the new-born babe, personifying Pity, has been replaced by the demonic apparition of 'a bloody child'. In the earlier vision the forces of good are triumphant but in the later speech it is the victory of Satan to which Macbeth looks forward. He seems to envisage the prospect with equanimity if not the delight which Dover Wilson detects[8] and if he is not actually possessed diabolically at this moment he is surely in an extreme state of 'deep damnation'.

Macbeth's curse later in the scene on all those who put their trust in the Sisters (l. 139) has particularly ironic point therefore and it is not surprising that immediately following this meeting with the Sisters he formulates his most despicable crime—the murder of Lady Macduff and her children. The initial horror and ensuing hesitancy with which he contemplates the killing of Duncan after his first encounter with the Sisters is replaced by the vow: 'From this moment / The very first firstlings of my heart shall be / The firstlings of my hand' (IV.i. 146–8). He is acting 'before this purpose cool' partly perhaps to escape the need for any further dealings with the Sisters. His cry, 'But no more sights' (l. 155) is answered for he is no longer pursued by supernatural phenomena. However, the Sisters have no need to reappear or to continue their torment by indirect means. The Apparitions' prophecies are seen to be illusory; Macbeth's trust in them cannot save him and almost his final words are to acknowledge the deception of the 'juggling fiends' whose paltering with him in a double sense has guided him to his destruction.

## Notes to Chapter 4

1    Kittredge, *Witchcraft in Old and New England*, p. 30.
2    See the New Arden *Macbeth*, pp. lxvii–lxviii.
3    Quoted in Murray, *Witch-Cult*, p. 54.
4    Jean Bodin, *La Demonomanie des Sorciers* I.i, p. 49, and William Perkins, *A Discourse of the Damned Art of Witchcraft*, V, p. 636. Leslie A. Fiedler in *The Stranger in Shakespeare* (1973) argues that 'the real witch of the play . . . is, of course, Lady Macbeth herself' (p. 60). This conclusion is based on the view that Lady Macbeth is an unnatural woman and a bad mother 'in the Jungian analysis of the witch archetype'.
5    J. B. Harcourt, 'I pray you, remember the porter' in *Shakespeare Quarterly*, 12 (1961), pp. 393–402; and Glynne Wickham, 'Hell-Castle and its door-keeper' in *Shakespeare Survey*, 19 (1966), pp. 68–74.
6    See Emrys Jones, *The Origins of Shakespeare* (1977), pp. 81–3.
7    Kittredge, pp. 155–8.
8    New Cambridge *Macbeth*, Introduction, p. lxiii.

# CHAPTER 5

# THE SCOURGE OF MEN AND LANDS

## NEO-CLASSICAL WITCHCRAFT IN *SOPHONISBA* AND *THE MASQUE OF QUEENES*

*Dame:* You Fiendes, and Furies ...

haue yo$^r$ selues disarmd,
And, to our powers, resign'd yo$^r$ Whipps, & brands,
When we went forth, the Scourge of Men, & Lands.

[*The Masque of Queenes*, ll. 218–23]

### I

Apart from Forman's account of the production at the Globe in 1611 there is no record of the early performances of *Macbeth* but its immediate success is suggested by its apparent influence on several subsequent works, especially Jonson's *The Masque of Queenes* (1609) and Middleton's *The Witch* (1609–17). The play's treatment of witchcraft as an overtly evil force and the portrayal of some of its more grotesque aspects might also have been the inspiration for the witchcraft elements in Marston's *Sophonisba*, where the witch Erictho indulges in even more repellent activities than do Shakespeare's Weird Sisters.

*Sophonisba* was first entered in the Stationers' Register on 17 March 1606 and was probably first performed at about this date by the Children of the Queen's Revels at the second Blackfriars Theatre. *Macbeth* cannot be dated so precisely although 1605–6 is usually considered the most likely period for its composition. Therefore it is possible that *Sophonisba* predates *Macbeth* and even inspired the latter. As Bradley points out in

*Shakespearean Tragedy* (p. 471), there are numerous verbal parallels between the two plays and Muir, in his Introduction to the new Arden *Macbeth* (pp. xxii–xxiv), argues that these suggest that Shakespeare was the debtor. On the other hand, whilst the witchcraft elements in *Macbeth* are fully integrated within the work and play an essential part in its overall structure, the witch Erictho appears only briefly in Marston's work and makes no significant contribution to the play's development. The two scenes in which she appears could even have been grafted on to the work prior to its first performance in an effort to compete with the current success at the rival Globe Theatre—*Macbeth*.

Whichever work influenced the other, it is certainly true that both plays give prominence to the less salubrious aspects of witchcraft. Erictho is similar to the Weird Sisters in that Marston, like Shakespeare, has modelled his creation on a mixture of Classical and contemporary witch beliefs and also his portrayal exhibits a blend of human and supernatural qualities. Erictho is closely based on the figure of the same name in Lucan's *Pharsalia* (book VI) and like her ancient forerunner many of her rituals are necrophiliac in character and involve the desecration of newly buried corpses. (Her defilement of the dead is paralleled by the threat made by Syphax to the virtuous Sophonisba in V.i that if she kills herself to escape him he will sexually abuse her corpse.) Erictho's practices are described in repulsive detail, in terms very close to those found in Lucan:

> but when she finds a corpse
> But newly graved, whose entrails are not turn'd
> To slimy filth, with greedy havock then
> She makes fierce spoil, and swells with wicked triumph
> To bury her lean knuckles in his eyes.
>
> [IV.i.113–17][1]

The Weird Sisters also desecrate the dead, using a pilot's thumb and a 'finger of birth-strangled babe' in their rites, and it will be recalled that the anti-witchcraft Statute of 1604 had expressly forbidden such practices.

Erictho lives in a cave whose mouth is choked with yew—a tree that had provided one of the elements in the Weird Sisters' charm and here a reminder of the tree's pagan associations—and which was formerly a charnel house. It lies beside the ruins of a temple of Jove which is now wholly desecrated—in part by the age-old practice of defilement by graffiti:

> Where statues and Jove's acts were vively lim'd
> Boys with black coals draw the veil'd parts of nature,
> And lecherous actions of imagin'd lust.
>
> [IV.i.156–8]

Her dwelling by this once sacred place 'where holy flamens wont to sing' stresses the perverted and diabolic aspects of her nature. She is not introduced until IV.i, when Syphax enlists her aid in his attempts to win the love of Sophonisba. Unknown to Syphax, Erictho has long harboured a 'covetous lust' for him and she tricks him into making love to her in Sophonisba's stead. Her method of substituting herself for Sophonisba is not made entirely clear. The stage direction reads, 'Enter Erictho in the shape of Sophonisba', which suggests that the witch has actually assumed the form of her rival. However, the direction adds that Erictho's face is veiled and she has previously stressed to Syphax that the success of her charm depends on his maintaining absolute silence and meeting his beloved in complete darkness, into which he must not admit 'one light, one light'. This suggests that Erictho has merely disguised herself as Sophonisba and has not actually taken her outward form in the manner of a genuine shape-shifting operation.

The episode also seems to be based in part on the concept of the succubus demon which assumes human female form to betray a human lover sexually. The notion of such a demonic activity—and of its masculine equivalent, the incubus—was the subject of much controversy. Most Roman Catholic writers, including Thomas Aquinas and the authors of *Malleus Maleficarum*, held that devils could assume this form in order to gain fuller control over their victims, and many of those suspected of witchcraft, particularly on the Continent, were accused of harbouring such spirits. Reginald Scot, on the other hand, rejected the concept, arguing that the devil was a wholly spiritual creature and had no means of achieving physical union with a human being.

The orthodox view is represented in *Doctor Faustus* where the succubus in the form of Helen of Troy ensures Faustus's damnation. Firestone in *The Witch* and Caliban in *The Tempest* are both the children of witches and devils in incubus form. Merlin in *The Birth of Merlin* (c. 1622) is also the son of an incubus demon and in this play there is perhaps an unconscious echo of *Sophonisba* when the devil, in requesting diabolic gifts for his child, invokes the aid of 'Squint-eyed Erichtho, midnight incubus' (III.iii.13). Such births are counter to orthodox theological teaching, which held that if such intercourse was possible, no offspring could result from the union. Scot reflects this view, arguing that: 'the power of generation consisteth not onlie in members, but chieflie of vitall spirits, and of the hart: which spirits are never in such a bodie as Incubus hath, being but a bodie assumed as they themselves saie' (*Discoverie*, book IV, chapter x). The problem of Erictho's means of seducing Syphax is compounded by her admission that because her 'filters and Hell's charms' were not strong enough to arouse his desires she has had to deceive him by means of 'brain sleights' (V.i.18–20). This suggests straightforward trickery rather than the use of supernatural means, and her acknowledgement of the weakness of her occult art conforms to the established concept that whilst witchcraft could be used to destroy love it lacked the positive power to create it against a person's will.

The impression of the demonic element in Erictho's nature is reinforced by her escaping from Syphax's sword when he discovers her deception. The stage direction states that she 'slips into the ground'. This was presumably achieved by the actor descending through a trap-door but the intention is clearly to suggest that Erictho, like Ariel and his fellow spirits in *The Tempest* (III.iii), is invulnerable to the 'bemocked-at stabs' of weapons and also that she was capable of vanishing at will.[2] Having satisfied her desires and hoisted Syphax with his own lustful petard, Erictho thus departs and plays no further part in the drama.

## II

Apart from the verbal echoes and the parallel themes of witchcraft and the downfall of those who seek its aid, there is little common ground between *Sophonisba* and *Macbeth*. The influence of the latter play is much more evident in Jonson's *The Masque of Queenes*, which both structurally and thematically bears close resemblances to Shakespeare's work. In each play demonic forces are embodied in the forms of witches who perform elaborate rituals and incantation ceremonies aimed at creating both universal discord and the destruction of specific persons. They are opposed in each case by Christian powers symbolised by the figures of divinely appointed monarchs. If King James was present at a performance of *Macbeth* he would have had no difficulty in equating his own person with the composite ideal of kingship embodied in the portrayals of Duncan, Malcolm and Edward. He certainly attended the court performance of the masque and the work concludes with an elaborate act of homage to the monarch whose virtues have proved too powerful for the Satanic forces which have conspired to destroy the harmony of his kingdom.

*The Masque of Queenes* was performed at the Banqueting House, Whitehall, on 2 February 1609. It was, as Jonson states in his prefatory remarks, 'the third time of my being us'd in these services to her Majesties personall presentatio's with the ladyes whome she pleaseth to honor'.[3] In the early years of James's reign masques had been commissioned from various writers, notably the poet Samuel Daniel, but by 1609 Jonson seems to have established himself as unofficial Master of the Court Masques, a role he retained despite increasing criticism from his rivals and quarrels with his collaborators until James's death in 1625. With few exceptions, a Jonsonian masque formed part of the Court's annual Christmas celebrations and he also continued to create them to mark other royal festive occasions.

*The Masque of Queenes* is a particularly interesting example of the genre for several reasons. Firstly, we have preserved (in Royal MS18AXIV in the British Museum) a holograph copy of the text, including the extensive annotations, which Jonson presented to James's eldest son, Prince Henry. This fine manuscript, running to some twenty folio sheets, provides a unique opportunity to study a complete work of Jonson's exactly as he wrote it. (In an attempt to convey something of the flavour of the holograph text, quotations from the Masque are given in their original form, rather than in a modernised version.)

The Masque is also of interest in that it embodies the first fully developed example of the anti-masque (or ante-masque, or antick-masque—Jonson uses all three forms). The witchcraft elements are contained in this preliminary section of some 357 lines, with the Dame and her eleven hags acting as foils to the twelve Queens who perform the Masque proper. Jonson pays fulsome tribute to Queen Anne because, 'best knowing, that a principall part of life in these Spectacles lay in theyr variety', she suggested that the Masque should be preceded by 'some Daunce, or shew, that might ... have the place of a foyle, or false-Masque' (ll. 10–13). Jonson is at pains to stress that this prelude is not a masque 'but a spectacle of strangenesse' (l. 20), and if the device was indeed the result of the Queen's command, he has brilliantly taken up the idea and developed it into a most successful application of his dictum, expressed in *Pleasure Reconciled to Virtue*, that virtue is 'more seene, more knowne, when Vice stands by' (l. 342).[4]

In addition to the holograph manuscript, there are also preserved (in the Chatsworth Collection) Inigo Jones's original costume sketches and also his design for the House of Fame, which is featured in the Masque proper.[5] The structure embodied an elaborate example of Jones's most spectacular stage effect—the turning machine or 'machina versatilis'. This 'glorious and magnificent building', as Jonson described it (ll. 359–60), must have been of considerable size for on the upper section of one side were positioned the twelve Queens 'sitting upon a Throne triumphall, erected in forme of a Pyramide, and circled with all store of light' (ll. 362–3). The structure revolved for, following Virtue's speech, 'the Throne wherein they

**7** Inigo Jones's design for the House of Fame, the 'machina versatilis' used in *The Masque of Queenes*. The upper section, with the trefoil arch, was the turning structure on which the twelve masquers would have been seated. The doors at stage level would have opened for the Queens to ride through, mounted on their chariots. Underneath are draft designs for Fame's throne of clouds and for the 'store of light' that illuminated the scene.

sate, being Machina versatilis, sodaynely chang'd; and in the place of it appeared Fama bona' (ll. 446–8).

In his description of the scenic effects Jonson gives high praise to his collaborator but in subsequent years the two were to differ bitterly over the increasing emphasis on the spectacle in the masques, a development which Jonson was to deplore, seeing in it the triumph of the 'body' or outward form over the 'soul' or inner meaning of the work. Despite the strong visual impact that *The Masque of Queenes* must have had, it is, paradoxically, one of Jonson's most powerful affirmations, both in performance and its printed version, of his belief that the masque should have a predominantly literary and intellectual basis.

There was a clear division of opinion at Court over the nature and function of the masque. For some, including Daniel, Inigo Jones and Francis Bacon (who begins his essay *On Masques and Triumphs* with the patronising words: 'These Things are but Toyes to come amongst such Serious Observations'), the spectacle was what mattered; for others, and Jonson was foremost amongst these, the masque deserved the status of a literary form in its own right. In performance, the masque was indeed an ephemeral 'dream or shewe'. However elaborate the spectacle, it was essentially an occasional piece, receiving in nearly every instance a single performance and then being, as Jonson describes his own anti-masque in *The Masque of Queenes*, 'quite vanish'd . . . scarse suff'ring the memory of any such thing' (ll. 357–9).[6] It was in an attempt to preserve the memory of such insubstantial pageants that Jonson printed his individual masques in quartos and included them in the folio editions of his collected works of 1616 and 1640. He clearly wished his masques, which he described habitually as 'poemes', to be placed on the same level of literary respectability as his full-length dramatic works.

He was at great pains to establish the accuracy of the scholarship contained in his masques. Several of them, in their printed forms, are fully annotated, with Jonson recording in great detail the Classical and Renaissance sources for the characters and events portrayed in the works. With the single exception of *Hymenaei*, *The Masque of Queenes* is the most fully annotated of all Jonson's masques. In the forty-four annotations, he cites or quotes from fifty-four writers, giving 126 quotations in Latin or English translation, together with seventy-three citations. However, this impressive display of erudition has been considerably undermined by close scrutiny of his alleged sources.[7] It is clear that Jonson took many short cuts in his pursuit of a scholarly reputation. For example, he uses a chain of quotations in many of the notes, citing a series of authorities, where a single source has provided all the material. However, it must be remembered that such an approach was not at all uncommon amongst Jonson's contemporaries, where what might seem plagiarism or deception was merely a time-saving device, quite acceptable to Renaissance scholars. Indeed, Jonson's learning and, more importantly, his respect for knowledge and his conviction of its supreme value in human affairs are beyond dispute. He insisted that the masque ought to be 'grounded upon antiquitie and solide learninge'[8] and *The Masque of Queenes* is a major illustration of this belief.

In his dedication Jonson had singled out for specific praise Prince Henry's 'favor to letters and these gentler studies that goe under the title of Humanitye' (ll. 21–2), and the basic theme of the work is the triumph of Virtue, which for Jonson was synonymous with knowledge, over the vice and ignorance symbolised by the witches. The victorious Virtue, Fame and the twelve Queens (and by implication King James himself, to whom they pay homage) are equated with learning, whilst, again implicitly, the detractors of scholarship are linked with the vanquished, ignorant witches.

All Jonson's masques are fully imbued with the spirit of Renaissance humanism, where the preservation of Classical learning and values was of paramount importance.[9] A fundamental precept of Renaissance thought was the necessity of harmony and order, both within the individual and within the state. Such stability was frequently expressed symbolically in terms of music and dance[10] and Jonson has brilliantly employed these basic elements of the masque form to give a dramatic demonstration of this theme. This is nowhere seen more effectively than in *The Masque of Queenes*, for in the anti-masque Jonson has adopted many of the current concepts of witchcraft practices to contrast with the virtues extolled in the Masque itself, thereby giving an added dimension to the symbolic function of such elements as the music, which accompanies both the dances and the songs.

The witches are intent on creating disorder, destroying the harmony that they see around them and replacing it with that state of misrule so feared by the Renaissance mind, and which is established in Scotland under Macbeth's tyrannical rule when the Satanic forces gain temporary power. The Dame urges her followers to 'Shew orselves truely envious; and let rise our wonted rages' and she declares, in a clear reference to James's pacific policies:

> Ill lives not, but in us.
> I hate to see these fruicts of a soft peace,

And curse the piety gives it such increase.                    [136–45]

To give visual expression of the discord the witches seek to create Jonson includes two dances in the anti-masque, performed, as he recounts: 'full of praeposterous change, and gesticulation, but most applying to theyr property: who, at theyr meetings, do all thinges contrary to the custome of Men, dauncing, back to back, hip to hip, theyr handes joyn'd and making theyr circles backward' (ll. 345–9). This is an accurate description of the dances popularly associated with witches' rites,[11] but these grotesque antics take on a fuller significance in Jonson's drama when they are contrasted with the elegance and symmetry of the four dances which form an integral part of the Masque itself. The precision of these is made evident by Jonson's descriptions. The first two were 'both right curious, and full of subtile' (l. 733), whilst the third was even more elaborate:

> then which a more numerous composition could not be seene; graphically dispos'd into letters, and honoring the Name of the most sweete and ingenious Prince, Charles, Duke of Yorke Wherin, beside that principall grace of perspecuity, the motions were so even, and apt, and theyr expression so just; as if Mathematicians had lost proportion, they might there have found it.                    [749–56]

The linking of the dance in this description with one of the great areas of Classical learning, Mathematics, makes the contrast with the witches' dances even more pointed. Similarly, the crude and malevolent spells and chants of the hags are paralleled by the harmonious and 'exact' songs in praise of Virtue and Fame which are featured in the Masque. The witches accompany their dances 'with a kind of hollow and infernall musique' (ll. 29–30), played on 'timbrells, rattles, or other veneficall instruments, making a confused noise' (ll. 43–6). The dramatic disappearance of the witches at the onset of Virtue is heralded by 'a sound of loud Musique, as if many Instruments had given one blast' (ll. 354–5), and the final appearance of the vanquished hags, dragging the masquers' chariots, is accompanied by 'a full triumphant Musique' (l. 729).

The symbolic equation of light with virtue and knowledge and of darkness with vice and ignorance is another common Renaissance theme that Jonson employs in *The Masque of Queenes*. He develops the contrasting images in a similar manner to that of Shakespeare in *Macbeth*. The early productions of the latter almost certainly took place at the open-air Globe Theatre and therefore Shakespeare had to rely on the power of his imagery to create the impression of darkness so essential to much of the play. (One can imagine that such scenes as the events on the night of Duncan's murder, the cavern sequence and, above all, Lady Macbeth's sleep-walking were much more effective visually in any revivals of the play once the King's Men had taken over the indoor and much more intimate Blackfriars Theatre in 1608.)

However, although Jonson had much more sophisticated technical resources at his disposal than had Shakespeare, he too creates elaborate verbal motifs on the themes of light and darkness. Like the Weird Sisters, his hags are creatures of the night, emerging from an 'ougly Hell: which, flaming beneath, smoak'd unto the top of the Roofe' (ll. 24–6). They harbour such nocturnal creatures as owls, moles and bats (ll. 75–7), and many of the ingredients in their spell-making rites have been gathered by night. In fact, it seems essential that this should be so. The Second Hag reports:

> I have been gathering Wolves hayres,
> The mad Doggs foame, and the Adders eares;
> The spurging of a dead mans eyes,
> And all, since the Evening Starre did rise.          [159–62]

The Fifth Witch declares:

> Under a cradle I did creepe,
> By day; and, when the Child was a-sleepe,
> At night, I suck'd the breath; and rose,
> And pluck'd the nodding nurse, by the nose.          [171–4]

The brain of a 'black cat' is also added to the spell and even the names of the herbal ingredients, such as nightshade and moonswort, increase the nocturnal atmosphere. The Dame proclaims that they are 'faythfull Opposites to Fame and Glory' and she demands, 'Let not these bright Nights / Of Honor blaze, thus, to offend or eyes' (ll. 132–4). In destroying the harmony that so offends them, they will 'blast the light' and she implores Hecate, 'thou three-formed-star', to:

> Darken all this roofe,
> With present fogges. Exhale Earth's rott'nest.
> And strike a blindnesse, through these blazing tapers.          [241–3]

Apart from the obvious allegorical intent here, Jonson is also making full use of the impressive lighting effects that were employed during the performance of the Masque. In brilliant contrast to the darkness enveloping the witches, the victory of Fame and Virtue is signalled, not only by the triumphant music, but by a sudden eruption of light, the very light that the witches have unsuccessfully sought to extinguish. The hags are replaced by the 'glorious and magnificent' House of Fame, surmounted by the twelve masquers 'sitting upon a Throne triumphall . . . and circled with all store of light' (ll. 359–63), an effect amplified by Jonson's subsequent description: 'The Freezes, both below, and above, were filled with severall colour'd Lights, like Emeralds, Rubies, Sapphires, Carbuncles, etc. The reflexe of which, with other lights plac'd in ye concave, upon the Masquers habites, was full of glory' (ll. 695–9). The figure of Virtue descends from the structure and his speech begins: 'So should, at Fames loud sound, and Vertues sight / All poore, and envious Witchcraft fly the light' (ll. 367–8).

Following his oration, the masquers' throne revolves to reveal Fame 'attir'd in white with white Wings, having a collar of Gold, about her neck' (ll. 449–50). The brilliance of the scene and the physical manifestation of the triumph of light over darkness would have been completed by the final effect of the 'bright Bevie' of Queens in their chariots, drawn by the captive hags, and accompanied by fourteen torchbearers.

It is true, as Jonson generously indicates in his descriptive notes, that these elements were the work of his collaborators: Jones, Thomas Giles, who was responsible for the choreography of the dances, and Alfonso Ferrabosco, the composer of the songs. But it is clear, from the manner in which the text complements the stage effects, that Jonson's was the guiding hand and that he was utilising the full potential of such physical displays to underline the basic intellectual theme of the Masque.

It might be imagined that the combined effects of the elaborate symbolism and the scaffolding of erudite annotation which, literally, surrounds the text on the printed page would extinguish any potential vitality in the work itself, but this is very far from true. Admittedly, in the Masque proper, the modern reader has to rely heavily on his imagination to bring it to life, even with the help of Jonson's descriptions and Jones's drawings. The Masque is presented primarily in visual terms for, apart from the three songs, the text consists solely of the two conventional orations by Fame and Virtue. The Queens themselves, played by Queen Anne and ladies of the court, are, as was customary, not allotted speeches but merely perform the dances and process in their chariots.

The Masque itself, in fact, is much closer to the form favoured by Jonson's predecessors and contemporary rivals than are most of his works of this kind. It is in the anti-masque that we find a much greater emphasis on the text and are, paradoxically, more aware of the 'soul' of the work, compared with the 'bodily' spectacle of the second section. It must be borne in mind, however, that although the hags have more than twice the amount of dialogue given to the characters in the Masque proper, this would not have been reflected in the work's 'playing-time', for much of the action of the second part is taken up with the spectacular effects of the 'machina versatilis' and the songs and dances with which the performance would have ended. Nevertheless, a significant proportion of the work is devoted to the witches' anti-masque, for they also have their spectacle and their musical interludes.

Jonson's choice of witches to represent the 'faythfull opposites' of the virtues extolled in the Masque is most apt. We have already seen how the antitheses give visual and auricular expression of Jonson's theme but, for the triumph of Virtue to be fully effective, the defeated vices must present a sufficiently formidable foe. This Jonson has achieved, for the witches, embodying Ignorance and the other vanquished ills, have a sombre and powerful vitality.

The rhetoric of the Dame occasionally achieves a measured intensity, particularly in her impressive invocation to Hecate. Clearly based, as Jonson acknowledges, on the familiar Medea speech from Ovid's *Metamorphoses*, VII, it compares not unfavourably with Shakespeare's rendering of the lines in *The Tempest*. The Dame declares that their triumph will be complete:

> When we have set the Elements at warres;
> Made Mid-night see the Sunne; and Day the starres;
> When the wing'd Lightning, in the course, hath stay'd;
> And swiftest Rivers have runne back, afrayd
> To see the Corne remove, the Groves to range,
> Whole places alter, and the Seasons change.          [228–33]

Throughout the work Jonson demonstrates great metrical flexibility, employing a wide variety of rhythmical forms. At times these seem to reflect the frequent changes of pace of the dances, 'full of praeposterous change', which presumably accompanied the witches' chants. The ponderous 'Comes she not, yet? / Strike another heate' is immediately followed by the jaunty 'The Weather is fayre, the wind is good, / Up, Dame, o' yor Horse of Wood' (ll. 61–3). The variations, irregularities and, at times, laboured speech rhythms reflect the disorder that the witches embody. The syntactically superfluous punctuation of the following lines, present in the holograph text and the original printed versions, illustrates the unnatural effects Jonson was seeking:

> Quickly, come away:
> For we, all stay.
> Nor yet? Nay, then,

Wee'll try her agen. [70–3]

Similarly, although in this case the effect is more apparent on the printed page than it would have been in performance, many of the Dame's speeches contain a series of run-on lines, with irregularly placed pauses, which undermine the effect of the rhyming couplets and contrast strongly with the stately heroic couplets of the speeches of Fame and Virtue. The Dame addresses her hags thus:

> Joyne, now, our hearts, we faythfull Opposites
> To Fame, and Glory. Let not these bright Nights
> Of Honor blaze, thus, to offend our eyes.
> Shew ourselves truely envious; and let rise
> Our wonted rages. Do what may beseeme
> Such names, and natures. [133–8]

Jonson needed to create as strongly as he could the impression of potential discord, because the Masque lacks any dramatic confrontation between the opposing forces. At the first onset of Virtue the hags 'quite vanish'd; and the whole face of the Scene alterd; scarse suffring the memory of any such thing' (ll. 355–9). This device is more effective as allegory than drama. The witches and the Queens are mutually exclusive and the former cannot be converted to the service of Good Fame—as the Satyrs serve Oberon in the masque *Oberon, the Fairy Prince* (1611) —except as enslaved chariot-bearers. Therefore it was all the more vital for Jonson to convey the impression that the witches and the vices they represent are very real dangers to the peace and harmony reigning in the House of Fame (and thus at James's court), before their unresisting admission of inevitable defeat by the superior forces of Virtue.

### Notes to Chapter 5

1   *Sophonisba* is included in vol. 2 of Marston's *Works*, edited in three volumes by A. H. Bullen (1887).

2   Both of these powers were also attributed to fairies, further evidence of the close links between witchcraft and fairy lore.

3   All quotations from *The Masque of Queenes* and other masques by Jonson are taken from vol. VII (1941) of the *Complete Works of Ben Jonson*, edited by C. H. Herford, Percy and Evelyn Simpson in eleven volumes (1925–52).

4   Herford and Simpson *Works*, vol. VII, p. 491. The masque is dated 1618.

5   All Jones's designs are reproduced in Stephen Orgel and Roy Strong, *Inigo Jones: the Theatre of the Stuart Court*, 2 vols. (1973).

6   For full discussions of the development of the English masque see E. Welsford, *The Court Masque* (1927) and Allardyce Nicoll, *Stuart Masques and the Renaissance Stage* (1937).

7    See E. W. Talbert, 'New light on Ben Jonson's workmanship', *Studies in Philology*, XL (1943); and W. Todd Furniss, 'The annotation of Ben Jonson's *Masque of Queenes*', *The Review of English Studies*, vol. V, no. 20 (1954).

8    Prefatory note to *Hymenaei* (1606).

9    For a full discussion of this aspect of the masque see J. C. Meagher, *Method and Meaning in Jonson's Masques* (1966).

10   See, for example, Sir John Davies's *Orchestra, a Poem of Dancing* (1596).

11   A similar account to that of Jonson's is found in the anonymous *A Pleasant Treatise of Witches* (1673): 'The dance is strange and wonderful, as well as diabolical, for turning themselves back to back, they take one another by the arms and raise each other from the ground, then shake their heads to and fro like Antiks, and turn themselves as if they were mad.'

# CHAPTER 6

# THE TUNE OF DAMNATION

## SQUALID GRANDEUR IN *THE WITCH*

*Hecate:*                                     **I'm so light**
**At any mischief! there's no villainy**
**But is a tune, methinks.**

*Firestone:* **A tune? 'tis to the tune of damnation then I warrant you,**
**and that song hath a villainous burden.**

[*The Witch*, V.ii.80–4]

### I

Court records show that the cost of staging *The Masque of Queenes* was at least £3,000[1]—and this was for the masque proper. There is no record of the expenses incurred in the anti-masque but Jonson's notes indicate that this also required highly elaborate—and expensive—properties and costumes. It was partly on these grounds that W. J. Lawrence developed his ingenious hypothesis linking *The Masque of Queenes* with *Macbeth* and Middleton's *The Witch*.[2] He argued that the King's Men had probably performed the anti-masque for Jonson's work and had also given the first performance of Middleton's play, utilising the elaborate witchcraft paraphernalia that had received just a single airing in the masque. However, *The Witch* does not seem to have been a success. In Crane's transcript of the play, made between 1620 and 1627,[3] the dedicatory epistle refers to it as having long lain 'in an imprisond—Obscuritie' and the title page declares that it had been 'long since Acted by his Ma[ties] Servants at the Black-Friers'. Lawrence argues that in a second attempt to put their

78

witchcraft properties to fuller use, the King's Men produced *Macbeth* in a revised form, incorporating the songs and dances and other spectacular effects which had proved some of the few popular elements in Middleton's play.

This attractive theory has not received complete acceptance but it does help to explain the unheralded appearance of Hecate in *Macbeth* (III.v) and the brief references in the First Folio text to the two songs—'Come away, come away etc.' (III.v.33) and 'Black spirits etc.' (IV.i.43)—which appear in full in Middleton's work.

It certainly seems clear that *The Witch* was written to capitalise on the current interest in the supernatural and on the increasing vogue for the dramatic representation of the more repellent aspects of magic—and of witchcraft in particular. In addition to the probable links with *Macbeth* and *The Masque of Queenes* the play has several elements in common with *Sophonisba*, which may or may not be fortuitous. Erictho and Hecate are both grandiose and at the same time squalid creatures in the Classical tradition. They are both consulted by persons seeking love charms and they each harbour secret desires for their 'clients'. Whilst Erictho satisfies her lust for Syphax, Middleton does not develop the dramatic potential of Hecate's aside when Almachildes consults her:

> 'Tis Almachildes—fresh blood stirs in me—
> The man that I have lusted to enjoy;
> I've had him thrice in incubus already.        [I.ii.196–8]

Middleton presumably means that Hecate has taken the form of a succubus, rather than incubus, here. In the same scene there are other references to the concept. Hecate reminds her minion, Stadlin, that: 'Last night thou got'st the mayor of Whelplie's son; . . . I think thou'st spoil'd the youth, he's but seventeen: I'll have him the next mounting' (ll. 29–32). Firestone, himself the result of Hecate's demonic sexual practices, asks: 'Mother, I pray, give me leave to ramble abroad tonight with the Nightmare, for I have a great mind to overlay a fat parson's daughter' (ll. 90–2). We see here how closely linked were the demonic concepts of the nightmare and the incubus, and the impression of the witches' concupiscence and depravity is completed by Hecate's response to her son's plea:

> And who shall lie with me, then? . . .
> You had rather hunt after strange women still
> Than lie with your own mothers.        [93–8]

Just as the Erictho episode gives the impression of having been inserted into *Sophonisba* so the three witchcraft scenes in Middleton's play—despite its title—seem to have been clumsily and hastily added on to the basic material of the work. It could well be that Middleton adapted a recently completed play—a typical Jacobean tragi-comedy of intrigue and revenge in an Italian setting—to accommodate the witchcraft sequences commissioned by the King's Men.

The play is primarily concerned with the attempts by the Duchess to gain vengeance on her husband, who has humiliated her by forcing her to drink a toast at a banquet from a cup made from her father's skull. It also tells of her subsequent amatory involvement with Almachildes. This story is found in Machiavelli's *Florentine History* and perhaps came to Middleton through the medium of Belleforest's *Histoires Tragiques*.[4] There are no supernatural elements in the original versions and the Duchess's recourse to the witches in V.ii is startling in that hitherto there has been no indication of her awareness of their existence. The decision, made to secure her lover's 'sudden and subtle' death, seems primarily a device for Middleton to provide the audience with his own version of a cauldron scene, complete with incantations and suitably nauseating ingredients, for in the subsequent, and final scene, the Duchess's plan is rapidly thwarted, despite Hecate's confident promise that the deed will be 'dispatched this night'.

A minimal effect on the development of the plot is also achieved by Almachildes's own earlier and equally unexpected visit to the witches. He acquires from them a love-charm in the form of a ribbon, through which he hopes to satisfy his desires for Amoretta, the Duchess's serving-woman. He thrusts the charm into her bosom, but it is rapidly displaced and she then resumes her former hostile attitude towards him, as is required for the furtherance of the plot. It can be argued that there is a certain irony in the equally unsuccessful attempts by the two faithless lovers to enlist supernatural aid to further their selfish aims, and Almachildes's failure to win Amoretta is in line with the concept already noted in relation to Erictho that, because of their basically evil natures, the witches cannot create genuine or lasting love.

The subsidiary plot concerns Sebastian's efforts to destroy the marriage of Antonio and his former betrothed, Isabella. The witches' successful response to his request for the means to induce Antonio's impotence contrasts with their inability to create positive love and reinforces the impression of their greater power for negative or disruptive actions. Their behaviour here does contribute more significantly to the main theme, although Antonio's innate weakness and viciousness could well have led to his speedy estrangement from Isabella without supernatural interference. It is none the less noteworthy that the witches' principal contribution to the plot is the success of this essentially malevolent spell, springing from Sebastian's feelings of jealousy and desire for revenge.

A further indication of the hasty composition of the supernatural elements is Middleton's heavy reliance for his material on Scot's *The Discoverie of Witchcraft*. As the nineteenth-century editors Bullen and Dyce both note in their Mermaid editions of *The Witch*, entire sections of Scot's work were transcribed and inserted into the play. Sometimes there is a superficial rearrangement of the material or a veneer of versification, but frequently the parallels are so close that one feels Middleton must have been working directly from a copy of Scot's text. In taking his material, Middleton completely ignores the questioning spirit of the original—in fact, it is a constant irony that the main source for his witchcraft episodes should be the leading sceptic of the period.

One example of Middleton's borrowings from Scot which throws interesting light on his working method occurs when Hecate, for no apparent reason, launches into a declamatory roll-call of unearthly creatures: 'Urchins, Elves, Hags, Satyrs, Pans, Fawns, Sylvans, Kitt-with-the-candlestick, Tritons, Centaurs, Dwarfs, Imps, the Spoorn, the Mare, the Man-i'-the-oak, the Hellwain, the Fire-drake, the Puckle! a ab hur hus!' (I.ii.117–20). The last phrase is especially incongruous if one is aware, with Scot, that this is a traditional charm against the toothache! (book XII, chapter xiv). The remainder of the speech is identical, with a few random omissions, to Scot's famous enumeration of spirits with which 'in our childhood our mothers' maids have so fraied us' (book VII, chapter xv). The names of two of Hecate's hags, who make two appearances in this scene, are also taken from this list of spirits—Hellwain and Puckle. This presumably unintentional duplication suggests undue speed on Middleton's part. In addition, neither name is appropriate to be applied to witches. Puckle is a diminutive of Puck, whilst the Hellwain was the waggon in which the souls of the dead were carried to the next world.

The superficiality of Middleton's knowledge of the subject is also shown by the fact that Hecate, traditionally a divine personage, is portrayed as a human witch. She is listed in the Dramatis Personae as 'ye cheif Witch' and her first appearance—in I.ii—is indicated by the direction 'Enter Hecate: and other witches.' Because of Middleton's heavy reliance on Scot, who in turn drew largely on Continental authorities—including Le Loyer, another of Middleton's sources[5]—Hecate displays many of the sensational features that were more frequently applied to the European witch than to the English equivalent. She and her fellow hags are creatures of the night, gathering their magic herbs and flying for thousands of miles through the air on moonlit nights. Hecate's final words suggest that they indulge in some form of lunar worship: 'Come, my sweet sisters; let the air strike our tune, / Whilst we show reverence to yond peeping moon' (V.ii.96–7). She and her companions possess familiar spirits in such traditional forms as cats, toads and bats and they allow these to suck their blood. Stadlin reports that: 'There was a bat hung at my lips three times / As we came through the woods, and drank her fill' (III.iii.11–12).

They are dedicated to evil, eagerly plotting harm both for their own purposes and on behalf of those who consult them. Hecate agrees to Sebastian's request for help, declaring: ''Tis for love of mischief I do this, / And that we're sworn to the first oath we take' (I.ii.199–200). The oath is presumably a reference to the diabolic compact, and Hecate also informs her son Firestone that her death 'will be / Even just at twelve o'clock at night come three year' (I.ii.75–6). Although this can be seen merely as evidence of prophetic powers, it is more probably a reference to the predetermined time of settlement of her hellish bargain. They willingly commit murder, killing an unbaptised child in the performance of their rites, and they also practise image-magic. Hecate asks:

> Is the heart of wax
> Stuck full of magic needles? . . .
> And is the farmer's picture and his wife's
> Laid down to the fire yet?

[I.ii.49–53]

As well as bringing about death, such images could be used to cause infertility and impotence and Hecate, eagerly anticipating Sebastian's request for a charm, asks: 'Is it to starve up generation? / To strike a barrenness in man or woman?' (I.ii.165–6). Conversely, she cannot create genuine or lasting love. As with Erictho, her powers are entirely negative, as she admits to Sebastian:

> We cannot disjoin wedlock;
> 'Tis of Heaven's fastening. Well may we raise jars,
> Jealousies, strifes, and heart-burning disagreements,
> Like a thick scurf o'er life.

[I.ii.188–91]

Her minion, Stadlin, can raise actual storms 'That shipwreck barks, and tears up growing oaks' (I.ii.148), whilst Hoppo can 'Blast vineyards, orchards, meadows' (I.ii.158). She plans to do this as part of the witches' vengeance on the farmer and his wife who 'denied me often flour, barm, and milk / Goose-grease and tar' (I.ii.57–8). This is similar to the Weird Sisters' revenge on the sailor's wife and, as was noted in that connection, trial accounts of the period abound with cases of such alleged acts following some petty insult. Hecate's planned vengeance follows the traditional pattern: in revenge for the supposed slight she vows to bewitch the farmer's stock, laming various animals and sending snakes to suck the milk from his cows[6] before finally bringing about the deaths of the farmer and his wife.

## II

Hecate and her minions have obvious superficial affinities with the witches in both *Macbeth* and *The Masque of Queenes*. This is particularly evident in their total devotion to evil, planning upheaval and destruction in both the natural and mortal spheres. There are, however, vital differences among the creations. Jonson's hags have no direct contact with their human victims and the dealings between Macbeth and the Weird Sisters differ significantly from those between the principal characters and Hecate in *The Witch*. The latter is consulted *after* individuals have chosen their courses of action and taken their moral decisions. In the cases of Sebastian, Almachildes and the Duchess, the witches are sought out to provide the means to achieve ends that have already been decided upon. On the other hand, the Weird Sisters appear to single out Macbeth as a chosen victim. He may well have the seeds of evil lodged within him but it is their 'supernatural soliciting' that brings them so swiftly to fruition.

It is perhaps significant that it is in the later scenes in *Macbeth*, with the intrusion of Hecate, that the nature of the Sisters and Macbeth's relationship with them appears to undergo a fundamental change. As G. K. Hunter remarks in the New Penguin *Macbeth*, in III.v Macbeth is 'viewed as an adept or disciple of the witches, not a victim' (p. 167). It is certainly true that it is Macbeth who seeks out the witches in IV.i and his decision that he 'will tomorrow ... to the weird sisters' (III.iv.131–2) is similar to Almachildes's declaration, 'I will to the witches' in Middleton' play, (I.i.105). However, Macbeth's action, in view of the previous events of the play and coming as it does immediately after the visions of Banquo's ghost, is a wholly natural step, whereas Almachildes's decision is as abrupt and unexpected as is the Duchess's similar resolve later in the play. Moreover, there remains the fundamental distinction that even though Macbeth visits the Weird Sisters for their second encounter, his purpose is not to enlist their aid in an enterprise he has already decided upon, as with Middleton's characters, but to make use of their already proven gifts of prophecy—'to know / By the worst means the worst' (III.iv.133–4). Indeed, his decision to kill Macduff and, failing this, his family and retainers, is taken in spite of the Sisters' apparent reassurances.

Hecate and her followers exert none of the pervasive influence evident in the power of the Weird Sisters in *Macbeth*. However, despite Middleton's heavy reliance on Scot and his other sources, the incongruities, the ill-judged attempts at humour, and their minimal contribution to the development of the play, there is a degree of sombre intensity in the witchcraft sequences and the current of evil running through the play is reinforced by these scenes. The distasteful qualities of the principal characters, especially their hypocritical obsession with 'reputation', which is a recurring theme in the play, are thrown into greater relief when set against the unashamed relish of evil and the pursuit of self-gratification openly displayed by the witches. In fact, despite their apparently superfluous nature, the witches' main function can be seen as providing grotesque parallels with the behaviour of the principal characters in the play. The hags are obsessed with achieving satisfaction through sexual indulgence and acts of vengeance and these are also the main preoccupations of the leading characters. However, the hypocrisy and covert maliciousness of the latter is contrasted, to their detriment, with the uninhibited and uncomplicated viciousness displayed by Hecate and her minions. The fact that they turn for aid to such squalid and preposterous creatures serves only to underline their own depravity.

Although the witches lack control over the human will and cannot force a man unwillingly into sin, they can greatly facilitate his pursuit of evil. Here, too, they have affinities with the Weird Sisters' relationship with Macbeth; whilst a further quality that they share is that, despite their limited powers, they have the ability to corrupt and pervert the naturally attractive or innocent. Banquo seems to have been tarnished by his contact with the Sisters and in *The Witch* Hecate, in seeking vengeance on the farmer, vows:

> the dew-skirted dairy-wenches
> Shall stroke dry dugs for this, and go home cursing;
> I'll mar their sillabubs, and swathy feastings
> Under cows' bellies with the parish-youths.        [I.ii.59–62]

In addition to these thematic parallels *The Witch* contains numerous verbal echoes of Shakespeare's and Jonson's plays.[7] All three works depict

84

elaborate incantation ceremonies which are conducted around cauldrons, and a comparison of these scenes throws interesting light on the approaches of the three writers. In *Macbeth* the Sisters are concocting the 'hell-broth' as an integral part of the 'charm of powerful trouble' which they are creating to hasten Macbeth on his path of delusion and destruction. In the comparable sequence in *The Masque of Queenes* (ll. 155–204) the hags, under the command of the Dame, have been gathering items to produce a charm that will:

> blast the light;
> Mixe Hell, with Heaven; and make Nature fight
> Within her selfe; loose the whole henge of Things;
> And cause the Endes runne back into theyr Springs.

[146–9]

Their aim, therefore, is a more universal upheaval than the loss of a single soul envisaged by the Weird Sisters, and the apocalyptic nature of their intentions is akin to the destruction foreseen by Macbeth when he demands:

> though the treasure
> Of nature's germens tumble all together,
> Even till destruction sicken, answer me
> To what I ask you.                                          [IV.i.58–61]

Jonson's image of the loosening of 'the whole henge of things' is reminiscent of Macbeth's 'Let the frame of things disjoint, both the worlds suffer' in III.ii.16.

In *The Witch* there are two cauldron scenes. In the first (I.ii) Hecate is producing an ointment which will facilitate her flying powers—the ingredients being taken largely from Scot's account of 'John Bapt. Neap's ... receipts for the miraculous transportation of witches' (*Discoverie*, book II, chapter i)—and in the second (V.ii) she mixes a concoction that she assures the Duchess will bring about the speedy death of Almachildes. The main element in the first brew is the fat of an 'unbaptized brat' and the second also contains a human relic—'three ounces of the red-haired girl / I killed last midnight' (V.ii.65–6). Jonson's hags also commit murder to obtain their ingredients. The Sixth Witch boasts: 'I had a dagger, what did I with that? / Kill'd an infant, to have his fat' (ll. 175–6). Although the Weird Sisters would scarcely shrink from direct killing, their comparable ingredient has been taken from a child who died at birth: 'Finger of birth-strangled babe, / Ditch-deliver'd by a drab' (IV.i.30–1). They summon the Apparitions by adding 'grease that's sweaten / From the murderer's gibbet' (ll. 65–6), whilst Jonson's Seventh Hag reports:

> A Murd'rer, yonder, was hung in Chaines,
> The Sunne, and the Wind had shrunke his vaynes;
> I bit of a sinew, I clipp'd his hayre,
> I brought of his ragges, yt daunc'd i' the ayre.          [179–82]

In addition to the two cauldron scenes in *The Witch*, Firestone tells Hecate in III.iii that he has been gathering herbs, together with 'six lizards and three serpentine eggs' (l. 34), which are presumably intended for some later ritual. The herbs have all been 'cropped by moonlight' and the hags in *The Masque of Queenes* have also collected their items at night—'And all, since the Evening Starre did rise' (l. 162). The Weird Sisters are creatures of even greater darkness, for their hemlock was 'digg'd i' th' dark' (l. 25) and the slips of yew have been 'sliver'd in the moon's eclipse' (l. 28). Middleton's linking of Hecate with the moon is in accord with many witchcraft beliefs but the fact that the Weird Sisters avoid even its eerie light emphasises their evil natures and is an additional element in the dark/light pattern running through the play. As Katharine Briggs comments in *Pale Hecate's Team*, 'Black witchcraft is the magic of sterility; the moon's waxing time has always been counted the time of growth, and the moon's eclipse therefore would be the time of complete negation' (p. 80).

In addition to the children's remains, there are several other ingredients that are common to all three works. These include portions of toads, bats and snakes—all of which have strong witchcraft associations. The witches in *The Masque of Queenes* and *Macbeth* also derive their material from frogs, owls, wolves and hemlock, whilst Shakespeare's mythological 'scale of a dragon' is comparable with the 'basilisk's blood' in Jonson's scene. The creatures of both Middleton and Shakespeare use lizards, and those of Jonson and Middleton employ the herb libbard's bane. Nearly all of the elements featured by the latter writers were taken from authoritative writings on witchcraft. As elsewhere, Middleton borrows freely from Scot and Le Loyer whilst Jonson is at pains, through his annotations, to establish the authenticity of his material. Some of the materials he shares with Shakespeare can be explained by the fact that both authors have drawn on the same Classical sources. Ovid's Medea (*Metamorphoses*, VII) uses owl's feathers and wolves' entrails whilst in Studley's version of Seneca's play Medea employs the 'durtye stynking guttes' of a screech-owl, 'the squesed clootered blood / Of serpents' and a herb 'snepped of in depe of sylent nyght'. Jonson gives Lucan as one of his sources for the molesting of the murderer's body and in his *De Bello Civili*, VI, Lucan describes how the witch Erichtho attacks the bodies of criminals and scrapes the grease from the crosses on which they have been crucified.[8]

However, the majority of Shakespeare's ingredients appear to be his own invention. For example, the Jew's liver, nose of Turk and Tartar's lips are not found in any other accounts of incantations and were almost certainly never used in reality. These gruesome objects add to the noxious impression of the scene and the traditional cruelty of the Turks and Tartars would make such elements attractive to the Sisters, their supposed viciousness entering the spell by ritual transference. The three victims also share with the ditch-delivered babe the fact that they have not experienced Christian baptism. The horrific nature of the Sisters' ingredients is heightened by Shakespeare's rendering of the two common—and harmless—herbs hound's tongue and adder's tongue as the seemingly more sinister 'tongue of dog' and 'adder's fork'. On the other hand, both he and Jonson include hemlock, which is described in Gerard's *Herbal* (1597) as 'a very evil, dangerous, hurtfull, and poysonous herbe'. Gerard also quotes Galen in stating that yew 'is of a venemous qualitie, and against man's nature'.[9] The Weird Sisters have presumably gathered their slips, or seedlings, from a churchyard and the plant had ancient associations with funeral ceremonies, a factor that would strengthen the appropriateness of its inclusion in their fatal brew.

The elemental nature of Shakespeare's ingredients is matched by the basic style of his cauldron scene, which is composed of rhyming couplets, except for the initial three unrhymed lines and lines 30 to 32, where the rhyme is repeated, for no apparent reason. The predominant rhythm is trochaic, most lines containing seven syllables, four of which are stressed. This basic pattern, with its deliberately limited and insistent tone, is the same as that set for the Sisters' speeches in I.i and I.iii. The section in *The Masque of Queenes* is also in rhyming couplets, with each of the eleven hags speaking four lines and the Dame concluding the sequence with a speech of six lines. There is some trochaic rhythm and some lines are identical to the *Macbeth* form. Line 200, for example, is: 'Horned poppie, Cypresse boughs.' However, there is no basic metre, many variations being rung on a blend of iambic and anapaestic rhythms. This irregularity is maintained in the lengths of lines, which range between seven and ten syllables, and in the disruptive punctuation which was discussed previously.

This disjointed effect was clearly deliberate on Jonson's part. The cauldron episodes in *The Witch* also bear little evidence of coherence or regularity of style but this may be due to Middleton's speedy composition of these sections rather than a conscious stylistic device. The first scene (I.ii) contains a mixture of blank verse (ll. 20–48) and rhyming couplets (ll. 14–27), the latter forming Hecate's opening speech. This has a predominant rhythm of iambic quatrameter and, in view of the controversy over the authorship of the Hecate speeches in *Macbeth*, it is perhaps significant that the latter take this precise form. Middleton's second scene (V.ii) also has a mixture of blank verse and rhyming couplets, the latter occurring during the actual incantation sequence.

Although there are inevitable distinctions, particularly in style, the cauldron scenes are alike in that they epitomise the evil embodied in the witches of the three plays. The rites are all performed to achieve deeds of 'maleficia' and the grotesque rituals, with their gruesome ingredients, add immensely to the aura of superhuman wickedness that surrounds the witches. Their enactment gives physical expression to the horrors that must have lain in the imaginations of the great majority of Jacobeans, from King James and his Court to the groundlings of the Globe. The rationalism and humanity expressed by Scot and Gifford had not yet found general acceptance and all three playwrights reflect if not pander to the most widely held fears and prejudices. The incantation scenes exemplify their basic approaches, for the emphasis in each is on the more horrific and sensational aspects of witchcraft. Following the rituals, attention is focused on their effects on the potential victims, with no interest or concern shown in the ultimate and inevitable fates of the performers of the rites themselves.

### Notes to Chapter 6

1   Herford and Simpson (*Works*, vol. X, pp. 491–3). James answered Parliamentary criticism of such expenditure by declaring in 1609: 'It is true I have spent much: but yet if I had spared any of those things, which caused a great part of my expense, I should have dishonoured the kingdom, myself, and the late Queen.' (Quoted in Meagher, *Method and Meaning in Jonson's Masques*, p. 34).

2   'Notes on a collection of masque music', *Music and Letters* (1922) and 'The mystery of *Macbeth*' in *Shakespeare's Workshop* (1928).

3   The quarto is now in the Bodleian Library. It was first published by Steevens in 1778 and all modern editions are based on this text. Quotations from *The Witch* are taken from the Mermaid edition of *The Works of Thomas Middleton*, vol. V, edited by A. H. Bullen (1885).

4   Bullen reprints an English translation of 1674 of the relevant section from *Florentine History* in the above edition, pp. 353–4.

5   Gareth Roberts in 'A re-examination of the magical material in Middleton's *The Witch*', *Notes and Queries* (May–June 1976) indicates some additional

borrowings from Scot and also argues convincingly for another source in Le
Loyer's *A Treatise of Specters* (Angers, 1586).

6    For examples of this belief see *Notes and Queries*, 10th series, X (1908), pp.
265 and 316–17.

7    Some of the echoes of *Macbeth* are indicated by Muir in the New Arden
*Macbeth* (pp. xxxvii–xxxviii). Hecate's speech in *The Witch*, III.iii.82–5, has
affinities with ll. 53–60 in *The Masque of Queenes*.

8    Marston uses similar material in his description in *Sophonisba* of the
activities of Erictho, who is also, of course, based on Lucan.

9    John Gerard, *The Herbal or General History of Plants* (1597).

# CHAPTER 7

# INSTRUMENT OF MISCHIEF

## TRAGI-COMEDY IN *THE WITCH OF EDMONTON*

*Old Carter:* **The witch, that instrument of mischief!**
[*The Witch of Edmonton*, V.iii.21]

### I

As was noted in Chapter One, there were only five recorded executions for witchcraft in the last nine years of James I's reign, compared with thirty-five during the first thirteen years. The magistrates seem to have taken their cue from James's own increasing reluctance to accept many of the claims and accusations of occult powers. However, this more humane—or sceptical—attitude would clearly have taken much longer to filter through to the general populace. One of the five executions was that of Elizabeth Sawyer, who was hanged for witchcraft at Tyburn on 19 April 1621. *The Witch of Edmonton* recounts this real-life case in dramatised form and it reflects the slowly developing attitude to witchcraft in that it is the first play to contain a full-scale portrayal of a witch where the protagonist is treated with any measure of sympathy or understanding.

Although the play was not printed until 1658, the first recorded production was at Court on 29 December 1621 when it was presented by the Prince's Men. It had almost certainly been performed earlier in that

# The Witch of Edmonton

## A known true STORY.

### Compoſed into

# A TRAGI-COMED

### By divers well-eſteemed Poets;

## William Rowley, Thomas Dekker, John Ford, &

Acted by the Princes Servants, often at the Cock-Pit in *Drury-Lane*,
once at Court, with ſingular Applauſe.

*Never printed till now.*

**8** The title page of the earliest printed quarto of *The Witch of Edmonton* (1658). The woodcut combines two separate scenes from the play: the first meeting of Mother Sawyer and her dog spirit; and the ducking suffered by Cuddy Banks in his pursuit of a spirit in the shape of his beloved Katherine.

year at the company's Cock-Pit Theatre, as is suggested by the lines 'Villains are strip't naked, the witch must be beaten out of her Cock-pit' (V.i.47–8). The title page of the 1658 quarto describes the work as 'A known true Story. Composed into a Tragi-Comedy' and it was clearly written to capitalise on the excitement generated by the recent witchcraft trial. The affair seems to have been something of a nine-days' wonder, for in addition to the play it was also the subject of popular ballads, now lost, which, according to Henry Goodcole, 'were sung at the time of our returning from the witches execution'. Goodcole was the chaplain of Newgate Gaol, where Elizabeth had been imprisoned, and he wrote an account of the case justifying her execution, if any such defence were needed. His work was entitled: *The Wonderfull discoverie of Elizabeth Sawyer a Witch, late of Edmonton, her conviction and condemnation and death. Together with the relation of the Divels accesse to her and their conference together.* This pamphlet was entered in the Stationers' Register on 27 April 1621, just eight days after the execution. In view of the speed with which the account was produced, it is remarkably free from the printing errors evident in many of the pamphlets of the period, especially those that have clearly been produced to coincide with currently sensational cases. At one point Agnes Ratcliffe, one of the witch's alleged victims, is referred to as Elizabeth, but generally the document is a clear and painstakingly accurate, if biassed, account of Elizabeth Sawyer's trial and subsequent confession.[1]

*The Witch of Edmonton* follows the pamphlet account very closely, and also seems to make use of material from the ballads, which Goodcole refers to but dismisses as inaccurate. In dramatising the events, elements are introduced into the play which are not present in the historical account. There are two major plots apart from the Elizabeth Sawyer episodes, but the three themes are quite skilfully blended and the other sections reinforce and complement the witchcraft sequences, in a far more successful manner than, for example, Middleton achieves in *The Witch.*

The quarto states that the work was composed 'by divers well-esteemed Poets; William Rowley, Thomas Dekker, John Ford etc.' Modern scholars ignore the 'etcetera' and are generally agreed in assigning the Mother Sawyer scenes to Dekker, the Cuddy Banks episodes to Rowley, and in giving overall responsibility for the Frank Thorney/Winnifride/Susan plot to Ford (with help from Dekker). Such arbitrary divisions are, of course, a gross over-simplification. From what we know of Jacobean collaborative techniques, such clear-cut divisions are most unlikely, particularly where the plots overlap within single scenes, but on grounds of style and character treatment, the witchcraft scenes are generally felt to bear most clearly the stamp of Dekker.[2]

Just as, despite the title, the supernatural scenes in *The Witch* are a comparatively minor element in the play, so the main theme of *The Witch of Edmonton* is concerned with the life and death of Frank Thorney. This plot is a typical Jacobean domestic tragedy, telling how Frank secretly marries Winnifride, a serving-maid who is pregnant. Whether Frank is responsible for this or whether the father is in fact Winnifride's master, Sir Arthur Clarington, is not made clear but, once married, Winnifride rebuffs all advances from her aged former lover. Frank, through a combination of greed and weakness, is persuaded by his father into a bigamous union with a minor heiress, Susan Carter. The affair is resolved when Frank murders Susan and feigns an attack on his own life. His treachery is unmasked by Susan's sister, Katharine, and he goes to his death, seeking and gaining forgiveness from his wife and from Susan's father.

The dramatists use several obvious devices to link this plot with the Elizabeth Sawyer sections. Old Carter declares that Frank has been bewitched by her into murdering Susan, and Thorney's progress to the scaffold in V.iii is divided into two parts, with Elizabeth Sawyer's execution journey interposed. In both cases the prisoners make final speeches of repentance, although the witch does not receive the ready forgiveness that Frank is accorded.

A major element in the historical case was the dog which reputedly acted as Mother Sawyer's familiar spirit. In the play, the dog also appears to Frank and seems to encourage his murderous designs. It is also present when his treachery is discovered in IV.ii and in fact seems to play a part in his unmasking. This parallels its relationship with Mother Sawyer, which begins in apparent accord and ends with the spirit's desertion of the old woman. The black dog is also featured in the third plot, for it appears to Cuddy Banks, 'the Clown', who is organising a May Day morris dance at the homes of Sir Arthur and Old Carter—which, in itself, is a further linking element. However, Cuddy treats the dog as a pet rather than an evil spirit and does not fall prey to it in the same manner as do its other two victims.

Adherents of the Margaret Murray school of thought concerning the origins of witchcraft might find an ironic link in the fact that Cuddy is preparing a morris dance to celebrate May Day. To those who trace the origins of witchcraft back to the ancient religions, May Day Eve, the date of the major Spring festival, is of special significance. The morris dance itself is regarded as retaining vestiges of primitive fertility rites. The hobbyhorse which Cuddy rides is aligned with witches' broomsticks and other symbolic flying devices, whilst Maid Marion, one of the leading characters in the morris, is identified by such writers with the queen of the coven at witchcraft gatherings.

However, the links between the May Day/morris revels and witchcraft are far from universally accepted, and it is almost certainly over-subtle to see deliberate parallels between these scenes and the witchcraft sections of the play. On the other hand, there are certain clear linking devices in this episode: the morris dancers want a witch to be included in their ranks (a request turned down by Cuddy on the grounds, significantly, that this would be a break with tradition), and the dog spirit's intervention, marring the festivities, complements the havoc he wreaks in other quarters. But apart from this, it is difficult to see intentional ironic parallels between the innocent revels and the sombre witchcraft scenes.[3]

Dramatic irony is used in other sections of the play to provide less disputable links. There are several references to devils and fiends in relationship to Frank Thorney—for example, his father calls him 'a devil like a man' (I.ii.156) and Frank himself describes beggary and want as 'Two devils that are occasions to enforce / A shameful end' (I.i. 19–20). Such references are obvious complements to the dog–devil with which Elizabeth Sawyer becomes embroiled.

Winnifride rebukes Sir Arthur for swearing by the sun (traditionally a symbol of goodness and Christian virtue):

> Can you name
> That syllable of good, and yet not tremble
> To think to what a foul and black intent
> You use it for an oath? [I.i.180–3]

This is mirrored by the dog's insistence that Mother Sawyer should turn her back on the sun before uttering her diabolical incantation in II.i. Much emphasis is laid in the first scene on the marriage vows which Frank reiterates to convince Winnifride of his good faith. In particular, the Christian aspect of these vows is stressed. Winnifride rejects Sir Arthur's approaches with the words: 'And shall I then for my part / Unfile the sacred oath set on record / In Heaven's book? (I.i.200–2).

These vows contrast with the diabolical pact which Elizabeth Sawyer makes with the dog-spirit. Neither Frank nor the dog remains faithful to the bonds, and deception and infidelity are themes common to all three plots. Frank betrays both Winnifride and Susan and persuades Sir Arthur to join him in the deception of his father. Frank, in turn, is deceived by Winnifride and Sir Arthur who hide their liaison from him. Similarly, Cuddy Banks is tricked by the devil–dog into pursuing a spirit in the form of Katharine and he receives a ducking for his pains. More tragically, Mother Sawyer is also the victim of the dog's deception, for the creature, having enticed her into the devilish pact, finally forsakes her and, gloating over her downfall, leaves her to her fate: 'Out, witch! Thy trial is at hand. / Our prey being had, the devil does laughing stand' (V.i.73–4).

In contrast, Cuddy Banks, despite his apparent simplicity, is too shrewd to become similarly ensnared. His comical insistence on treating the spirit as a dog rather than a devil seems to ensure his immunity from its wiles. He rejects the dog's offer of a pact with the words: 'No, I'll see thee hang'd; thou shalt be damned first. / I know thy qualities too well. I'll give no suck to such whelps' (V.i.178–9).

Contrasting with the treachery and deception are the constancy and fidelity exhibited by both Winnifride and Susan towards Frank, despite his treatment of them. Likewise, there is the genuine affection, amounting to love, which Elizabeth develops for her dog-spirit. This devotion arises out of her intense loneliness, for she is reviled and abused on all sides. It is particularly pathetic that her clearest expression of these feelings comes shortly before the dog's treachery is revealed:

> Kiss me, my Tommy,
> And rub away some wrinkles on my brow
> By making my old ribs to shrug for joy
> Of thy fine tricks.                                [IV.i.157–60]

In addition to these inter-related themes of constancy/infidelity and loyalty/betrayal, the last-minute repentances of Frank and Mother Sawyer are foreshadowed in the first scene by Winnifride's expressions of penitence for her deception of Frank, inspired by his apparently honourable action in marrying her. He has done so to save her from the fear of 'what the tattling gossips in their cups / Can speak against thy fame' (I.i.–4). In contrast, Elizabeth Sawyer has had no one to protect her from the gossip and slander which has been the major cause of her turning to witchcraft.

The various portrayals of corruption and repentance are aspects of the principle theme of the play, which is a consideration of individual moral responsibility. This is seen most clearly in the increasing corruption of Mother Sawyer and Frank Thorney, who both try to excuse their crimes. The witch blames the unkindness of her neighbours, declaring that she has become a witch only after enduring their unjust slanders and physical cruelty. Her first words are:

And why on me? why should the envious world
Throw all their scandalous malice upon me? ...
                 Some call me witch,
And being ignorant of myself, they go
About to teach me how to be one.                [II.i.1–10]

Frank blames destiny for his misdeeds, linking this with a Macbeth-like acceptance of his increasing involvement in sinful acts:

              On every side I am distracted,
Am waded deeper into mischief
Than virtue can avoid. But on I must,
Fate leads me, I will follow.                [I.ii.190–3]

The devil–dog plays a crucial part in the ultimate crimes that each commits. It persuades Mother Sawyer to make her satanic pact and, at her behest, it brings about the death of her enemy, Anne Ratcliff; it also appears to help Frank make up his mind to murder Susan. However, it is extremely significant that the dog materialises only after the two characters have already begun to contemplate such acts. Elizabeth Sawyer, desiring revenge on her tormentors, prays for a familiar spirit which will help her to:

Abjure all goodness, be at hate with prayer,
And study curses, imprecations,
Blasphemous speeches, oaths, detested oaths,
Or anything that's ill.                [II.i.109–12]

Thorney's involvement with the dog is of a different nature. Whilst exerting influence over him, it remains invisible during the murder of Susan. Frank seems unaware of the dog's prompting—in fact, he is anxious to impress on his victim that the crime is unpremeditated. The heavy-handed irony behind his words appears to confirm the unseen influence of the spirit, despite his avowal that:

The Devil did not prompt me. Till this minute
You might have safe returned; now you cannot;
You have dogg'd your own death.           [III.iii.37–9]

However, the dog's words at the beginning of the scene put a different complexion on Frank's apparently spontaneous action. These suggest that the spirit has insight into Frank's mind and recognises an opportunity for evil in very much the same manner as do the Weird Sisters in their dealings with Macbeth:

Now for an early mischief and a sudden.
The mind's about it now; one touch from me

Soon sets the body forward. [III.iii.1–3]

As long as Elizabeth Sawyer and Thorney remain innocent of sinful thoughts the dog cannot influence them. Thus the moral responsibility for their actions remains their own. This is highlighted by the fact that the simple but essentially good-hearted Cuddy Banks remains uncorrupted by the dog's temptations. Having failed to seduce Cuddy, the dog openly explains its function and methods to him, showing clearly how the devil is ready to take advantage of any inherent weakness in its prospective victims:

> I'll thus much tell thee: thou never art so distant
> From an evil spirit, but that thy oaths,
> Curses, and blasphemies pull him to thine elbow.
> Thou never tell'st a lie, but that a devil
> Is within hearing it. Thy evil purposes
> Are ever haunted, but when they come to act,
> As thy tongue slandering, bearing false witness,
> Thy hand stabbing, stealing, cozening, cheating,
> He's then within thee. Thou play'st; he bets upon thy part.
> Although thou lose, yet he will gain by thee. [V.i.128–37]

It is possible to see the dog as a symbolic device, introduced to reinforce the theme of moral responsibility. Mark Stevig, in *John Ford and the Traditional Moral Order* (1968), declares that, 'the handling of the dog is in fact an instructive illustration of the ways in which symbolism, realism, psychology and morality are often linked in seventeenth century plays' (p. 48). Nevertheless, the dog–devil is not wholly successful in theatrical terms. In dramatising a well-known contemporary case in which the dog-spirit was an essential element, the playwrights were more or less obliged to portray the devil in this form but it presents practical problems, and in performance it would be difficult to create and sustain the essentially sinister qualities that a malevolent devil should possess. The humorous episodes with Cuddy Banks would be easier to handle but these might conflict with rather than complement the horrific effects necessary in other sections.

Marlowe faced a similar problem in *Doctor Faustus*, where a demonic figure is a major 'character', but his sources were more helpful in this respect and the presentation of the evil spirit in priestly form is dramatically effective. It enables the audience to respond to the human feelings of anguish and regret for his fallen state which Mephistophilis expresses and the priestly guise introduces various paradoxical and symbolic undertones.

James I, in his *Daemonologie* (book I), declares that while Satan will

97

reveal himself to the greatest magicians and fulfil their behests, lesser practitioners of the occult have to be content with demons in the forms of dogs, apes or vermin, which give brief answers and swift abuse. Mother Sawyer clearly comes into the second category and therefore her devil companion takes an appropriate shape.

There are, however, certain parallels between the Faustus–Mephistophilis relationship and that of Elizabeth Sawyer and her dog. Both spirits appear when their prospective victims are practising blasphemy and are already inclined mentally towards diabolism. As Mephistophilis says:

> For when we hear one rack the name of God,
> Abjure the scriptures and his saviour Christ,
> We fly, in hope to get his glorious soul. [iii.49–52]

This is also in accord with the view propounded by James I in *Daemonologie* (book II). He asserts that the devil only approaches a witch who is already ignorant or contemptuous of God and when she is solitary, in bed or in the fields. It is in just such a situation that Mother Sawyer is first tempted by the devil–dog. Both the dog and Mephistophilis trap their prey by pretending friendship and tempting them with promises of supernatural powers. They both make compacts sealed with blood, compacts which are immediately broken. Mephistophilis refuses Faustus's request for a wife—a hint that he is as isolated and as much in need of companionship as is Mother Sawyer—on the grounds that 'Marriage is but a ceremonial toy'. The dog admits his inability to inflict death on Old Carter who, incredibly, in view of his brutality towards Mother Sawyer, is apparently living in love and charity with all his other neighbours. The two spirits become companions to their victims, encouraging them along their primrose paths before finally deserting them and leaving them to their fates.

Such chains of events are typical of the traditional concepts of the inevitable consequences of diabolic pacts as propounded in many of the prose writings of the period, so it is not surprising that the two relationships follow such similar lines. More significant perhaps are the verbal echoes in *The Witch of Edmonton* of the earlier play. These are especially evident in II.i where the fatal pact is made. The following exchange is very close to the equivalent scenes in *Doctor Faustus*

> *Sawyer*: May I believe thee?
> *Dog*:                  To confirm 't, command me
>     Do any mischief unto man or beast,
>     And I'll effect it, on condition
>     That uncompell'd, thou make a deed of gift

```
        Of soul and body to me.
Sawyer:                        Out, alas!
        My soul and body?
Dog:                           And that instantly
        And seal it with thy blood. If thou deniest,
        I'll tear thy body in a thousand pieces.        [II.i. 128–35]⁴
```

However, even these similarities might be fortuitous, for the dialogue in
*The Witch of Edmonton* at this point is also very close to Goodcole's
description of this incident. In her confession to him, made in the
condemned cell, Elizabeth Sawyer gave her own account of the pact she
had made with the dog-spirit. She stated that the creature:

> Demanded of mee my soule and body; threatning then to teare me in
> pieces if that I did not grant unto him my soule and my bodie when he
> asked of me ... to seale this my promise I gave him leave to sucke of
> my blood, the which he asked of me.

## II

The dramatists adhere very closely to Goodcole's narrative throughout the
witchcraft sections of the play. In both the dramatic and the prose accounts
the devil–dog first appears to Mother Sawyer whilst she is uttering
blasphemous imprecations. The dog's first words to her, as recorded in her
confession, were: 'Oh! Have I now found you cursing, swearing and
blaspheming? Now you are mine.' These appear in the drama as: 'Ho!
Have I found thee cursing? Now thou art / Mine own' (II.i.118–19).
Mother Sawyer admitted to Goodcole that she was at first frightened by
the apparition but 'hee did bid me not to feare him at all, for hee would do
me no hurt at all, but would do for mee whatsoever I should require of
him'. In the play the dog calms Elizabeth's fears with the words: 'Come, do
not fear; I love thee much too well / To hurt or fright thee' (II.i.122–3). As
in Goodcole's version, it then proceeds to tempt its victim with promises of
revenge over her enemies.

The blasphemous prayer that the dog teaches Mother Sawyer is identical
in each work ('Sanctibicetur nomen tuum'), but the playwrights create a
rhyming couplet by preceding the phrase with the line: 'If thou to death or
shame pursue 'em' (II.i.173). The circumstances in which the prayer is
taught are different in the two versions. Whereas in the play the witch
learns the words during her first encounter with the dog, as part of its
preliminary instructions to her, in the prose version the prayer is imparted
on a later occasion, after the devil has caught Mother Sawyer praying to

Christ. She declares: 'He charged me then to pray no more to Jesus Christ but to him the Divell.' The playwrights have ignored here the chance to introduce dramatic tension, which is present in *Doctor Faustus*, arising from the victim's desperate but unavailing attempts to turn back from the diabolic path.

On other occasions, however, the dramatists have developed points from the prose account to give an added dimension to the drama. For example, in Goodcole's version Elizabeth admits that she has 'handled' the dog: 'Yes, I did stroake him on the backe, and then he would becke unto me and wagge his tayle as being therewith contented.' This hint of mutual affection is built up into the pathetic picture of the friendless old woman of the play, developing the genuine love for her treacherous dog-spirit which was noted previously.

**9**                    'Ho, ho, my dainty,
          My little pearl! No lady loves her hound,
          Monkey, or parakeet, as I do thee.'
Melvyn Hayes as the dog-spirit and Ruby Head in the title role in *The Witch of Edmonton*, directed by Bernard Miles at the Mermaid Theatre, London, in 1960.

The dog's ultimate betrayal is present in both versions. In Goodcole's account, Elizabeth asserts that she has not seen the spirit for three weeks and that it has not visited her in prison. As her confessor notes, the dog has deserted her for, 'being descried in his waies and workes, immediately he fled, leaving her to shift and answere for herselfe'. In the play the desertion is quite fully developed throughout V.i. Mother Sawyer, beginning to fear that the dog has left her, summons it with her prayer. The dog appears but its colour has changed from black to white. This transformation signals the creature's new attitude to her and it proceeds to taunt her openly with her impending death: 'My whiteness puts thee in mind of thy winding sheet . . . When the devil comes to thee as a lamb, have at thy throat' (V.i.34–8).

The colour change has been adapted from the witch's declaration to Goodcole that the spirit came to her 'always in the shape of a dogge and of two collars [colours], sometimes of blacke and sometimes of white'. She also stated that the dog was usually black but 'when I was praying hee would come unto me in the white colour'. From these bare details the playwrights have created the theatrically effective symbol of the dog's dramatic change of colour, which heralds its victim's final downfall. The dog is in fact one of the most common forms for familiar spirits as they were described in contemporary witch confessions and in such accounts the colours black and white often recur. Cats were also frequent companions and the creatures were often spoken of as being 'parti-coloured'. According to Edward Fairfax in his *Daemonologia* (1621), Margaret Waite's spirit was 'a white cat spotted with black'. Although an actual colour change was a much rarer feature, Margaret Johnson, who was one of the accused in the second Lancashire witch-scare of 1633, confessed that 'when her devill did come to sucke her pappe, hee usually came to her in ye liknes of a cat, sometymes of one colour, and somtymes on [sic] an other. And yt since this trouble befell her, her spirit hath left her, and shee never sawe him since.'[5] The latter point was also a common feature of such cases and is present in Mother Sawyer's relationship with her spirit.

Elizabeth Sawyer's confession of guilt, made two days before her execution and fully recorded in the pamphlet, is also given an added dimension in the drama, which subtly reinforces the impression of the dog-spirit's power over its victim. Just before her arrest, Mother Sawyer vows that she will never confess and the dog retorts that 'ere the executioner catch thee / Full in 's claws, thou'lt confess all' (V.i.71–2). When she is accused of bewitching Frank Thorney into killing Susan (a palpably absurd charge of which she is clearly innocent) she replies as if under a fatally hypnotic spell, incriminating herself in her attempted denial:

> is every devil mine?
> Would I had one now whom I might command
> To tear you all in pieces: Tom would have done't
> Before he left me. [V.iii.28–31]

A further variation between the prose and dramatic works is that Goodcole's pamphlet describes the single trial at which Mother Sawyer was indicted and condemned for causing the death of Agnes Ratcliffe. In the play she faces two separate hearings—in IV.i and V.ii. The first is not an official trial but is closer to such pre-trial hearings as that recorded in the St Osyth pamphlet, where an attempt was made to determine whether there was sufficient evidence for the accused to be sent for trial. The scene is most effective in dramatic terms. It begins with a group of incensed townsmen, led by Old Banks, who display the frightening blend of credulity, fear and malice of a lynch mob. They see Mother Sawyer as the scapegoat for all the sins and misfortunes of the neighbourhood: 'Our cattle fall, our wives fall, our daughters fall, and maid-servants fall; and we ourselves shall not be able to stand if this beast be suffered to graze amongst us' (IV.i.12–14).

To 'prove' her guilt they use the device of thatch-burning. This involves the taking of a handful of thatch from her roof and burning it. If Mother Sawyer is a witch, she will immediately come to the spot. This was a common method of testing for witchcraft,[6] and Goodcole states that 'an old ridiculouse custome was used, which was to plucke the Thatch of her house, and to burne it, and it being so burnt, the author of such mischiefe should presently come'. In the play, Mother Sawyer does of course enter, although the text does not make it clear whether her arrival is fortuitous or has indeed been supernaturally induced. She is surrounded, amidst cries of 'Beat her, kick her, set fire on her.' Fortunately, Sir Arthur Clarington arrives, conveniently accompanied by a Justice who shares Goodcole's scepticism, and he roundly condemns the townsmen for their folly in taking the law into their own hands.

Old Banks then accuses the old woman of being responsible for his own perverted behaviour. He confesses that:

> So, sir, ever since, having a dun cow tied up in my backside, let me go thither or but cast mine eye at her, and if I should be hang'd, I cannot choose, though it be ten times in an hour, but run to the cow and, taking up her tail, kiss—saving your worship's reverence—my cow behind, that the whole town of Edmonton has been ready to bepiss themselves with laughing me to scorn. [52–8]

There is a possible vestige here of the anal kiss, whereby witches were popularly supposed to salute the devil, whether in human or animal form. No mention of this charge is to be found in Goodcole, but Gifford, in his *A Dialogue Concerning Witches and Witchcraftes* (1593), mentions a similar case in the section where he is ridiculing the flimsy nature of much of the St Osyth pre-trial testimony. Samuel, a credulous rustic, reports that:

> A third man came in, and he sayd she [the accused] was once angry with him, he had a dun cow which was tyed up in a house, for it was in winter, he feared that some evill would follow, and for his life he could not come in where she was, but he must needes take up her tayle and kisse under it. Two or three other came in and sayd she was by common fame accounted a witch: We found her giltie, and she was condemned to prison, and to the pillorie, but [she] stood stiffe in it that she was no witch.
>
> *Daniel*: And are you sure she was one? . . .
> *Samuel*: But what can you say to the other? The man which could not chuse but kisse under his cowes tayle?
> *Daniel*: I say he was farre in love with his cow.[7]

The Justice seems to share Daniel's opinion and he ignores Banks's evidence. However, he proceeds to interrogate Mother Sawyer, who responds to his 'mild questions' with a stream of abuse. This corresponds with Goodcole's statement that her only defence was to curse her accusers. The playwright (almost certainly Dekker, in view of the social comment involved) takes the opportunity to put into the old woman's mouth charges of hypocrisy and moral laxity against the higher classes which, she claims, are as near to witchcraft and devilish behaviour as anything of which she has been accused. She demands:

> What are your painted things in princes' courts,
> Upon whose eyelids lust sits, blowing fires
> To burn men's souls in sensual, hot desires,
> Upon whose naked paps a lecher's thought
> Acts sin in fouler shapes than can be wrought?          [105–9]

She ironically declares:

> The man of law
> Whose honeyed hopes the credulous client draws—
> As bees to tinkling basins—to swarm to him
> From his own hive, to work the wax in his—
> He is no witch, not he!          [130–4]

This outburst is over-sophisticated in its expression, coming from such a simple and uneducated person, but is otherwise highly effective. A further, ironic dimension is added to this scene when Mother Sawyer cries:

> Dare any swear I ever temped maiden
> With golden hooks flung at her chastity,
> To come and lose her honour, and being lost
> To pay not a denier for 't? [140–3][8]

Her words have particular significance for Sir Arthur and her apparent insight into his seduction of Winnifride convinces him of her guilt.[9] However, the Justice rightly concludes that there is no evidence to sustain the charges and he contents himself with advising Mother Sawyer to 'mend thy life, get home and pray' (l. 149). The sympathy that has been evoked for the old woman during the early part of this scene is considerable, but it is largely dissipated when we see that, far from repenting and taking the Justice's advice, she immediately renews her relationship with her dog-spirit and turns her malicious attentions to:

> That jade, that foul-tongu'd whore, Nan Ratcliffe,
> Who for a little soap lick'd by my sow,
> Struck and almost had lam'd it; did not I charge thee
> To pinch that quean to th' heart? [IV.i.170–3]

This formed the basis of the main charge brought against her at the trial, where it was alleged that she 'did witch unto death Agnes Ratcleife ... because that Elizabeth [sic] Ratcleife did strike a Sowe of hers in her Sight for licking up a little Soape where shee had laide it'. In the play, at the witch's instigation, the dog turns the woman mad and, in an insanity scene typical of the period, Anne Ratcliffe confronts her enemy:

> *Ratcliffe*: Are you not Mother Sawyer?
> *Sawyer*: No, I am a lawyer.
> *Ratcliffe*: Art thou? I prithee let me scratch thy face, for thy pen has
> flay'd off a great many men's skins. [IV.i.180–3]

The face-scratching reference is not present in Goodcole but, like the thatch-burning, this was a crude method of dealing with suspected witchcraft. It was commonly believed that scratching a witch (usually 'above the breath') and so drawing blood would temporarily break an evil spell. Amongst the pre-trial brutality to which the 'Witches of Northamptonshire' of 1612 were subjected was scratching, performed by two of their supposed victims: 'This Gentleman and his Sister being brought to the gaole where these Witches were detained, having once gotten sight of them, in their fits the Witches being held, by scratching they drew blwd of them, and were sodainely delivered of their paine.'[10] Anne Ratcliffe fails to scratch Elizabeth Sawyer, breaks free from her husband

and others who attempt to restrain her, and beats out her brains. This incident, according to Goodcole, was untrue but was featured in the current ballads inspired by the case. The madness element was developed by the dramatists from the account in the indictment, given by her husband, of Agnes Ratcliffe's fatal illness following her supposed bewitchment: 'That evening Agnes Ratcleife fell very sicke, and was extraordinarily vexed, and in a most strange manner in her sicknesse was tormented ... she lay foaming at the mouth and was extraordinarily distempered.'

Amongst the evidence of Elizabeth Sawyer's guilt produced at the actual trial was the testimony of three women who had physically examined the accused and had found that she 'had a private and strange marke on her body'. This of course was held to be the teat with which she suckled with blood her dog familiar. This feature is also included in the play when Mother Sawyer turns to her dog after the stress of her first unofficial trial:

> *Sawyer*: Comfort me: thou shalt have the teat anon.
> *Dog*: Bow wow: I'll have it now.
> *Sawyer*:                  I am dri'd up
> With cursing and with madness; and have yet
> No blood to moisten these sweet lips of thine.    [IV.i.151–4]

Additional evidence based on her physical appearance spoke of her habitually downcast countenance (which was hardly surprising in view of the abuse to which she was constantly subjected) and crooked, deformed body. In popular belief such an aspect could betoken a witch and the Elizabeth Sawyer of the play is portrayed in a similar manner. Goodcole states that she was partially blind in one eye, the result of an accidental injury involving 'a sticke which one of my children had in the hand'.[11] However, the playwrights make only passing reference to this disability when one of Cuddy Banks's fellow morris-dancers says of her, 'Bless us, Cuddy, and let her curse t'other eye out' (II.i.85).

In the first speech Mother Sawyer describes herself as 'poor, deform'd, and ignorant, / And like a bow buckl'd and bent together' (II.i.3–4). Similarly, the witch Sycorax in *The Tempest* was, through age and envy, 'grown into a hoop' and Samuel Harsnett in his *A Declaration of Egregious Popishe Impostures* (1603/4) describes the typical witch as being 'an olde weather-beaten Croane, having her chinne, and her knees meeting for age, walking like a bow leaning on a shaft' (p. 136).

In their treatments of Mother Sawyer's appearance, the essential difference between Goodcole and the playwrights is that whereas in the former's account the old woman's repellent aspect is merely additional proof of her guilt, in the drama it is made the cause of her first venture into witchcraft. Whatever her subsequent crimes, the first evil was inflicted on her. Because of her ugliness she has been made an outcast, the subject of malicious gossip and 'a common sink / For all the filth and rubbish of men's tongues / To fall and run into' (II.i.6–8).

Because her neighbours treat her as a witch, Elizabeth Sawyer responds by becoming one. The psychological insight displayed by the dramatists here is very much in accord with Reginald Scot's explanation of one of the principal causes of apparent witchcraft. In *The Discoverie of Witchcraft* he writes:

> One sort of such as are said to bee witches, are women which be commonly old, lame, bleare-eied, pale, fowle, and full of wrinkles ... They are leane and deformed, shewing melancholie in their faces, to the horror of all that see them ... These miserable wretches are so odious unto all their neighbours, and so feared, as few dare offend them, or denie them anie thing they aske: whereby they take upon them; yea, and sometimes thinke, that they can doo such things as are beyond the abilitie of humane nature ... The witch, exspecting hir neighbours mischances, and seeing things sometimes come to passe according to her wishes, cursses and incantations ... confesseth that she (as a goddes) hath brought such things to passe.
>
> [Book I, Chapter iii]

In Goodcole's account, Elizabeth Sawyer's motives for engaging in witchcraft are given as springing simply from her 'malice and envy'. He limits himself to a straightforward, unemotional description of the woman's downfall, taking the opportunity to point out the moral dangers of her unchristian behaviour but not committing himself to an opinion of the actual witchcraft powers, either as they are ascribed to Elizabeth Sawyer in particular or in a wider sense.

In the play there is no question of Mother Sawyer's guilt and the dog is without doubt a diabolical spirit through which she works her evil, but the whole tenor of the dramatists' treatment of the theme is akin to the humanity and rationalism expressed by Scot. Witchcraft is portrayed as a reality and is condemned and the witch is held up as an example of the dangers of meddling with the occult. Nevertheless, the playwrights show great compassion for the simple creature who, initially through the malice of others and at first committing no greater wrong than foolishness, becomes enmeshed in the devil's toils. It is an indication of King James's changing attitude to witchcraft that the play should have been given a court performance when its portrayal of the witch figure is so much in accord with the compassionate views of Scot, whom James had previously so bitterly condemned.

The dramatists are at least as concerned with Mother Sawyer's fate as with portraying her evil deeds. This emphasis on the witch's destiny contrasts with the portrayal of 'maleficia' in such works as *Macbeth*, *The Witch* and *The Masque of Queenes*—and as it is described in *The Tempest*. In all these plays we merely see instances of 'maleficia' presented as manifestations of superhuman wickedness, rather than their being principally the means of destroying the performers of the deeds. The evil-doers in these plays are portrayed as supernatural creatures in their own right, allies of the devil and working with him towards the destruction of human souls, whereas Mother Sawyer remains pathetically human to the end. She is essentially the tool or 'instrument of mischief': the 'maleficia' she performs are clearly activated by the devil in order to achieve more certainly her damnation and her fate constitutes the major tragic element in the play.

In this respect the play is similar to *Doctor Faustus* and, as in Marlowe's play, the audience witnesses the actual making and destruction of a witch. We see the events leading up to the fatal demonic contract and we are left in no doubt that the devil has made this pact primarily to gain Mother Sawyer's soul. The devil–dog proclaims, 'See, now I dare call thee mine' (I.ii.145) and it finally leaves her with the taunt, 'Thy time is come to curse and rave and die; / The glass of thy sins is full, and it must run out at gallows' (V.i.62–3). This is similar to Mephistophilis's relationship with Faustus but whereas the latter is a blend of scholar and magician in the esoteric Renaissance tradition, Mother Sawyer is a much humbler figure. However, her portrayal provides us with a thoroughly convincing picture of the witch as she must have been most frequently in reality—old, solitary, and embittered but an essentially pathetic figure, brutally persecuted by her neighbours through a blend of prejudice and ill-founded suspicion. She is the helpless scapegoat for her fellow townspeople's barely suppressed feelings of guilt at their own superstitions and irrational fears. She is too wary and embittered to recognise genuine kindness when it is shown to her by Cuddy Banks but the sympathy evoked for her, particularly in the early stages of the play, leads one to hope that her final plea for divine forgiveness does not go unheard.

### Notes to Chapter 7

1   Goodcole's pamphlet is reprinted in A. H. Bullen's revision (1895) of A.

Dyce's edition of Ford's *Dramatic Works* (1869). Quotations from *The Witch of Edmonton* are taken from *Jacobean and Caroline Comedies*, edited by R. G. Lawrence (1973).

2   See, for example, the essays edited by E. G. Fogel and D. V. Erdman in *Evidence for Authorship* (1966) and for specific discussion of Dekker's collaborative techniques see C. J. Sisson, *Lost Plays of Shakespeare's Age* (1936), pp. 110–14, together with his articles in *The Library*, fourth series, vol. VIII (1927), pp. 39–57 and 233–59. See also G. R. Price, *Thomas Dekker* (1969), pp. 104–5, and M. Joan Sargeaunt, *John Ford* (1935), pp. 34–9

3   For a discussion of possible links between such activities and witchcraft see, for example, Pennethorne Hughes, *Witchcraft* (1952), chapters 8 and 9.

4   Faustus also makes 'A deed of gift of body and soul ... with thine own blood' (scene v) and is warned by the Bad Angel, 'If thou repent, devils will tear thee in pieces' (scene vi). The play also contains numerous echoes of Shakespeare, including Sir Arthur's scornful cry to Winnifride, 'Get you to your nunnery' (I.i.209) and there are also references to Lyly's *Mother Bombie* (IV.i.198) and to *Gammer Gurton's Needle* (IV.i.253–4).

5   Quoted in Murray, *Witch-Cult*, p. 213.

6   Kittredge, pp. 102 and 434.

7   An amusing reversal of this situation occurs in an apocryphal tale which exists in several versions, one of which is recounted in *Newes From Scotland* as an instance of the youthful follies of Dr Fian. In an attempt to arouse the love of a 'gentlewoman', Fian allegedly asked her brother, who was a pupil of his, to obtain 'three haires of his sisters privities'. Instead, the boy took three hairs from the udder of a cow 'which never had borne Calfe nor gone to the Bull'. Taking the hairs to a church, Fian 'wrought his arte upon them', in response to which the cow appeared 'and made towards the Schoolemaister, leaping and dauncing upon him, and following him foorth of the church and to what place so ever he went to the great admiration of all the townes men of Saltpans, and many other who did beholde the same'.

8   These lines provide further evidence of Dekker's authorship of this scene, for the image is very similar to that in Hippolito's speech in *The Honest Whore, Part One*, I.i:

> Were I but o'er your threshold, a next man,
> And after him a next, and then a fourth,
> Should have this golden hook, and lascivious bait,
> Thrown out to the full-length.

9   This ability to read innermost thoughts is also displayed by Erictho in *Sophonisba* (IV.i). James I's initial reaction to the confessions of the North Berwick witches was that they were 'extreame lyars' but he was convinced of the guilt of Agnes Sampson (Tompson) when she showed similar powers by recounting his wedding-night conversation with his bride, Anne of Denmark.

10   The pamphlet is reprinted in modernised form in Rosen, *Witchcraft*, pp. 344–56.

11   There is no indication in the play (apart from her name) that Mother Sawyer has any children. Their presence would presumably have created an unnecessary complication, just as Lady Macbeth's apparent motherhood is ignored after her single reference to her knowing 'how tender 'tis to love the babe that milks me' in I.vii.

108

# CHAPTER 8

---

# SECRET SPELLS OF ART

## MAGICIANS AND CONJURORS

> *Bacon*: Masters, for that learned Burden's skill is deep,
> And sore he doubts of Bacon's cabbalism,
> I'll show you why he haunts to Henley oft;
> Not, doctors, for to taste the fragrant air,
> But there to spend the night in alchemy,
> To multiply with secret spells of art;
> Thus private steals he leaning from us all.
>
> [*Friar Bacon and Friar Bungay*, ii.104–10]

### I

It is impossible to draw clear distinctions between witchcraft and the other magical arts practised in the sixteenth and seventeenth centuries. Both within the intellectual spheres of alchemy, astrology and theurgy and between these and the humbler activities of the village witch and conjuror there was a constant overlap of beliefs and practices. Many 'black' witches of the humbler sort seem to have combined their malicious roles with those of wise women or healers; often, in fact, they appear to have begun their occult careers as practitioners of the more beneficent skills before being tempted to move on to the less innocuous arts. Ursula Kemp, one of the St Osyth witches, was credited with curing Grace Thurlow's son, Davy, who was 'strangelie taken and tormented'. The two women subsequently quarrelled and Thurlow accused the other of inflicting sickness on herself and her infant daughter. Agnes Tompson (or Sampson), the most prominent of the North Berwick witches who plotted against King James, had previously gained a reputation as a healer and a charm is ascribed to her which begins: 'All kinds of ills that ever may be, / In Christ's name, I conjure ye.'[1]   Conversely, most village wizards were fully conversant with the 'black' arts, in theory if not in practice. Every locality had its wise man or woman, whose skills were largely based on traditional lore, often handed on from one generation to the next. Their main function was the dispensing of herbal remedies for a wide range of maladies, physical and psychological. They were reputedly able to counter the powers of bewitchment; many also practised fortune-telling and their aid was frequently sought in a search for lost or stolen goods. Their divination activities usually involved ancient rituals performed with sieve and shears or key and book (a psalter or Bible) and these were often accompanied by pseudo-religious rites involving the chanting of spells and the tracing of symbolic patterns with magic rods.[2]

It was to such persons that the majority of the populace turned in times of sickness, trouble or any other adversity. It was for this reason that many of the clergy complained of their activities, seeing them as rivals and intruders within their spiritual domains.[3] The suspicion with which such healing activities were viewed in some quarters is indicated by the episode related in *Newes From Scotland* concerning one of the accused, Gillis Duncan, who was a maidservant to one David Seaton, a deputy bailiff in the town of Tranent. Seaton became aware that Gillis was going out secretly at night. On investigation, he found that she had 'took in hand to help all such as were troubled or greeved with any kinde of sicknes or infirmitie. . . . Seaton had his maide in some great suspition, that she did not those things by naturall and lawfull wayes, but rather supposed it to be doone by some extraordinary and unlawfull meanes.' Gillis refused to confess to this, despite various tortures, but her body was searched and the devil's mark was discovered, 'which being found, she confessed that all her doings was doone by the wicked allurements and inticements of the Divell, and that she did them by witchcraft.'

William Perkins, it will be recalled, condemned all such practices, arguing that no magical activities, 'black' or 'white', were innocent; they were all dependent on diabolical aid and indeed the 'white' magician, through the seductive nature of his seemingly beneficent arts, was even more dangerous than the openly malevolent 'black' witch. 'The most horrible and detestable monster', he declared, 'is the good witch.'[4]

However, the general populace does not seem to have shared this view. Scot affirmed, to his 'greefe', that every parish had its miracle worker and some had as many as seventeen or eighteen 'at one instant'.[5] As long as their activities remained harmless, the healing wizards were at the very least tolerated and there are very few records of trials of 'white' witches, either before secular or ecclesiastical courts, even though many of their practices contravened the anti-witchcraft statutes of the sixteenth and seventeenth centuries. This fact strengthens the view that in England most witchcraft prosecutions began at 'grass-roots' level; as long as the general populace did not feel threatened by occult activities, there was no impetus to suppress them.

One case which did reach the stage of a judicial hearing was that of John Walsh in 1566, and this enquiry seems to have been instigated from above. Walsh was summoned to appear before an ecclesiastical court 'upon certayne Interrogatories touchyng Wytchcrafte and Sorcerye'. This was a preliminary examination held before a commissary to the Bishop of Exeter but although the hearing clearly reveals Walsh to have been a conjuror, guilty by his own admission of raising spirits, there is no record of any subsequent trial. Walsh admitted practising 'physique or surgerie' but claimed that he did so 'by Arte, naturallye practised by him as he sayth, and not by anye other ill or secrete meanes'. [6] He also confessed to having a book, given him by his master, Sir Robert Drayton, a Roman Catholic. This book:

> had great circles in it, wherein he would set two waxe candels acrosse of virgin waxe, to raise the familiar spirite, of whom he woulde then aske for any thing stollen, who did it, and where the thing stollen was left, and thereby did know and also by the Feiries he knoweth who be bewitched.

The familiar was not a witch's demon but a spirit summoned by conjuring ceremonies and Walsh stressed that it 'serveth for no purpose but to search out things theft-stollen and for no other purpose at all'. However, he went on to reveal a detailed knowledge of the less innocent aspects of familiar spirits and also of image magic, although he strongly denied any practical experience of such activities. Despite these denials of personal involvement, he was clearly moving in the shadowy borderland between conjuring and 'black' magic. There is no record of his fate but in his testimony he comes across as an honest, if naive, figure, genuinely believing in both the efficacy and innocence of his art.

However, there can be no doubt that many so-called conjurors were quacks and tricksters, plying their trade with a blend of sleight of hand and native cunning to deceive their gullible clients. It was for this reason that Scot condemned their activities in *The Discoverie of Witchcraft*. He wrote scathingly of the 'counterfet art which they professe' and which they shared with 'couseners or witches', and added that 'when they have either learning, eloquence, or nimblenesse of hands to accompanie their confederacie, or rather knaverie, then (forsooth) they passe the degree of witches, and intitle themselves to the name of conjurors' (book xv, chapter i).

Popular works such as Greene's *A Disputation betweene a Hee Conny-catcher and a Shee Conny-catcher* (1592) and Chettle's *Kind-Harts Dreame* (1592?) contain detailed exposés of the practices of such cheats and swindlers. A favourite device was to promise the victim an introduction to the Queen of the Fairies, through whose supernatural ministrations fabulous wealth would be acquired. Chettle gives an account of such a fraud and the same case is narrated in the pamphlet describing 'The Brideling, Sadling and Ryding, of a rich Churle in Hampshire, by the subtill practise of one Judeth Philips, a professed cunning woman, or Fortune teller'. The trickster was formerly married to a man named Pope, and so was able to assure her victims that she had 'but come now from the Pope and know more of his mind than anie woman in the world'! She persuaded the Hampshire merchant to prepare a room in his house for the reception of the Fairy Queen, the arrangements entailing the provision of fine white linen, together with the setting out of five candlesticks, under each of which was placed an 'angel of gold'. She then made her victim attire himself with saddle, girths and bridle, rode him three times round his yard, and then ordered him and his wife to lie prostrate under a holly tree for three hours to await the arrival of the Queen of the Fairies. Meanwhile, Philips removed the linen and gold coins, appeared briefly before the 'quaking' couple clad in 'a faire white smock, somewhat disguised with a thing on her head all white, and a stick in her hand ... using some dalliance, as old wives say, spirits with night-spelles do, she vanished away, and againe entered the chamber where her pack laie ready and so roundly went away, leaving the churle and his wife in their cold lodging'. For this and other ingenious swindles Philips was tried at Newgate in February 1594/5 and sentenced to be 'whipped through the Citie'.[7]

Another such trickster was popularly known as the Wise Woman of Hogsdon. Her alleged activities feature in several tracts and she is also the subject of Heywood's play of that name, which is conjecturally dated at 1604. She combines her 'occult' hoaxes with playing the bawd and she lists her occupations thus:

> Let me see how many trades have I to live by: first, I am a wise woman, and a fortune-teller, and under that I deal in physic and fore-speaking, in palmistry, and recovering of things lost; next, I undertake to cure mad folks; then I keep gentlewomen lodgers, to furnish such

chambers as I let out by the night; then I am provided for bringing young wenches to bed; and, for a need, you see I can play the matchmaker. [III.i.54–61][8]

However, she strongly denies having any dealings with spirits or with the devil. The play reveals many of the tricks of her trade and the folly of her victims is summed up by young Luce:

'Tis strange the ignorant should be thus fooled!
What can this witch, this wizard, or old trot,
Do by enchantment, or by magic spell?
Such as profess that art should be deep scholars.
What reading can this simple woman have?
'Tis palpable gross foolery. [II.i.37–42]

A devastating exposure of fraud based on the trappings and pseudo-learning of 'deep scholars' is contained in Jonson's *The Alchemist* (1610). Amongst the many victims of the title-figure's trickery is Dapper, who is hoaxed into a supposed meeting with the Queen of the Fairies, but Subtle deceives most of his dupes through a dazzling display of the superficial trappings of the mystical art of alchemy. The genuine alchemist was a scholar, whose researches into the natural world were the precursors of much subsequent scientific investigation. However misguided he might have been in his basic aims, he was following a highly developed academic tradition which stretched back into classical times, and in which the search for the philosopher's stone, whereby all metals could be transformed into gold, was often subjugated to an intense spiritual and unworldly way of life.

A comparable intellectual and ascetic discipline was practised by the magus or theurgist who, following the precepts of such Renaissance scholars as Cornelius Agrippa and Paracelsus, believed that a full understanding of the mysteries of God could be gained through the practice of magic in its highest forms. The theurgist regarded himself as a man capable of practising magic because of the purity of his life. He had been specially prepared by instruction, experience and ceremonial consecration and this priest-like figure could extend his influence into realms far beyond those of ordinary mortals. By devoting his life to his art, he could gradually ascend through the scale of creation until he was in full spiritual communion with God.[9]

The theurgists' magical activities were devoted largely to the performance of elaborate rituals, as they were set out in such a work as Ficino's Latin translation of the supposedly pre-Christian *Corpus Hermeticum*. By means of these ceremonies, spirits were summoned and commanded to reveal aspects of the hidden secrets of life. This apparent ability to gain knowledge through supernatural revelation rather than study led to the widespread practice of a debased form of theurgy at many European universities during the Renaissance era, but in its purest form it was undoubtedly a mental and spiritual discipline of the most demanding kind.

The close bonds between the academic pursuits of alchemy, astrology and theurgy are evident in the careers of such figures as John Dee, Simon Forman and Abraham Savory. Forman, for example, practised medicine in London from 1583 until his death in 1611 but, as his case-books show, he was frequently consulted on matters of astrology, for which he had drawn up a complex set of rules. His aid was also enlisted by clients seeking the philosopher's stone and others sought his help in the inducement of love by means of magic charms. However, Forman certainly did not live up to the high ideals of theurgy; he was no ascetic, as the frank accounts of his sexual exploits in his private journal reveal. His activities brought him into conflict with the establishment and he was imprisoned on several occasions on charges brought by the Church and by the Royal College of Physicians.

Although recent research has sought, with some success, to establish John Dee as the prime English exemplar of the Rosicrucian ideal of the magico-scientist, his reputation amongst his contemporaries was far from unalloyed.[10] He resolutely affirmed that none of his occult activities was in contravention of God's will, but he, like Forman, suffered several terms of imprisonment and died in disgrace and penury in 1608, four years after King James had refused to help him refute 'that horrible and damnable, and to him most grievous and dammageable sclaunder ... that he is or hath been a conjuror or caller or invocator of divels'. Dee's unpopularity was due in part to the widespread suspicions of fraud surrounding his activities—especially the spiritualist seances he conducted with his companion, Edward Kelly—but as his plea to James indicates, the principal objection to his practices was that he had dealings with spirits. It was this aspect of the magical activities of both the intellectual and the lowly wizards that was regarded as the most potentially harmful by opponents of their arts.

In all spheres of conjuring elaborate rituals were performed in order to raise spirits. Whilst the academic followed the rites laid down in the scholarly works, his village counterpart enacted the spells and rites prescribed in such popular manuals as *The Key of Solomon* and *The Constitution of Honorius*. It was presumably such a volume that John Walsh used in the spirit-raising ceremonies that he described at his examination. Practitioners of 'black' magic also claimed the power to

114

summon spirits but the theurgists and conjurors believed that their magic was superior, in that the 'black' magician had gained his power through the taking of the demonic oath and was therefore subject to the beings he apparently commanded. Exponents of 'white' magic, on the other hand, claimed that their art came from God and they had the power not only to summon but also to control spirits. Moreover, the theurgist believed that the spirits with whom he dealt came, not from Hell, but from a sphere mid-way between Heaven and earth and were either angels or members of a division of spirits who were neither angels nor demons.

However, not all scholars agreed with this sanguine view. St Augustine condemned all magical practices as evil and Jean Bodin bitterly attacked Agrippa's view that theurgy was in accordance with God's will, affirming that the magus's attempts to extend his powers beyond human limitations, for whatever ends, were in defiance of God and a challenge to His omnipotence. Scot agreed with this view and wrote in *The Discoverie of Witchcraft*:

> There is yet another art professed by these cousening conjurors, which some fond divines affirme to be more honest and lawfull than necromancie, which is called Theurgie; wherein they worke by good angels ... But the more divine these arts seeme to the ignorant, the more damnable they be.       [book XV, chapter xlii]

For once, James I was in agreement with Scot and he too condemned such practices as, at best, dangerous folly. He declared in his *Daemonologie* (book I):

> For although, as none can be schollers in a schole, and not be subject to the master thereof: so none can studie and put in practize ... the circles and art of Magie, without committing an horrible defection from God ... These practiques, which I cal the devilles rudiments, unknowing them to be baites, casten out by him, for trapping such as God will permit to fall in his handes.

## II

This is of course an accurate account of the career of John Faustus, the legendary scholar and principal exemplar of the man of learning who, in his insatiable search for knowledge, practises a debased form of theurgy, falls to the temptation of the illusory promise of the demonic pact and thus crosses the tenuous borderline between magic and witchcraft.

In Marlowe's play we first see Faustus reviewing the traditional areas of study which he has hitherto pursued with increasing dissatisfaction. In his intellectual frustration he turns to the 'metaphysics of magicians', confident that the dominion of the latter 'stretcheth as far as doth the mind of man'. This is an unexceptionable statement both of the Renaissance attitude to learning and of the theurgists's principal purpose but even in this opening scene it is made clear that Faustus's motives are entirely egocentric. Through his magical practices he hopes to gain 'a world of profit and delight, / Of power, of honour, of omnipotence' (i.52–3). The degenerate nature of Faustus's purposes is stressed later when he rejects the theurgic vow of chastity in his first request of Mephistophilis—for a wife, 'for I am wanton and lascivious and cannot live without a wife' (v.142–3).

In his first conjuring experiment Faustus attempts to raise a spirit through the construction of a circle within which 'is Jehovah's name / Forward and backward anagrammatiz'd' (iii.8–9). In his incantation he abjures the Trinity, sprinkles holy water and makes the sign of the cross but these acts, however blasphemous, were not in themselves considered damnable and were fully in accord with established magical practice. However, the dangers inherent in such actions are made clear when Mephistophilis declares that he has answered Faustus's summons, not because of the potency of the ritual, but:

> For when we hear one rack the name of God,
> Abjure the scriptures and his saviour Christ,
> We fly, in hope to get his glorious soul.                [iii,49–51]

This assertion, coupled with Mephistophilis's declaration that he can serve Faustus only with the agreement of Lucifer, conflicts with the comforting concept of the theurgist's control over the spirits that he raises. Furthermore, Mephistophilis freely admits that he is a spirit of Hell—unlike the angelic beings that theurgists claimed to command. At this stage of the play, before the taking of the demonic oath, Faustus's actions (if not his aims) have been wholly acceptable in theurgic terms but the exchanges between Faustus and Mephistophilis indicate the playwright's view of the fallacious and self-deluding nature of the magus's beliefs.

However, it is not until Faustus takes the demonic pact that he is in fact damned. Henceforth, despite the occasional ventures into such intellectual spheres as astrology and cosmography, his activities become increasingly aligned with witchcraft, with Faustus becoming more and more deeply entwined in the devil's toils. He has moments of illusory grandeur, such as when he is graciously received by the Duke of Vanholt and by Charles, the

**10**    'Lo, Mephistophilis, for love of thee
Faustus hath cut his arm, and with his proper blood
Assures his soul to be great Lucifer's,
Chief lord and regent of perpetual night.'
Eric Porter as Faustus and Terrence Hardiman as Mephistophilis in the
Royal Shakespeare Company's production of *Doctor Faustus* in 1968,
which was directed by Clifford Williams.

German Emperor, who addresses him as 'Wonder of men, renown'd
magician, / Thrice-learned Faustus' (xii.1–2). Such an attitude is in accord
with the spirit of the romantic comedies of the early sixteenth century,
where wizards and enchanters were honoured and the legality of their
magical practices was unquestioned.

Despite such episodes, both Faustus and the audience are constantly
aware of the presence of Mephistophilis and the inexorable approach of the
expiration of the pact. In his final hour the learning that had apparently
underpinned his magic cannot save him. In the first scene Cornelius had
assured Faustus that:

> He that is grounded in astrology,
> Enrich'd with tongues, well seen in minerals,
> Hath all the principles magic doth require.          [137–9]

117

However, Faustus's desperate utterance of the Ovidian 'O lente lente currite noctis equi!' (xix.142) and his unavailing command 'Stand still, you ever-moving spheres of heaven' (l. 136) demonstrate the limitations of his scholarship. Too late he acknowledges the perversion of his learning and intellect and the self-deluding nature of the theurgist's view of his art in his moving admission, 'Though my heart pants and quivers to remember that I have been a student here these thirty years, O, would I had never seen Wittenberg, never read book!' (ll. 44–6).

Faustus is just one of many magicians and conjurors portrayed on the English stage in the sixteenth and seventeenth centuries. Such figures can be divided into three main groups: those who, like Faustus, persist with their occult practices until they enter the realms of witchcraft; others who manage to keep their activities within safer limits and who escape damnation, usually through an eleventh-hour renunciation of their magical powers; and a third group who seem able to practise their art with complete impunity.

Apart from Faustus, the most significant of the first type is Pope Alexander VI, as he is portrayed in Barnabe Barnes's *The Devil's Charter* (1606). The notoriety of Alexander, formerly Roderigo Borgia, had made him the focus of much anti-Catholic propaganda in the sixteenth century.[11] He was accused of a multiplicity of crimes, ranging from usury to murder by way of sodomy and incest. Barnes's play, which is strongly anti-papist in tone, portrays all these activities and it begins with a dumb-show in which we see Alexander being seduced into conjuring by 'a monk with a magical book and rod'. Two devils are raised, both of whom Alexander 'disliketh' but then a third appears 'in robes pontifical, with a triple crown on his head and cross keys in his hand'. Thus tempted, Alexander signs the demonic bond with his blood and in return receives the papal insignia, together with a 'magical book'.[12]

Before the opening of the play proper, therefore, Alexander has already embraced witchcraft and the work consists of a melodramatic catalogue of the crimes he commits, either to satisfy his perverted lusts or to expand and retain his worldly possessions. There is no attempt to portray him as a theurgist or scholar manqué. He is, in fact, no more than an elevated conjuror, with none of Faustus's pretensions of extending his learning or becoming a 'demi-God' through his magical practices. The emphasis throughout is on his misdeeds but even these are not in the main acts of 'maleficia' arising from his occult powers; they are merely sordid crimes committed through entirely natural means. He effects the deaths of his enemies by dint of various poisons and in this respect one is reminded of

Scot's assertion that the majority of deaths attributed to witchcraft were in reality achieved through the use of poisons.[13]

Apart from the introductory dumb-show, the major supernatural element of the play is contained in IV.i. where Alexander performs a conjuring ritual in order to discover the identity of the murderer of his son, the Duke of Candie. (He learns that the killer was his other son, Caesar Borgia, who has murdered his brother in order to be his father's sole heir!) The performance of these rites embodies the most detailed portrayal of a magical ceremony in the drama of the period. Barnes took much of his material for this scene from *The Heptameron*, a book of practical magic ascribed to the fourteenth-century scholar, Peter of Albano, but probably forged early in the sixteenth century and translated into English in 1600. It is probably this work which is recommended by Valdes to Faustus as an aid to his early conjuring ventures (i.153). *The Heptameron* contains a great deal of pseudo-Christian ritual for it presupposes that the rites it prescribes are not in conflict with divine will. Before performing his ceremony Alexander dons 'white robes of sanctity' and refers to the setting as 'this sanctified place', but during the ritual itself all overtly Christian references are omitted. For example, God is addressed only through obscure Hebrew versions of his name. The omission of such elements from the stage ceremony was no doubt due in part to the likely intervention of the censor if such references were too explicit, but the fact that a Pope, even such a Pope as Alexander, can perform his conjuring rites with all recognisably Christian aspects omitted reinforces the impression of his divorce from God and his complete affinity with the devil.

Until the final scene there is minimal interest in Alexander's ultimate and inevitable fate. Throughout the play he is a more melodramatic and less tragic figure than Faustus but as he is dying he at last utters words of regret similar to those of Faustus and the final stage direction is also reminiscent of the climax of Marlowe's play: 'Thunder and lightning. With fearful noise the devils thrust him down and go triumphing.'

A significant example of the second group of stage conjurors—those who become aware of the potentially damnable nature of their practices and renounce their magical art—is Friar Bacon, as he is portrayed in Greene's *Friar Bacon and Friar Bungay* (c. 1589/90). The play has affinities with *Doctor Faustus* but because of the uncertain dating of both works it is impossible to determine which influenced the other. Friar Bacon, like Faustus and Pope Alexander, was an historical figure around whom an elaborate mythos had been created. He lived from approximately 1220 to 1292, residing mainly in Oxford, and was renowned throughout Europe for

# THE
# HONORABLE
# HISTORIE OF
## FRIER *BACON*, AND
### FRIER *BONGAY*.

**As** it was lately plaid by the Prince *Palatine* his Seruants.

Made by *Robert Greene*, Maſter of Arts.

## LONDON,
Printed. by ELIZABETH ALLDE dwelling
neere Chriſt-Church. 16,0.

**11**    The title page of the 1630 quarto of *Friar Bacon and Friar Bungay*. The
illustration depicts the scene where Bacon and his servant, Miles, sleep
through the oracular utterances of the Brazen Head. The woodcut was
taken from the 1629 edition of the prose history, which was also printed by
Elizabeth Allende, and it is clearly based on the prose version of the
incident, where Bacon and Bungay are both present and Miles keeps himself
awake by playing on a pipe and tabor.

his studies in philosophy and experimental science. His learning was popularly ascribed to occult practices, although he himself denied any involvement in such activities. His reputation in this sphere is indicated in *Doctor Faustus* when Faustus is urged to consult 'wise Bacon's' works when he is embarking on his magical experiments (i.153).

Greene based his play closely on the prose work, probably written in the middle of the sixteenth century, *The Famous Historie of Fryer Bacon. Containing the wonderfull things that he did in his Life … Very pleasant and delightfull to be read.* This work stresses that Bacon's powers were derived from his learning, particularly in the realms of natural science, rather than from diabolic agencies. He was, therefore, potentially a theurgic figure, with a priestly vocation and devotion to learning but Greene does not develop his character in this form. Very little is made of either his scholarship or his priesthood; instead, he is depicted as a stock figure from the mediaeval romances, a blend of enchanter and conjuror, who performs his magical deeds in part through the invocation of spirits.

Bacon does not deny the accusation that he achieves his marvels 'by the help of devils and ghastly fiends' (ii.27). There is, however, no suggestion that he has taken the diabolic pact and he asserts throughout that he retains control over the demons he raises. He declares:

> The great arch-ruler, potentate of hell,
> Trembles, when Bacon bids him or his fiends
> Bow to the force of his pentageron. [ii.47–50][14]

However, like Faustus, he lacks the humility and discipline of the magus; he too is motivated largely by a desire for fame and honour. He revels in his reputation as 'a man supposed the wonder of the world' (ii.37) and he constructs a gigantic head of brass, which he hopes will utter hitherto unknown truths. This is apparently in line with the theurgist's search for knowledge but his primary aim is to increase 'Bacon's glory and his fame' (xi.36).

Although the brazen head is destroyed before it can reveal its secrets Bacon does succeed to some extent in his quest for honour. His magical combat with the German conjuror Vandermast (scene ix) is treated in strongly nationalistic terms with Bacon routing his foreign rival and being informed by King Henry: 'Bacon, thou hast honoured England with thy skill, / And made fair Oxford famous by thine art' (ll. 165–6). His reception by Henry is similar to the treatment of Faustus by Vanholt and the German Emperor and throughout the play his occult powers are fully accepted by the society in which he moves, with no overt condemnation of his activities voiced until his own final speech of renunciation.

However, Greene's treatment of the magical elements is at best ambiguous. The play is essentially a comedy and most of the demonic manifestations are humorous. This is particularly evident in scene xv where Bacon's servant Miles is carried off to Hell by a devil. The comic treatment of this scene, in which the clownish Miles positively welcomes his fate, contrasts with the horrific portrayal of similar events in the final scenes of *Doctor Faustus* and *The Devil's Charter*—and indeed of such episodes in mediaeval works such as *The Massacre of the Innocents* and *The Last Judgment*.

On the other hand, Greene makes a significant adjustment in his treatment of one of the comic elements in his prose source. In the original, Bacon, in the manner of a typical mediaeval enchanter, uses his magic to help a pair of young lovers thwart the designs of the girl's father, who wants to marry her off to a wealthy knight. In the play, Bacon's role is reversed and he promises to 'strain out my magic spells' (v.97) to help Prince Edward (the equivalent of the knight) seduce the virtuous Margaret. However, Bacon's efforts fail; when confronted by the force of true love his magic has no more power than the aphrodisiac charms of witchcraft.

Intertwined with the comedy and romance are more tragic elements and these arise directly from Bacon's occult practices. In scene xiii two scholars use his 'prospective glass' (a crystal ball) to witness a doubly fatal duel fought by their fathers over Margaret. The two young men then kill each other and in a fit of remorse Bacon breaks his glass and renounces his magic, declaring to his fellow conjuror:

> I tell thee, Bungay, it repents me sore
> That ever Bacon meddled in this art.
> The hours I have spent in pyromantic spells,
> The fearful tossing in the latest night
> Of papers full of nigromantic charms,
> Conjuring and adjuring devils and fiends
> With stole and alb and strange pentaganon,
> The wresting of the holy name of God . . .
> Are instances that Bacon must be damned
> For using devils to countervail his God. [xiii.85–97]

In his repentance he seeks consolation in a belief in the mercy of God, and he vows:

> Bungay, I'll spend the remnant of my life
> In pure devotion, praying to my God
> That he would save what Bacon vainly lost. [106–8]

Thus Bacon escapes the fate of Faustus who, in his extremity, believes that his offence 'can ne'er be pardon'd', but the overall impression of Bacon's magical dealings is that without doubt they are potentially damnable and that it is only through his renunciation of his art that Bacon escapes the fate that befalls Faustus and Alexander.

*Friar Bacon and Friar Bungay* seems to have been a commercial success (there are several references to performances of the play between 1592 and 1602 in Henslowe's diary) and it was followed in about 1590 by a sequel entitled *John of Bordeaux; or, The Second Part of Friar Bacon*, which was possibly also written by Greene. Despite his previous renunciation of magic, Bacon returns to his conjuring practices. By supernatural means he helps to defeat the Turks who are besieging Ravenna and he also renews his contest with Vandermast. Like most sequels, the play is greatly inferior to its predecessor but it is ironic that here Bacon's attitude to his magic is much closer to the theurgic ideal than it is in the earlier play. In contrast with his willing complicity with Prince Edward's rapaciousness, Bacon uses his magic to protect the chastity of the faithful Rossalin. Vandermast, who has been using his magic on behalf of her would-be seducer, is loftily reprimanded:

> Stay, uncivil scholar, that abusest art
> And turn'st thy skill to prejudice the just.
> Was magic therefore meant to maintain wrong,
> To force chaste ladies yield to foolish lust?          [661–4][5]

Bacon also expresses the theurgist's respect for humility and dedication to learning when he praises a young scholar for studying Aristotle. He declares:

> Herein I like thy mind and humble bent,
> For whoso wanders in philosophy
> Must read and think, and thinking read again.
> For more the soil is tilled, the better fruit,
> And more a man doth study, more his skill.          [729–33]

Bacon's magical powers are aligned throughout with Christian forces. He uses them to defeat the infidel Turks and two devils summoned by Vandermast turn against him and side with Bacon, because, as they inform the German, 'thou hast no power over a Christian faith' (l. 1146). The play ends with unalloyed triumph for Bacon and there is no suggestion here or at any other stage of the play of an abjuration of his magical powers. In this sequel he has, therefore, been transformed into a magician of the third kind, able to practise his magic hampered by neither self-doubts nor final condemnation.

One of the most interesting examples of this type is portrayed in the late Jacobean play, *The Birth of Merlin* (*c.* 1622). The title page of the earliest surviving quarto of 1662 claims that it was 'Written by William Shakespear and William Rowley' but it is now wholly ascribed to the latter. The intensely patriotic plot is concerned with the semi-legendary events immediately prior to the birth of King Arthur. They revolve around the conflict among Aurelius, King of Britain, his brother Uter Pendragon, the Welsh King Vortiger and the Saxon invaders, led by Ostorius. Three magicians appear: Anselme, a hermit; Proximus, a Saxon wizard; and Merlin. In the early part of the play Anselme and Proximus are depicted as the champions of their respective forces, competing through their magical prowess in much the same way as do Friar Bacon and the German Vandermast.

Anselme seems to have acquired his powers entirely through the strength of his saintliness. He is described as 'a man of rare esteem for holiness' (I.i.72)[16] and he faces the Saxon forces armed merely with his cross and staff. He is distinguished from such priestly conjurors as Bacon and Friar Comolet in Chapman's *Bussy D'Ambois* in that he has gained his powers directly from God. Through his holiness he has achieved the close affinity with God sought by the theurgist but he has gained this without the study or magical rituals required by the magus. He embodies the ideal envisaged by Agrippa whereby man's soul is purified by faith to the extent that he gains superhuman powers. Agrippa cites the miracles performed by the Apostles as instances of the direct manifestation of God's powers through human agencies[17] and Anselme's defeat of the Saxon forces with a host of angels in the form of armed men is clearly in this tradition. Aurelius affirms that 'it was the hand of heaven / That in his virtue gave us victory' (II.iii.41–2).[18]

Proximus, the Saxon—and therefore pagan—magician, attempts to demonstrate his superior magical ability by raising two spirits in the forms of Hector and Achilles but Anselme routs them merely by stepping between them. In a similar manner Bacon defeats Vandermast by exerting his powers against the spirit of Hercules that the German has raised (*Friar Bacon*, scene ix). The Christian source of Anselme's magic is reiterated when he informs the discomfited Proximus:

> Know, mis-believing pagan, even that power,
> That overthrew your forces, still lets you see
> He only can control both hell and thee.                [II.iii.108–10]

In the later stages of the play the hermit's patriotic role is taken over by Merlin, who uses his magical arts in the defence of Uter Pendragon. The play's account of Merlin's origins follows tradition in that his father is an incubus/devil. His mother is a simple country girl named Joan Go To't who spends much of the early part of the work seeking the gentleman in 'most rich attire' who has fathered her child. One of the play's many inconsistencies is that throughout the first three acts there is no suggestion that Joan is a witch or that the devil appeared at her deliberate summons but in V.i she does give some indication as to why the devil selected her as the recipient of his 'infernal seed'. She rejects the advances of her former demon-lover, asking:

> Why shouldst thou now appear? I had no pride
> Nor lustful thought about me, to conjure
> And call thee to my ruin, when as at first
> Thy cursed person became visible.      [30–3]

'Conjure' seems to be used metaphorically here but her acknowledgement of pride and lust is reminiscent of Mephistophilis's admission that he has appeared in the hope of gaining Faustus's soul. Similarly, the Weird Sisters see in Macbeth a prospective victim and the devil–dog first approaches Mother Sawyer in *The Witch of Edmonton*—of which Rowley was part-author—when she is in a prime condition to be tempted.

When Merlin is born he is fully grown, complete with beard and teeth, in the manner of the monstrous births recorded in the contemporary ballads. The birth itself is heralded by the devil / father, who prays to the infernal trilogy of Lucina, Hecate and Proserpine. In terms reminiscent of the Dame in *The Masque of Queenes* he demands that they:

> Mix light and darkness, earth and heaven dissolve,
> Be of one piece again, and turn to Chaos;
> Break all your works, you powers, and spoil the world.   [III.iii.1–3]

From such unpromising origins arises Merlin, the prophet and magician who is to exert all his powers for his country's well-being. The play's uneasy juxtaposition of the two apparently contradictory elements—the noble, wholly admirable magician descended from the devil—is typified by the conclusion of the brief scene accompanying Merlin's birth. The devil ends his ritual by summoning the three Fates and Lucina, who foretells that they shall bring:

> All their assisting powers of Knowledge, Arts,

> Learning, Wisdom, all the hidden parts
> Of all-admiring Prophecy, to foresee
> The event of times to come: his Art shall stand
> A wall of brass to guard the Britain land. [25–9]

This latter project was also one of the ambitions of Friar Bacon, and Faustus planned to defend his native Germany by similar means, but in none of these instances does this miraculous feat actually materialise. However, Merlin does proceed to complete the tasks begun by Anselme. He vanquishes Proximus by causing a stone to fall and deal him a fatal blow; he wins Vortiger to the British side and ensures the final defeat of the Saxons. He is not too engrossed in such nationalistic affairs to neglect family concerns. He rescues Joan from a renewed assault by his devil/father by confining him within a rock and he promises to erect Stonehenge as a monument to his penitent mother.[19]

Although Merlin is, dramatically, a more dominant figure than Anselme and although he completes the hermit's patriotic endeavours, his magic is of a less exalted nature. It is difficult to place Merlin within any distinct category of magician, especially as Rowley adheres far more closely to traditional rather than orthodox beliefs about magic, but he does seem to owe his powers in part to the results of study. On his first appearance, immediately after his birth, he is reading a book in order 'to sound the depth / Of Arts, of Learning, Wisdom, Knowledge' (III.iv.23–4). Later, he promises Uter that he will devote 'all my studies for my country's safety' (IV.v.140). He shares many characteristics with his dramatic forerunners. He uses a wand to perform such a magical feat as striking the Clown dumb, in much the same way as Bacon deals with Bungay in *Friar Bacon*, scene vi. His honoured position at court is similar to the respect accorded to Bacon and Faustus but it is significant that, whereas Aurelius declares confidently that Anselme's powers are a manifestation of God's will, no such claim is made for Merlin's art. He is firmly cast as a beneficent magician, defeating the powers of evil—both natural and supernatural—but he is much closer than is the saintly Anselme, in both the nature and execution of his magical powers, to the magicians in the mainstream of the dramatic tradition.

## Notes to Chapter 8

1  Grace Thurlow's evidence is reproduced in Barbara Rosen's modernised version of the St Osyth pamphlet in *Witchcraft*, pp. 107–8. Agnes Tompson's charm is quoted in Christina Hole, *A Mirror of Witchcraft* (1957), p. 237.

2  Scot describes some of the most favoured techniques in *Discoverie*, book XVI, chapter v.

3  A character in Gifford's *A Dialogue concerning Witches and Witchcraftes* (1593) declares of her local wise woman that 'she doeth more good in one yeare than all these scripture men will doe as long as they live'.

4  Perkins, *Discourse*, p. 174.

5  *Discoverie*, book I, chapter ii.

6  The hearing is described in the blackletter pamphlet printed on 23 December 1566, entitled *The Examination of John Walsh, before Maister Thomas Williams, Commissary to the Reverend father in God William bishop of Excester, upon certayne Interrogatories touchyng Wytchcrafte and Sorcerye ... the XX of August, 1566*. The pamphlet is reprinted in modernised form in Rosen, pp. 64–71.

7  The pamphlet is reproduced in Rosen, pp. 214–18.

8  *The Wise Woman of Hogsdon* is included in *Heywood: Dramatic Works*, edited by R. H. Shepherd, 6 vols. (1874), vol. 5.

9  Accounts of the theory and practice of theurgy can be found in D. P. Walker, *Spiritual and Demonic Magic From Ficino to Campanella* (1958) and F. A. Yates, *Giordano Bruno and the Hermetic Tradition* (1964).

10  See, for example, F. A. Yates, *Shakespeare's Last Plays: a New Approach* (1975). Dr Yates supports the view that Subtle in *The Alchemist* is a satirical depiction of Dee and she argues that in *The Tempest* Shakespeare was presenting the case for the defence by creating in Prospero an exemplar of the Rosicrucian ideal. She feels that 'Prospero might be a vindication of Dee; a reply to the censure of James' (p. 96). This last point seems particularly dubious; Shakespeare was not given to attacks, however veiled, on the existing establishment, and a court performance of *The Tempest* in 1611, presumably attended by James, passed without reports of royal displeasure.

11  The pamphlet recording the examination of John Walsh begins with a violently anti-Catholic preface which denounces the 'devilish practices' of Alexander VI and other Popes.

12  *The Devil's Charter* is printed in an Old English Drama Students' Facsimile Edition, 21 (1913). The title page of the 1607 quarto states that 'it was plaide before the Kings Majestie, upon Candlemasse night last: by his Majesties Servants'.

13  Scot follows Wier in this and argues that the correct translation of the Hebrew term 'chasaph' is 'poisoner' rather than 'witch' and that the Law of Moses should therefore read, 'You shall not suffer any *poisoner* to live' (*Discoverie*, book VI, chapter i). John Webster in his *Displaying of Supposed Witchcraft* (1677) states that there are persons, commonly called witches, who are so influenced by the Devil that they are full of 'hatred, malice, revenge and envy' and 'do secretly and by tradition learn strange poysons, philters and receipts whereby they do much hurt and mischief' (pp. 231 and 242).

14  *Friar Bacon and Friar Bungay* (The New Mermaids), edited by J. A. Lavin (1969).

15    *John of Bordeaux; or, The Second Part of Friar Bacon* is printed as a Malone Society Reprint, edited by W. L. Renwick and W. W. Greg (1935–6).

16    *The Birth of Merlin* is included in *The Shakespeare Apocrypha*, edited by C. F. Tucker Brooke (1908).

17    *Three Books of Occult Philosophy*, III.vi.

18    This miraculous phenomenon is reminiscent of the reputed manifestations of the Angels of Mons and the celestial forces witnessed at the Battle of Marathon in 491 B.C.

19    Merlin also promises Joan that he will conduct her:

                        to a place retir'd,
Which I by art have rais'd, called Merlin's Bower.
There shall you dwell with solitary sighs,
With groans and passions your companions,
To weep away this flesh you have offended with,
And leave all bare unto your aerial soul.       [V.i.92–7]

This is reminiscent of the tradition that the mother of Merlin, repenting of her foolish dealings with the Devil, became a nun.

# CHAPTER 9

# SO POTENT ART

## THE MAGIC OF PROSPERO

*Prospero*:               **Graves at my command,**
**Have wak'd their sleepers, op'd, and let 'em forth,**
**By my so potent art.**

[*The Tempest*, V.i.48–50]

### I

The most widely held view of Prospero's supernatural powers is that he is an embodiment of the theurgic ideal, practising a form of magic whose nature is wholly legitimate, sanctioned and even inspired by God. C. J. Sisson, for example, states of Prospero's magic that it 'in fact is philosophy, in its higher reaches. It is White Magic both in origin and purpose and effect'.[1] D. G. James agrees with this view. In *The Dream of Prospero* (1967) he argues that the theurgical concept 'rendered possible, in the early days of the seventeenth century, ... a Prospero conceived as a holy and priestly magus, whose mind was set upon divine things' (p. 61).

This is perhaps the immediate impression created by Prospero's magic, particularly when it is allied with the almost God-like stance that he maintains throughout most of the play, but it is extremely doubtful if the majority of Shakespeare's audience would have responded to his supernatural deeds with such approbation. There is certainly no question that Prospero does exhibit many of the qualities required of the magus.

129

**12**     'Prospero the prime duke, being so reputed
In dignity, and for the liberal arts
Without a parallel.'
John Gielgud in Peter Brook's prodution of *The Tempest* at the Shakespeare
Memorial Theatre, Stratford-upon-Avon, in 1957.

Before his exile he has devoted his life to 'secret studies' and it is implied that it is through his intellectual endeavours that he has obtained his magical powers. His studies seem to have included astrology—an essential element in the training of the theurgist—for he is warned of the proximity of his enemies by an 'auspicious star'.

Prospero has led the life of chastity required of the magus—during his sojourn on the island, at least. However, it must be admitted that if one discounts the incestuous interest in Miranda detected by some critics[2] his opportunities for sexual activity have been extremely circumscribed! Nevertheless, it is particularly apposite that the theme of chastity, which plays such a prominent role in all the late romances, should be a recurring motif in *The Tempest*, for it has close affinities with the theurgic ideal. Prospero is much concerned with imposing sexual restraint on others; he thwarts Caliban's rapacious designs on Miranda and is insistent that her purity be respected by Ferdinand. In this respect he can be seen as an instructor in the preliminary stages of the self-discipline essential to the magus. His despair at the frequent lapses of Caliban may be due to the apparent failure of his attempts to impart some of the basic theurgic qualities to this unrewarding pupil. Prospero describes him as 'A devil, a born devil, on whose nature / Nurture can never stick' (IV.i.188–9) but he is in fact a 'demi-devil', the child of the witch Sycorax and a devil/incubus, and the strand of humanity within his brutish form offers some hope for his redemption. Ironically, his final avowal that he will be 'wise hereafter, / And seek for grace' (V.i.294–5), with its suggestion that he is about to enter the first stage of the upward progression of the soul, comes when Prospero has apparently abandoned his own theurgic practices.

With the arrival of Ferdinand, Prospero finds more promising material. The youth willingly undertakes the menial labour of carrying logs, a task which Caliban, true to his *homme sauvage* role, performs only grudgingly.[3] In his acceptance of Prospero's authority, Ferdinand displays traces of the theurgic virtues of submission and humility. The control of the passions is a constant theme of the play and Prospero's attempts to curb his own rebellious emotions are in themselves a recurring element. This striving to remain true to the theurgic ideal is a vital humanising factor which leavens the almost deific impression his supernatural powers create. His efforts culminate in the declaration of his forgiveness of his enemies:

> Though with their high wrongs I am struck to th' quick,
> Yet with my nobler reason 'gainst my fury
> Do I take part; the rarer action is
> In virtue than in vengeance. [V.i.25–8]

Some critics have argued that, from the outset, Prospero is intent on exacting full vengeance on his foes and that it is only Ariel's prompting that causes him to opt for forgiveness.[4] This view is quite out of accord with the play's central themes of justice, mercy and forgiveness—themes which recur in all the late plays—and with Prospero's essential role in their exposition. He certainly exacts a limited form of revenge but this is of a strictly temporary nature and he is motivated primarily by a concern that his prisoners should recognise and acknowledge their wrongs in order that they may receive full forgiveness. There is no reason to question the sincerity of his declaration that 'they being penitent, / The sole drift of my purpose doth extend / Not a frown further' (V.i.28–30). In this respect Prospero exemplifies the argument expressed by Francis Bacon in his essay *Of Revenge*: 'Some, when they take Revenge, are Desirous the party should know, whence it commeth: This is the more Generous. For the Delight seemeth to be, not so much in doing the Hurt, as in Making the Party repent.'[5]

During Prospero's first appearance in I.ii great stress is placed on the fact that the storm he has raised will cause no lasting harm to those caught up in it. That 'there's no harm done' is specified on four occasions, with Prospero stressing that he has ensured this 'with such provision in mine Art' that Ariel can report that 'not a hair perished'. This concern for the physical well-being of the shipwrecked mariners is in sharp contrast with the maliciousness of the Weird Sisters' avowal in *Macbeth* that although they cannot destroy the 'tempest-tost' sailor he will endure months of bodily and mental suffering.

Prospero's name is very much in line with the symbolic titles given to several characters in the last plays—including of course Miranda, a name which Shakespeare seems to have invented.[6] The word 'prosperous' is derived from the Latin 'prosper-us' and as early as the fourteenth century had the meaning 'favourable, fortunate'.[7] This accords with the impression that Shakespeare seeks to create of Prospero and his actions. Although he is careful not to identify Prospero's motives and actions with exclusively Christian ethics, such allusions as those to the 'Providence divine' which guided him to the island and to the 'good angels' and 'Heavens' which protect Alonso from Antonio and Sebastian, when in fact it is Prospero who 'through his Art foresees the danger', give weight to the argument that on one level Prospero, if not a symbol for the deity itself, is acting as an instrument of divine providence, dispensing justice and mercy in an uneasy amalgam of Old and New Testament *mores*.

However, despite this impression, which is maintained consistently throughout the first four Acts, Prospero does finally abjure his magical practices. Not all critics have seen this act of renunciation as an acknowledgement of sin or error. W. C. Curry in *Shakespeare's Philosophical Patterns* argues that he does so because: 'His theurgical operations have accomplished their purpose. He wishes now to take the final step and to consummate the assimilation of his soul with the gods' (p. 196).

But this ignores the fact that Prospero is about to resume his position as Duke of Milan. He, at least as much as any other of the island's temporary inhabitants, has learnt the lesson of his previous failure and, even if one thought from henceforth will be of his grave, the remainder will surely be devoted to the practical concerns of government. If he has any other intention, he is inviting a further challenge to his position. At this moment of renunciation of his magic, Prospero replaces his robe and staff with the hat and rapier which he has presumably brought with him from Milan. This gesture reinforces his newly affirmed reliance on natural rather than metaphysical powers. From henceforth he will maintain his authority with the sword rather than the magical rod, whilst simultaneously the hat and rapier represent the crown and sceptre, dual symbols of temporal power.

Prospero is a final variation on the familiar Shakespearean theme of the ineffectual monarch. His former neglect and abuse of his regal responsibilities is comparable to the folly displayed by such diverse figures as Richard II, Lear and Duke Vincentio. In his account of his downfall Prospero betrays his own culpable negligence as he recalls how he spent his time 'rapt in secret studies'. These are clearly in the sphere of theurgy and the essentially egocentric nature of the ambitions of the magus is revealed in Prospero's description of himself as 'neglecting worldly ends, all dedicated / To closeness and the bettering of my mind' (I.ii.89–90). There is no suggestion that his endeavours will benefit his kingdom in any way. The hubris and desire for fame displayed by Faustus and Friar Bacon are also implicit in Prospero's complacent account of himself as 'being so reputed / In dignity, and for the liberal arts / Without a parallel' (I.ii.72–4). At this stage of the play it is clear that Prospero has not learnt from his misfortune; even in exile he still has his priorities wrong. Speaking of the books of magic he has brought with him, he uses the present tense when he describes them as 'volumes that / I prize above my dukedom' (ll. 167–8).

It was such a misguided and elitist attitude that had led Francis Bacon to condemn theurgy. In *The Refutation of Philosophies* he urges that the magician should forsake the 'remote and lofty tower' of his pride in order that he might come 'close to things'. He adds that this intellectual arrogance 'has brought men to such a pitch of madness that they prefer to commune with their own spirits rather than with the spirit of nature'. James I draws a similar distinction between natural and demonic magic in his *Daemonologie*, comparing 'unlawful charmes without naturall causes' with a philosophy that can 'abide the true toutche of naturall reason' (book I). [8]

James's main objection to theurgy was its reliance on spirits to effect its unnatural powers and there is no doubt that, however benevolent might be the ends to which Prospero employs his 'Art', he performs his magical deeds with the aid of spirits. [9] Indeed, he makes no attempt to disguise this fact, for he habitually addresses Ariel as 'spirit'. Nearly all Prospero's superhuman acts are executed through Ariel but he has other demonic beings at his command. 'Several strange shapes' bring in and remove the magical banquet in III.iii, and the performers of the 'insubstantial' masque in IV.i are, by Prospero's own admission, 'Spirits, which by mine art / I have from their confines call'd to enact / My present fancies' (ll. 120–2).

Later in the same scene Caliban and his fellow conspirators are pursued by 'divers Spirits, in shape of dogs and hounds, hunting them about' (l. 253). During the first four acts there is no indication that Prospero regards his dealings with spirits as being at all culpable. His relationship with Ariel in particular typifies the theurgist's confidence in his ability to control the spirits that he raises—and yet it is specifically to such creatures that Prospero bids farewell in his speech of abjuration in V.i. (ll. 33–57).

It is surely not by chance that Shakespeare modelled these lines on the familiar section in Ovid's *Metamorphoses*, book VII. The speech has caused considerable difficulty for those commentators who regard Prospero's art as being wholly 'white'. In the original, the lines are spoken by Medea, who in classical mythology was a blend of witch and sorceress, and the speakers of the parallel passages in *The Witch* and *The Masque of Queenes* are undoubtedly witches, practitioners of 'black' magic. Such literary associations are a clear indication of the culpable nature of the magical practices that Prospero reviews.

Early in the speech there is a passage whose apparent implications have not always been appreciated but which seems to indicate unexpectedly close links between Prospero's rites and those of witchcraft. Medea's reference to the elves 'of the night' (as they are referred to in Golding's translation, which was probably the main source of Shakespeare's lines) is developed into:

> You demi-puppets that
> By moonshine do the green sour ringlets make,

Whereof the ewe not bites; and you whose pastime
Is to make midnight mushrooms, that rejoice
To hear the solemn curfew.                    [V.i.36–40]

The emphasis on the nocturnal nature of their activities and their awaiting the curfew suggests that the spirits referred to are the demons who were believed to remain in their places of confinement all day but at its close were released. These spirits are identical with the 'night's black agents' which Macbeth describes as being abroad on the night of Banquo's murder. Prospero's references to these beings as 'weak masters' is reminiscent of the Weird Sisters' 'masters' (the Apparitions) which, like Prospero's spirits, are able to assume various shapes and in these forms communicate with human beings.

Regarding the supernatural powers that Prospero claims in the course of the speech, Frank Kermode states in the New Arden *The Tempest* (appendix D) that 'only those elements which are consistent with 'white' magic are taken over for Prospero' (p. 149). However, this is not the case. Prospero's assertions of his control of the elements are exemplified in the creation of such violent and potentially destructive phenomena as earthquakes and thunderbolts. Medea's ability to 'make the rough seas plain', as expressed in Golding's version, is not here transferred to Prospero, and his power to create calm seas as well as storms is not revealed until the very end of the play.

The impression that in this speech Shakespeare is stressing the dark side of Prospero's art is reinforced by the fact that Medea's necromantic powers are retained, for Prospero asserts that: 'graves at my command / Have wak'd their sleepers, op'd, and let 'em forth / By my so potent Art' (V.i.48–50). Sisson is sufficiently disconcerted by this claim to argue in his article 'The magic of Prospero' that 'the fact is that Shakespeare has been unwary in his borrowing from Ovid and has read too much of Medea into Prospero's speech' (*Shakespeare Survey*, XI, p. 76). However, throughout the rest of the speech Shakespeare seems to have been scrupulous in his apportionment of Medea's powers to Prospero. For example, her ability to 'darken the lightsome Moone' (in Golding's phrase) is transferred to Sycorax (V.i.269–71) and this is fitting in view of the close associations of the moon with witchcraft. It would be surprising if, in this highly significant speech, Shakespeare had been so casual as to give Prospero powers that conflicted with his overall vision of Prospero's art.

It is arguable that the ability to raise men from the dead is a metaphoric rather than a literal claim and refers to Prospero's engineering of the reunion of Ferdinand and Alonso, each of whom had thought the other had drowned. Also, it is true that in releasing Ariel from the pine tree Prospero had freed him from a living death. If Prospero's boast is to be taken literally, there is the problem of when he has performed such a feat. It is doubtful whether he has practised this art during his sojourn on the island for, as was noted previously, his powers seem to have distinct geographical limits. This raises the question of the degree which his commitment to magic had reached whilst he was still nominally Duke of Milan but as with so many other problems which extend beyond the play's textual boundaries, Shakespeare provides no answer.

Nevertheless, these lines provide a clear indication—the clearest in the entire play—of the almost indeterminate border-line between 'white' and 'black' magic. It is noteworthy that the necromantic assertion forms the climax to Prospero's review of his powers and it is followed immediately by his abjuration of 'this rough magic'. The epithet can be interpreted in several ways: it might indicate Prospero's final dissatisfaction with the limitations of his powers; or it might suggest that his art is not so pure or refined as he, the theurgist, would desire.

However, in view of the summary of his magic that immediately precedes this renunciation, it seems clear that Prospero is making an unequivocal, if belated, acknowledgment of the damnable nature of his art. This admission is reinforced by the Epilogue with which he closes the play. The rhyming couplets and conventional appeal for the audience's applause give the lines a platitudinous air but this should not be allowed to mask the serious intent behind Prospero's words. He declares:

> And my ending is despair
> Unless I be reliev'd by prayer,
> Which pierces so that it assaults
> Mercy itself, and frees all faults. [15–18]

His plea for forgiveness is given a specifically Christian emphasis in the last two lines, with their punning reference to the plea for divine forgiveness by means of indulgence: 'As you from crimes would pardon'd be, / Let your indulgence set me free'. (ll. 19–20).

Prospero, therefore, is acknowledging the sinful nature of his magical practices and, like Friar Bacon, seeking comfort in the mercy of God. Just as he has been able to forgive his enemies so now, in turn, he requests pardon for his own wrongs. Having turned away from his magic, he is able to seek this forgiveness with confidence and his optimism contrasts with the final despair of Faustus and Alexander. His measured declaration in his abjuration speech, 'I'll drown my book' is an echo of Faustus's anguished cry, 'I'll burn my books' as he tries desperately to escape his fate. Whereas Faustus's books are consumed by the same hell-fires that await him, Prospero is able to immerse his volume in the waters which throughout the play have had a mysteriously purifying effect. After the storm Gonzalo declares 'that our garments, being, as they were, drench'd in the sea, hold, notwithstanding, their freshness and glosses, being new-dy'd, than stain'd with salt water' (II.i.58–60). Such a power is reminiscent of the effect of the holy water used to remove original sin and to drive out evil spirits in the Christian ceremonies of baptism and exorcism and so it is particularly apposite that Prospero should perform this act of renunciation in such waters.

## II

These links with the earlier plays underline a point of fundamental importance in the assessment of Prospero's magical powers. They must be placed in the context of the established tradition of the dramatic portrayal of magicians and conjurors, for Shakespeare was working with absolute consistency within this form. Friar Bacon shares with Prospero a dedication to the 'liberal arts' whilst in the opening scene of *Doctor Faustus* we see Faustus 'rapt' in the 'secret studies' of Prospero's narrative. Nearly all of Prospero's supernatural exploits are within the powers of his fellow magicians. Faustus possesses his art of invisibility, whilst both Alexander and Bacon can detect secret guilt as effectively as does Prospero. The 'freezing' of Ferdinand's dagger is mirrored by similar feats performed by Bacon in both *Friar Bacon and Friar Bungay* and *John of Bordeaux*. Prospero's engineering of love between Ferdinand and Miranda is reminiscent of the role of the enchanter in the early romances.

He also shares this and other characteristics with Bomelio in the anonymous play *The Rare Triumphs of Love and Fortune* (1589). Bomelio is a nobleman who has been driven into exile by the treachery of 'fawning friends'. He has retired to a cell where he leads a hermit-like existence, devoting himself to improving his magical powers. He uses these to take vengeance on his enemies—he strikes Armenio, the Duke's son, dumb and only removes the affliction when he is restored to his rightful estate. However, like Prospero, he also uses his magic for more positive ends, promoting the love of his son, Hermione, and the Duke's daughter, Fidelia. The play is essentially a romance, with Bomelio playing the customary role of enchanter. However, there is one significant deviation from the romantic tradition in that the conventional unquestioning attitude to magic is not adhered to when Hermione finds his father's magic books. He is horrified and burns them, at which Bomelio goes temporarily insane. Hermione forcefully express his view of the dangers of magic and of his father's 'vile, blasphemous books'. He declares:

> My soul abhors as often as mine eyes upon them looks.
> What gain can countervail the danger that they bring?
> For man to sell his soul to sin, is't not a grievous thing;
> To captivate his mind and all the gifts therein
> To that which is of others all the most ungracious sin,
> Which so entangleth them that thereunto apply,
> As at the last forsaketh them in their extremity?
> Such is this art, such is the study of this skill,
> This supernatural device, this Magic such it will.                    [1357–65]

Shakespeare was probably familiar with the play—its plot has several affinities with *Cymbeline*—and it is therefore particularly noteworthy that the magic of Bomelio, a possible forerunner of Prospero, is attacked in such vehement terms.[10]

The major difference between Prospero and his dramatic predecessors is that although he conducts several magical rituals during the course of the play these are all performed off-stage. The rites that he must have enacted in order to raise the initial tempest itself have been completed before the play begins, although on his first appearance Prospero is wearing his magic robe, which he does not remove until the storm abates. Before his plans reach fruition by means of the magically induced banquet and hymeneal masque, Prospero has to renew his supernatural powers, but he leaves the stage with the words:

>                    I'll to my book,
> For yet, ere suppertime, must I perform
> Much business appertaining.                    [III.i.94–6]

Nearly all the supernatural happenings in the play, although clearly directed by Prospero, are in fact put into operation by Ariel, and on only two occasions do we actually witness Prospero personally performing magical acts. When Ferdinand draws his sword he is 'charmed from moving' as the stage direction instructs (I.ii.466). The direction for V.i.56, 'They all enter the circle which Prospero had made, and there stand charmed', implies that he has previously drawn such a circle but, significantly enough in a text notable for its detailed stage directions, there is no instruction for such an action. (In most productions of *The Tempest* the actor playing Prospero does in fact draw a circle with his rod at the beginning of this scene, in order to explicate the subsequent action, but it would violate the spirit of the play if this were accompanied by incantations or other elaborate ritualistic 'business'.)

Even in these cases, then, the magical act is not performed with intricate rites. We merely witness the end results of such unseen practices. This contrasts with the conjuring scenes in *Friar Bacon and Friar Bungay*; with Comolet's summoning of the devil Behemoth through Latin incantation in *Bussy D'Ambois*; and even more with the equivalent sequences in *The Devil's Charter* and *Doctor Faustus*.

Similarly, we are given no inkling as to how Prospero has obtained the book which he consults during the play and which he drowns at its conclusion. This might be a handbook such as *The Heptameron* or it might be a text provided by a demonic source. Faustus is given three such books by Mephistophilis, instructing him in astrology, natural science and magic, and during the dumb-show at the beginning of *The Devil's Charter* a devil presents Alexander with a 'magic book'. Shakespeare has presumably omitted such material in order to preserve the air of superficial beneficence that surrounds Prospero's actions but despite the absence of such overtly demonic elements his audience would have had no difficulty in placing Prospero in his dramatic context and in equating his magic with the potentially damnable practices of his fellows. Prospero is clearly a member of the group of magicians typified by Friar Bacon who renounce their art when they realise that its practice 'countervails' the will of God. That Prospero is part of a continuing tradition is indicated by the climax to the anonymous play *The Two Noble Ladies* (*c.* 1619–23) where the magician Cyprian abandons his magic with the words:

> And now in token of my love to heaven,
> This art, which heretofore I so esteem'd,
> Thus I abandon, and these curious books
> Thus sacrifice.
> [*Throws his charmed rod and his books under the stage;
> a flame riseth.*]

Of all the stage magicians who preceded Prospero perhaps the least sinister is another of Shakespeare's creations, Owen Glendower in *Henry IV, Part One*. He claims the theurgist's power both to summon and to command spirits, although the only magic he actually performs is to invoke spirits to play supernatural music, a comparatively innocuous feat which is also performed by Prospero. Despite Hotspur's scoffing rationalism,

Glendower is not a wholly ridiculous figure and his dignity is maintained in part because, as with Prospero, we do not witness any of his necromantic rituals.

However, Shakespeare's awareness of the potentially harmful nature of magic is suggested by Rosalind's reference in *As You Like It* to 'a magician, most profound in his art and yet not damnable' (V.ii.54–5). He had previously linked conjuring with 'black' magic in *Henry VI, Part Two*, when, in I.iv, the witch Margery Jourdain combines her powers with those of two priests and the conjuror Bolingbroke to perform 'the ceremonies belonging and make the circle' in order to summon the hellish spirit, Asmath.

Prior to *The Tempest*, Shakespeare's most extensive exploration of the power of magic had been in *A Midsummer-Night's Dream* (c. 1593–4) and the two works show many affinities in their treatments of the theme. In both plays groups of characters are temporarily removed from their customary civilised settings and the comparisons drawn between Prospero's former dukedom and his island and between the court of Theseus and the wood near Athens are variations on the traditional debate between the merits of a 'natural' existence and an ordered society. In *The Tempest* and *A Midsummer-Night's Dream* the theme has an added dimension in that the isolated characters are subjected to magical forces which release and maintain processes of change whereby they emerge transformed from their periods of physical and mental dislocation. In each case these changes are wrought within the span of a few hours and yet, beneath the romantic and pastoral elements in both plays, there is a strong impression that the characters have undergone a series of experiences which are profoundly disturbing but essential for their development.

After the magically induced interchanges of partners among the young and initially immature Athenian lovers they finally demonstrate that they have grown, as Hyppolita observes, 'to something of great constancy' (V.I.26). Their increased maturity is comparable with the final impression of the love of Ferdinand and Miranda and also with the degree of self-knowledge evident in Alonso's chastened admission of his guilt. As Gonzalo optimistically declares of the whole company, they have found 'all of us ourselves / When no man was his own' (V.i.212–13). When their purposes have been served both Prospero and Oberon have the power to remove the effects of their magic charms, but conversely neither is wholly immune to the powers of the magic they operate. Even though Oberon is a supernatural figure he responds in human fashion to the effects of his magic; he repents of the malicious trick that he plays on Titania and his

140

pity serves to deepen his love for her. Prospero is not unaffected by his own magical acts. Through the control he exerts over the creatures, both human and spiritual, at his command he learns to value the qualities required of him when he resumes his dukedom. Indeed, he has undergone the most profound change of all. Ironically, he now no longer prizes his books above his dukedom and has gained the wisdom and humility to abandon his magical book and staff in favour of the symbols of mortal rule.

In executing their supernatural acts Prospero and Oberon both use spirits and Ariel and Puck have many qualities in common. They can both travel with superhuman speed, assume various forms or become invisible. They can imitate human voices and they use all these arts to tantalise their mortal victims. Puck threatens to lead the mechanicals: 'Thorough bog, thorough bush, thorough brake, thorough briar, / Sometime a horse I'll be, sometime a fire' (III.i.101–3). This is similar to Ariel's Jack o' Lantern tormenting of Caliban, Stephano and Trinculo, who are led, as he tells Prospero,

> through
> Tooth'd briers, sharp furzes, pricking goss, and thorns,
> Which ent'red their frail shins. At last I left them
> I' th' filthy mantled pool beyond your cell.          [IV.i.179–82]

Both creatures are beyond the limits of mortality, but Puck's contemptuous 'Lord, what fools these mortals be' (III.ii.116) is complemented by Ariel's prompting of Prospero's 'nobler reason' with the declaration that his 'affections / Would become tender' (V.i.18–19) were he susceptible to human emotions. Katharine Briggs in *The Anatomy of Puck* (1959) comments on Ariel's exchange with Prospero thus:

> It is difficult to say why the simplicity and brevity of that reply ['Mine would, sir, were I human'] are so moving. It seems to contain in it the meaning behind all those stories of the Neck and the mermaid and the Scottish fairy who long for human souls, a sudden sharp reminder of the humanity we lose and insult by silly grudges. The marrow of a hundred fables is in it. [p. 53]

Ariel seems to be of a higher order of spirit than Puck for he is an essentially elemental creature which can be commanded only by the highest form of magician. Puck, on the other hand, is the minion of a fellow-spirit, Oberon, and is more fallible than Ariel. He sometimes blunders in executing Oberon's commands and fate can 'overrule' his actions, as he admits (III.ii.92), whereas Ariel can proudly proclaim himself and his fellow spirits to be the 'ministers of Fate' (III.iii.61).

141

In many respects both Puck and Ariel are in the English tradition of the 'knavish sprite', each being apparently more mischievous than evil. But both are capable of striking intense terror in their human victims and just as Puck's alternative name, Robin Goodfellow, links him with the devil, so Ariel has clear demonic affinities. For example, aeriel demons were thought to 'live in the air about us, sometimes descend into hell, appear to men, raise tempests',[11] a description which can well be applied to Ariel. Ferdinand's reaction to the fearful display of pyrotechnics during the storm is to cry, 'Hell is empty, / And all the devils are here' (I.ii.214–15), a response that would have been echoed by many in Shakespeare's audience. Although Prospero's description of Ariel as a 'malignant thing' (I.ii.257) is one of his milder taunts, this too is a reminder of his demonic and therefore potentially dangerous qualities.

Prospero controls Ariel in a theurgic manner but although he has certainly not made any Faustus-like pact with him, some form of agreement seems to have been entered into, whereby Ariel repays Prospero for freeing him from the cloven pine by serving him for a certain period of years. Ariel reminds his master that in return for his 'worthy service ... thou didst promise / To bate me a full year' (I.ii.247–50). He constantly chafes at his enforced servitude and Prospero has to control him with harshness and threats of punishment which are similar in tone to such spells as that prescribed for 'bringing a disobedient spirit into subjection'. This declares:

> By that power of Christ Jesus I cast thee into the tormenting pit of fire and brimstone there to be tormented untill the later day of judgement, except thou be obedient to fulfill my will and commandment in all things I have or shall aske or demaund of thee, without any deceit, falshood or delay.[12]

## III

Prospero's working with spirits is just one of many aspects of his supernatural activities that would have equated him in the popular mind not only with theurgy but also with the practices of the village conjuror and the witch. His ability to detect guilt, as in his presentiment of the plots being hatched by Sebastian and Antonio against Alonso and by Caliban, Stephano and Trinculo against himself, is comparable with the supposed power of cunning men to expose malefactors. Rituals were performed involving, for example, the tracing of astrological signs and the use of crystal balls and mirrors, but many of their methods were founded on elementary psychology, aimed at inducing confessions from persons whose guilt was already known or suspected. The rationale of the emotional pressures they exerted was similar to the thinking behind the mediaeval trials by ordeal and there is a reflection of these primitive but often successful means of revealing guilt in Prospero's treatment of his enemies. Ariel, in the terrifying garb of a harpy and with an accompaniment of thunder and lightning, accuses the 'three men of sin' of their crimes in III.iii and the continuing physical and mental torments that Prospero inflicts on them culminate in their being brought within his magic circle to be charged with their 'high wrongs' (V.i).[13]

The wise man's reputed ability to counteract the effects of 'black' magic is comparable with Prospero's freeing of Ariel from the cloven pine in which he had been imprisoned by Sycorax. She did this because Ariel refused to carry out her 'earthy and abhorr'd commands' (I.ii.273). However much he protests, Ariel has to perform Prospero's behests, thereby underlining the superiority of Prospero's magic. This is further stressed in that Sycorax, having confined Ariel, 'could not again undo' this act, whilst Prospero easily effects his release.

Whatever might be the geographical setting of *The Tempest*, Sycorax is clearly a witch of the Old World, composed of a blend of Classical and Renaissance witch-lore. Her magical rites involve such creatures as toads, beetles and bats, all of which are also employed by the hags in *The Masque of Queenes*. She worships the pagan devil Setebos, who was in reality a god of the Patagonians of the New World, described by Eden in his *History of Travaile* (1577). In contrast to this, she also seems to have links with Arabian necromancy (Suleiman ben David could summon and imprison spirits in a manner similar to hers), links which were established perhaps during her sojourn in Algiers. She escaped execution there 'for one thing she did' (I.ii.266). Charles Lamb took this to be a reference to the story of the witch who saved Algiers when it was besieged by Charles V in 1541, but the usually accepted explanation for this typically enigmatic phrase is that she was freed because she was pregnant. This was one of the few grounds for the reprieve of convicted witches in mediaeval Europe, and Shakespeare had previously made use of this custom in *Henry VI, Part One* (V.iv) where Joan la Pucelle unsuccessfully attempts to escape execution by falsely pleading pregnancy.

Sycorax also has certain affinities with Classical witches. She could 'control the moon, make flows and ebbs, / And deal in her command' (V.i.270–1). This power was ascribed to Medea, as the passage from *Metamorphoses* discussed above shows, and many other ancient sorceresses shared this trait. The ability to exercise control over the moon was also frequently held to be within the scope of mediaeval and later witches, a belief which forges one of the strongest links between ancient and Renaissance witchcraft. Scot, in his *Discoverie of Witchcraft* records the claim 'that they can pull downe the moone and the stars' (book I, chapter iv). There are also similarities between Sycorax and the enchantress Circe. She too was exiled to an island and was frequently portrayed as a symbol of the sensually seductive power which reduced men to beasts. Both Sycorax and Caliban are also representative of this force in the Nature / Nurture conflict which underlies much of the philosophical content of *The Tempest*.

Although Prospero's magic is clearly of a higher order than that of Sycorax, it is noteworthy that, in a work so rigorously designed around complementary themes and contrasting characters, the parallels between the two both unite them and highlight their essential differences. Both Prospero and Sycorax use dew as an element in their magical charms, as Caliban and Ariel inform us—within a hundred lines of each other in I.ii, ll. 227–9 and 321–3. Although the 'Bermoothes' constitute a more salubrious gathering-ground than the 'unwholesome fen' used by Sycorax, they were 'still-vexed' and Ariel fetched the dew for Prospero at midnight, the traditional time for witchcraft operations. Dew was an important element in many occult rituals. Kittredge in *Witchcraft in Old and New England* records a charm for stealing butter which was still practised in Ireland at the end of the last century, amongst whose ingredients were dew swept from the grass on a May morning, together with a dead man's hand (p. 168).

There are also superficial similarities in their past histories. Both have come to the island, accompanied by their only children, after being banished from Mediterranean countries; they practise and develop their magical arts during their enforced exiles, both of them employing demons to carry out their designs. It seems probable that the 'demi-puppets' who perform at Prospero's behest are the same spirits as the 'more potent ministers' that Sycorax invokes. It is certainly true that both use Ariel as their principal spirit/servant, with the important distinction noted previously, that whilst Prospero can both summon and command Ariel, Sycorax cannot force him to carry out her repellent demands against his will.

Although Prospero's release of Ariel from the cloven pine is further evidence of his superior powers, his threat to repeat this punishment by confining Ariel in the 'knotty entrails of an oak', which he himself describes as 'a torment / To lay upon the damn'd' (I.ii.289–90) is a further link between his magic and that of Sycorax. The confining of a human being or a spirit within a tree has strong witchcraft affinities. In the First Book of *The Fairie Queene* the Red Cross Knight encounters:

> once a man Fradubio, now a tree,
> Wretched man, wretched tree; whose nature weake,
> A cruell witch her cursed will to wreake,
> Hath thus transformed.                [canto II, xxxiii]

In one respect the fact that Sycorax has confined Ariel in a pine tree, whilst Prospero's threat is of imprisonment in an oak, underlines the essential difference between their magical arts. Since primaeval times the oak has been associated with ceremonies conducted by priest-like figures—such sacred groves existed in both ancient Greece and Celtic Europe, for example. In contrast, pine forests were regarded as the haunts of trolls and other demonic figures of North European mythology.

Trees were sometimes thought of as being animate and possessing souls; alternatively they were believed to be the abodes of demons. In each case, sacrifices were offered to the tree spirits and the legends of bodies being confined in trees by witchcraft might well be remnants of the folk-memories of these rituals. One such festival was practised in ancient Rome and was dedicated to Attis, the Phrygian equivalent of Adonis. He was believed to have been transformed into a pine tree and the latter featured prominently in the ceremonies dedicated to him. In many of the vegetation rites, particularly those associated with spring, there was a final stage of symbolic resurrection. *The Tempest* can, of course, be viewed as an allegory built around the Christian concept of rebirth, and Prospero's freeing of Ariel from his 'life in death' confinement can be seen as a variation on this major theme. Shakespeare, perhaps unconsciously, might have incorporated into this episode surviving traces of these ancient but complementary rituals.

Apart from their affinities with the powers of Sycorax, the magical arts of Prospero are, in many other respects, indistinguishable from those of 'black' witchcraft. His ability to cause madness was often ascribed to witches. Margaret Harknett, executed at Tyburn in 1585, was seen as the cause of the insanity of a bailiff with whom she had quarrelled;[14] Elizabeth Sawyer avenges herself on Anne Ratcliffe by sending her mad. Witches also shared with wise men the ability to read innermost thoughts, a power that Prospero demonstrates when he confronts Sebastian and Antonio with their intended treachery towards Alonso. To this display Sebastian makes the significant response that 'the devil speaks in him' (V.i.129). Prospero denies this but Agnes Sampson (Tompson) had given an equally impressive if ill-advised demonstration of apparent telepathic powers before James I, a display that had helped confirm his conviction of her guilt. Erictho in *Sophonisba*, Act IV, knows Syphax's purpose in seeking her and in response he addresses her as 'Deep knowing spirit, mother of all / Mysterious science'. Merlin in Rowley's play performs a similar feat for the Clown, who warns Joan: 'A witch, a witch, a witch, sister: rid him out of your company. He is either a witch or a conjuror; he could never have known else' (III.iv.44–7).

Prospero also seems to have the power of invisibility, a gift that was frequently ascribed to witches. The stage direction in III.iii describes him as witnessing the magical banquet 'on the top, invisible' and he may also be practising this art when he eavesdrops on Miranda and Ferdinand in III.i. James I, referring to witches, writes in *Daemonologie* (book I), 'And in this transporting they say themselves, that they are invisible to anie other, except amongst themselves; which may also be possible in my opinion.'

Witches were also thought capable of inflicting paralysis. One of the witnesses at the St Osyth trial of 1582, John Sayer, asserted that on one occasion 'his cart stood, that he could not make it forward nor backward by the space of one hour and more' and he claimed that this was due to the witchcraft of one Alice Manfield. This power is similar to the immobility with which Ferdinand and the 'three men of sin' are in turn stricken, when they are literally rendered 'spellbound' by the force of Prospero's magic.

Even Prospero's staff and cloak, essential items of the stock-in-trade of all magicians, were not associated exclusively with conjurors. Witches sometimes used them and they were also features of many apparent manifestations of the devil. John Fian of North Berwick declared that the devil appeared to him 'appareled all in blacke, with a white wand in his hande', and Major Weir, who was tried for witchcraft in Edinburgh in 1670, was described by a witness at his trial thus: 'His garb was still a cloak, and somewhat dark, and he never went without his staff'. Weir was convicted and burnt, together with his staff.[15]

Another characteristic that Prospero shares with witches is that despite his supernatural powers he is unable ultimately to control the human will. He can bring Ferdinand and Miranda together, but he cannot make them fall in love and is clearly relieved when this occurs. Of the 'three men of sin' only Alonso seems genuinely penitent and although Caliban finally vows to be 'wise hereafter', no firm assurance is held out for this, and he must be accounted another of Prospero's failures. W. H. Auden expresses well

Prospero's inadequacy in this respect. His poetic variations on *The Tempest*, *The Sea and the Mirror*, contain these lines ascribed to Antonio:

Your all is partial, Prospero;
My will is all my own:
Your need to love shall never know
Me: I am I, Antonio,
By choice myself, alone.[16]

Prospero's control over the elements is obviously akin to that ascribed to witches, particularly his ability to create storms. However, even here his powers are circumscribed. He has to await 'a most auspicious star' to bring his enemies within reach of his art and the storm itself is possibly limited in its potency, for the vessel is undamaged and its crew unharmed. Prospero, as was noted above, makes great play of these facts but he may be making a virtue of necessity in that the basic goodness of some of the mariners (especially Gonzalo, Ferdinand and Alonso) may be protecting them from greater hurt. The North Berwick witches believed they had failed to drown King James because of the strength of his Christian faith and the Weird Sisters in *Macbeth* cannot actually destroy the ship or the sailor caught up in their storm. Alonso's vessel, likewise, is not 'lost' despite its being 'tempest-tost'.

It is more likely, however, that Prospero deliberately ensures that the tempest does not inflict any lasting harm. The short-lived terror that it inspires is similar to the other punishments that he imposes on his enemies—they are physically and mentally distressing, but he remains in full command of their strictly limited duration. Nevertheless, all of the parallels with witchcraft, which would have been clearly recognised by Shakespeare's audience, confirm the inescapable fact that Prospero's magical practices, however elevated they might appear, are in the final analysis as damnable as the blackest witchcraft, and his only hope of salvation lies in their renunciation and a return to a life of prayer and faith in the forgiveness and mercy of God.

### Notes to Chapter 9

*1*    'The magic of Prospero', *Shakespeare Survey*, XI (1958), pp. 70–7.
*2*    See, for example, Leslie A. Fiedler, *The Stranger in Shakespeare* p. 196.
*3*    Frank Kermode develops this theme in his introduction to the New Arden *The Tempest* (1954), pp. xxxiv–lix.
*4*    See, for example, J. Dover Wilson, *The Meaning of 'The Tempest'* (1936).
*5*    *Essays*, The World's Classics series (Oxford, 1937).

6   *Oxford Dictionary of English Christian Names*, edited by E. G. Withycombe (1945).

7   *Oxford English Dictionary.*

8   For a discussion of this aspect of Prospero's powers see Patrick Grant, 'The magic of charity: a background to Prospero', *The Review of English Studies*, vol. XXVII, No. 105 (1976).

9   James's description of the powers of spirits in *Daemonologie* bears some resemblances with the acts performed by the spirits at Prospero's command. He states that a spirit has the ability to carry news 'from anie parte of the worlde' and he also refers to the 'faire banquets and daintie dishes, carryed in short space fra the farthest part of the worlde' His declaration that the devil can produce 'impressiones in the aire' of 'castles and fortes' is reminiscent of the 'cloud-capped towers' created in Prospero's masque. (See Jacqueline E. M. Latham, '*The Tempest* and King James' *Daemonologie*', *Shakespeare Survey*, 28 (1975), pp. 117–23).

10  The relevant sections of the play are printed in Bullough, *Sources*, vol. VIII, pp. 90–103.

11  Guazzo gives this definition, following the eleventh-century Psellos. (Quoted in R. H. West, *The Invisible World* p. 23.)

12  Brit. Mus. Add. MS. 36674, pp. 78ff. (Quoted in K. M. Briggs, *The Anatomy of Puck* (1959), pp. 253–4.) Although Caliban is hardly a disinterested observer, it is perhaps significant that he declares that Prospero's spirits 'all do hate him / As rootedly as I' (III.ii.90–1).

13  Keith Thomas in *Religion and the Decline of Magic*, pp. 252–64, summarises these aspects of the wizards' supposed powers.

14  Thomas, *op. cit.*, p. 663.

15  See Murray, *Witch-Cult*, p. 50.

16  *Selected Poems* (London, 1968), p. 62.

# CHAPTER 10

# SPECTACLE OF STRANGENESS

## THE STAGING OF THE SUPERNATURAL SCENES

> I had . . . devis'd that twelve Women, in the habite of Haggs, or Witches . . . should fill that part; not as a Masque, but a spectacle of strangenesse, producing multiplicity of Gesture, and not unaptly sorting w<sup>th</sup> the current, and whole fall of the Devise.
>
> [*The Masque of Queenes*, 15–22]

## I

The portrayal of supernatural phenomena had been established as one of the main sources of spectacle on the English stage long before the Elizabethan and Jacobean eras. Demonic figures were frequently represented in the mediaeval miracle and morality plays and magicians were stock figures in the pastoral romances of the early sixteenth century. These two traditional elements survived and were indeed intermingled in many dramas of the late sixteenth and early seventeenth centuries.

For example, both *Doctor Faustus* and *The Devil's Charter* conclude with magicians being carried off to Hell by devils. Before Faustus's final speech the stage direction reads 'Hell is discovered' (xix.115·1) whilst the final direction in Barnes's play indicates 'Thunder and lightning. With fearful noise the devils thrust him down and go triumphing' (V.vi). This effect is very similar to the account of the concluding scene in the twelfth-century Anglo-Norman drama *Jeu d'Adam*:

> Then shall the Devil come, and three or four other devils with him, bearing in their hands chains and iron shackles, which they shall place on the necks of Adam and Eve. And certain ones shall push them on, others shall drag them toward Hell; other devils, however, shall be close beside Hell, waiting for them as they come, and these shall make a great dancing and jubilation over their destruction; and other devils shall, one after another, point to them as they come; and they shall take them up and thrust them into Hell; and thereupon they shall cause a great smoke to arise, and they shall shout one to another in Hell, greatly rejoicing; and they shall dash together their pots and kettles, so that they may be heard without.[1]

This play was staged in the open air against the background of a church facade and the 'Hell' seems to have been positioned to one side of the main acting area. The fact that the devils thrust Alexander 'down' suggests that in *The Devil's Charter* the 'Hell' was situated beneath the main stage. Its presence was probably indicated by the opening of the mechanical trap-door which was a feature of most Jacobean playhouses—including the Globe, where the work had its first performance in 1602.[2]

During this period the large area underneath the main stage was commonly known as the 'hell', just as the uppermost section of the theatre was referred to as the 'heavens'. These terms could well be survivals of the symbolic use of these areas in the earlier dramas. Certainly, in most mediaeval plays Hell was traditionally situated beneath the stage. The Digby St Mary Magdalen plays of about 1480 required 'a stage and Helle ondyrneth that stage', whilst among the properties listed for the *Harrowing of Hell* and *Doomsday* dramas of the fifteenth-century Coventry Cycle was a 'hell-mouth'. This seems to have taken the form of a monstrous, gaping head, often in the form of a dragon, placed low down on one side of the stage. A description of such a device is contained in the *Wagner Book*, published in 1594. This purports to be an account of the staging of a magical performance of *Doctor Faustus* by his servant, Wagner. Although the authenticity of this anonymous work is the subject of much dispute,[3] the description of the portrayal of the demonic scenes provides us with our most detailed account of the probable staging of such episodes:

> There might you see the ground-worke at the one end of the Stage whereout the personated divels should enter in their fiery ornaments, made like the broad wide mouth of an huge Dragon, which with the continuall armies of smoake and flame breathed forth his angry stomackes rage, round about the eies grew haires not so horrible as men call brissels, but more horrible as long and stiffe speares, the teeth of this Hels mouth far out stretching, and such as a man might call

monstrous, and more than a man can by wordes signifie . . . Then out of this representation of Hels mouth, issued out whole Armies of fiery flames, and most thicke foggy smoakes, after which entred in a great batell of footemen Divels.[4]

The Coventry Cycle 'hell-mouth' required 'a fire kept at it' and the hell-fire effect was probably achieved by a method akin to that described by Nicola Sabbattini in *Pratica di fabricar scene e machine ne' teatri*. This work was not published until 1637 and is concerned with techniques used in the Italian theatre, particularly in the production of the masque, but it is very probable that the method he recommends was similar to that used to create comparable effects in the earlier English dramas. He instructed that:

Underneath the stage, four men are placed at each side of the trap . . . equipped with pots through which are passed torches, the pots filled with fine Greek resin. At the time of opening the Hell, these men must be at their places, each with his torch lighted, and now and again must throw flames of fire through the trap to the stage by raising the pots violently . . . the resin will come out through holes in the tops of the pots and catching fire will result in a big flame.[5]

That Sabbattini was describing established techniques to achieve these relatively simple effects is suggested by the fact that his method for simulating thunder and lightning is similar to that described by his compatriot, Sebastiano Serlio, whose *Regole generali di architettura* was published in 1545. The work was translated into English in 1611 and although the theatrical setting Serlio has in mind is clearly a typical sixteenth-century Italian structure, temporarily erected in a banqueting hall or palace courtyard, the technique he describes could easily have been employed in the English playhouses of the period.

You must make thunder in this manner: commonly all scenes are made at the end of a great Hall, whereas usually there is a Chamber above it, wherein you must roule a great Bullet of a Cannon or some other great Ordinance, and then counterfeit Thunder. Lightning must be made in this manner, there must be a man placed behind the Scene or Scaffold in a high place with a boxe in his hand, the cover whereof must be full with holes, and in the middle of that place there shall be a burning candle placed, the boxe must be filled with powder of vernis [resin] or sulphire, and casting his hand with the boxe upwards the powder flying in the candle, will shew as if it were lightning.[6]

Thunder and lightning almost invariably marked the appearances on stage of supernatural phenomena. Apart from the symbolic appropriateness of such effects, especially in relation to figures supposedly emanating from Hell, the accompanying sounds would help to mask or at least distract attention from the inevitable noises of the machinery employed in staging many of these scenes. Most Elizabethan theatres had at least one trap-door situated in the main stage, through which actors and properties could rise and descend by means of a mechanised structure operated by ropes attached to windlasses. Some of these traps were capable of carrying two or more actors simultaneously and ascents and descents could be achieved with considerable rapidity.

*The Devil's Charter* contains several spectacular sequences requiring the dextrous use of the trap. In the opening dumb-show two devils rise and descend in quick succession, to be followed by two more devils, who appear and descend together. Each of these entries is marked by the customary 'thunder and fearful fire'. Even more striking effects are required by the stage directions which accompany the incantation scene in IV.i. Following Alexander's conjurations there appear 'Fiery exhalations; lightning, thunder. Ascend a King, with a red face crowned imperial, riding upon a lion or dragon'. Alexander addresses the figure, after which 'The devil descendeth with thunder and lightning, and after more exhalations ascends another all in armour'. The demonic figures thus take symbolic forms and similarly the principal devil in the dumb-show, which tempts Alexander with the promise of the papacy, is attired 'in robes pontifical, with a triple crown on his head, and cross keys in his hand'.

Demons could of course assume any shape, human or animal, and in *Doctor Faustus* Mephistophilis adopts the form of a Franciscan friar after Faustus has commanded him 'to return and change thy shape' (iii.25). The title pages of the quartos of 1620 and 1624 depict this scene and Faustus, standing in his magic circle and holding his wand and book, is confronted by a devil with a human head and dragon-like body, complete with wings and tail. It is quite possible that Mephistophilis makes his initial entry in this form, for Faustus informs him, 'Thou art too ugly to attend on me' (l. 26). Later in the play demonic spirits appear in the forms of Alexander the Great, his paramour, King Darius and Helen of Troy. The minor demons who make several appearances in the course of the play also seem to have taken human shape, although presumably of a less stately form, for their unkempt appearance became a by-word. T. M.'s *Black Book* (1604) describes such a figure: 'Hee had a head of hayre like one of my Divells in *Dr Faustus* when the old theater crackt and frighted the audience'? In similar vein, John Melton in *Astrologaster* (1620) describes a production of the play at 'the Fortune in Golding-Lane' by the Palsgrave's Men, formerly Prince Henry's Men: 'There indeede a man may behold shagge-hayr'd

# of the Life and Death
## of Doctor F A V S T V S.

---

With new Additions.

---

Written by *Ch. Mar.*

**13**    From the title page of the 1624 quarto of *Doctor Faustus*. The illustration portrays the first appearance, possibly through a trap-door, of Mephistophilis, in the form of a dragon-like devil. It is following this entry that Faustus commands him 'to return and change thy shape'.

153

Devills runne roaring over the Stage with Squibs in their mouthes, while Drummers make Thunder in the Tyring-house, and the twelve-penny Hirelings make artificiall Lightning in their Heavens.[8]

Fireworks seem to have been an established means of indicating to the audience that devils were being represented. Faustus's request for a wife is answered by the entry of 'a Devil dressed like a woman with fireworks' (v.148·1); Mephistophilis and Faustus 'fling fireworks among' the friars at the Papal Court (ix.112·1), and in the so-called A2 text of 1609 Mephistophilis, having been summoned by Robin and the Vintner, 'sets squibs at their backs. They run about' (x.29·1).

Spectacular pyrotechnic effects were also provided by Greene in *Friar Bacon and Friar Bungay*, particularly in the scene featuring the magical disputation between the English friars, Bacon and Bungay, and the German magician, Vandermast (scene ix). Bungay begins the contest by conjuring a tree 'with the dragon shooting fire'. In response, Vandermast summons a spirit in the form of Hercules 'in his lion's skin' who proceeds to break off the tree's branches. Bacon then brings his superior magic into play and forces the spirit to withdraw, taking with him both the tree and the vanquished Vandermast. The initial effect in this sequence must have been accomplished by the appearance of the tree and dragon rising through a mechanised trap. Vandermast states that Bungay has 'mounted' the tree, by which he means that he has caused it to rise. The tree would have had to be sufficiently large and realistic for Hercules to dismember it without this provoking ridicule. The dragon was probably an artificial figure rather than an actor in costume for it has to be 'shooting fire'. Sabbattini describes precisely such an effect, achieved by a tube leading from the creature's mouth to the under-stage area, where an operator would blow aqua-vitae through it to reach a lighted candle previously placed in the dragon's mouth, at which small flames would be emitted.[9] (Sabbattini also describes a similar device to produce speech from an inanimate figure, with an actor speaking into the tube from below stage level. Such a method was probably used in scene xi of *Friar Bacon and Friar Bungay* when the brazen head voices its brief oracular utterances.)

On other occasions heraldic or animal figures seem to have been played by actors, for they are required to move freely about the stage. The spirits 'in shape of dogs and hounds' that pursue Caliban and his fellows in IV.i of *The Tempest* are clearly of this type, the effect probably being achieved mainly by means of masks. The cat that is summoned by Hecate in *The Witch* (I.ii) enters 'playing on a fiddle'[10] and of course the dog-spirit in *The Witch of Edmonton* not only has to move but also converses at length with the human characters.

Some of the most impressive effects involving fireworks are found in *The Birth of Merlin*. In IV.v there is the stage direction 'Blazing star appears'. This heralds a spectacular display which is described by the awe-struck onlookers:

> *Uter*: Look, Edol:
> Still this fiery exhalation shoots
> His frightful horrors on th'amazed world;
> See, in the beam that's 'bout his flaming ring,
> A dragon's head appears, from out whose mouth
> Two flaming flakes of fire stretch east and west.
> *Edol*: And see, from forth the body of the star
> Seven smaller blazing streams directly point
> On this affrighted kingdom.                            [1–9]

Merlin repeats this description and proceeds to interpret the vision as a portent of the coming of Arthur, together with the establishment and eventual destruction of the Round Table. The fact that Merlin repeats the verbal account suggests that the display is not visible to the audience, who perhaps have witnessed nothing more than the initial blazing star, which is the only effect actually required by the stage directions.

However, such elaborate displays were well within the capabilities of the pyrotechnicians of the period[11] and earlier in the play the directions demand an even more striking demonstration of their skill. In IV.i Merlin strikes his wand and after the inevitable thunder and lightning 'two dragons appear, a white and a red; they fight a while, and pause. . . . Thunder: the two dragons fight again, and the white dragon drives off the red'. The dragons, representing the Welsh king Vortiger and the Saxon leader Ostorius, could have been played by actors in costume, but it is more likely that this sequence was staged with the use of fireworks for a favourite set-piece of the time involved the portrayal of dragons fighting in the air.

The technique is described in detail in several of the firework handbooks of the seventeenth century. The otherwise anonymous 'J. W.' in *The School of Artificial Fireworks* (1651) describes 'how to make a Dragon, or the like, to run on the Line, spitting of fire'. The line referred to is explained by his instruction: 'You must make a hollow trunk through the body of each Figure, for a great Line to passe through, and likewise for a smaller Line to draw them to and fro from each other'. John Babington in *Pyrotechnia* (1635) describes 'how to make two Dragons to meete each other, from severall Caves, which shall send forth their fire to each other with great violence'. John Bate in *Mysteries of Nature and Art* (1634) warns that 'the

155

flying Dragon is somewhat troublesome to compose'. It should be constructed of 'dry and light wood' which is covered with canvas and painted. He adds:

> in the body thereof, there must bee a voyde cane to passe the rope through; unto the bottom of this cane must bee bound one or two large Rockets, according to the bignesse and weight of the Dragon shall require; the body must be filled with divers petrars, that may consume it, and a sparkling receipt must be so disposed upon it, that beeing fired, it may burne both at the mouth and at the tayle thereof.
>
> [pp. 117–18]

He also provides an illustration that shows a dragon flying along a line drawn between two windows, a device that could easily have been adapted for use in the theatre.

Such effects were ambitious developments of the technique described by

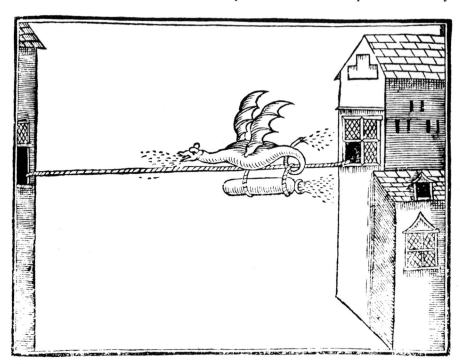

**14** A flying dragon, complete with fireworks, as portrayed in John Bate's *Mysteries of Nature and Art* (1634). Bate warns that the device is 'somewhat troublesome to compose' and suggests that the wings should be attached 'in such wise, that they may shake as the Dragon runnes along the line'.

Serlio in his account of the simulation of 'beames of the lightning' whereby

> you must draw a piece of wyre over the Scene, which must hang
> downewards, whereon you must put a squib covered over with pure
> gold or shining lattin [sheet tin] which you will: and while the Bullet is
> rouling, you must shoote of some piece of Ordinance, and with the
> same giving fire to the squibs, it will worke the effect which is desired.[12]

In Dekker's play *If It Be Not Good, The Devil Is In It*, performed at the
Red Bull Theatre in 1610–12, a stage direction reads 'Fireworks on lines'
(E2$^r$). In view of the Elizabethan and Jacobean audiences' predilection for
pyrotechnic displays it is a matter of some surprise that only two
playhouses—the first Globe in 1611 and the first Fortune in 1618—were
actually destroyed by fire.

## II

Despite the extensive dramatic portrayal of such diverse supernatural
phenomena, the Elizabethan playwrights made little use of the rich
potential for visual effects in their portrayal of witchcraft activities.
However, as was noted above, the representations of both magicians and
the demons they conjured were twin elements of established dramatic
traditions and no such tradition existed for the stage representation of
witchcraft. Moreover, the neglect of the obvious opportunities for spectacle
offered by witchcraft practices is part of the overall pattern of a low-key
approach to the subject. The principal exception is *Doctor Faustus* but
although Faustus is a witch his portrayal is closely allied to the conventions
of the stage magician. Likewise, the episode in *Henry VI, Part Two*, where
the spirit is summoned by Margery Jourdain and Bolingbroke (I.iv) is a
typical conjuration sequence, similar to many other such scenes of the
period.

However, during the early part of the seventeenth century the dramatic
portrayal of practices specifically related to witchcraft became a more
frequent occurrence. This might reflect a greater interest in the more
salacious aspects of the subject following the succession of James I, but the
dramatists also seem to have seen the opportunities witchcraft provided in
helping to satisfy their audiences' increasing demand for ever more
ambitious visual effects.

The scenes in *Macbeth* featuring the Weird Sisters are an early
indication of this growing trend. Any attempt to recreate the original
methods of staging these scenes must be highly conjectural. Compared

with many contemporary texts, the First Folio version contains few detailed stage directions, but it is possible to formulate a hypothesis, based on the hints given in the text coupled with our knowledge of Jacobean stage conditions.

There is one contemporary eye-witness account of *Macbeth* in performance—that by Simon Forman in his *Bocke of Plaies*, in which he describes seeing 'Macbeth at the Glob' on 20 April 1611.[13] Unfortunately, Forman virtually ignores the witchcraft elements in the play. He makes no reference to the opening scene or to Macbeth's visit to the Weird Sisters in their cavern and the Apparitions he witnesses there. These omissions are surprising in view of Forman's interest in astrology and the occult, but the whole account is completely unreliable and seems to have been based on imperfect recollection some time after the event—which he wrongly dates as 1610. Forman states, for example, that Macbeth is created Prince of Northumberland. He seems to have boosted his memory by reference to Holinshed's account, describing Macbeth's first encounter with the Weird Sisters in terms very close to those in the *Chronicles of Scotland*, where the meeting with the three 'nymphs or feiries' is set in a landscape of 'woods and fields'. Forman states: 'ther was to be observed, firste, how Mackbeth and Bancko, 2 noble men of Scotland, Ridinge thorowe a wod, the[r] stode before them 3 women feiries or Nimphes, And saluted Mackbeth, saying 3 tyms unto him, haille Mackbeth, king of Codon.'

It is thus very dangerous to place any reliance on Forman's account in assessing the staging of the play in 1611. For example, J. M. Nosworthy's assertion in *Shakespeare's Occasional Plays* (1965), in support of his dating of 1612 for the revised sections of *Macbeth*, that it is 'ludicrously impossible' to relate the 'secret, black and midnight hags' with the 'three women feiries or Nimphes' that Forman describes (p. 18) falls down on two counts. He ignores the fact that Forman has here clearly turned to Holinshed's account and he also disregards the plasticity of such terms in the Jacobean period, whereby both fairies and nymphs could be synonymous with the modern conception of witches and hags.[14] Similarly, some scholars have taken Forman's words literally and have argued that I.iii is set in a wood, with Macbeth and Banquo entering either on horseback or making 'skilled use of hobby-horses'.[15] Although horses were not unknown on the Elizabethan stage, their presence here would be an unnecessary complication and Forman once more seems to be relying on Holinshed—or perhaps recalling the woodcut illustration of the episode in the *Chronicles*.

Although the Weird Sisters are feminine—at least in their outward forms—it is likely that they were originally played by men, rather than the boys who normally took the female roles. Banquo's reference to beards in I.iii is, as we have seen, in accord with the traditional view of the witch's appearance, but it might also indicate masculine players. Certainly, by the Restoration period it was an established tradition that men played the witches' parts, a convention that persisted until the nineteenth century.

A matter of much debate has been whether the Weird Sisters in the first productions actually flew. The final line of I.i—'Hover through the fog and filthy air'—has led to conjecture that here, and elsewhere, they departed by means of a flying device. Such machinery was certainly available in some of the playhouses at the time of the first productions; characters and properties made descents and ascents suspended by wires. The earliest recorded use of such a device was in 1546 when John Dee contructed a machine for a performance of *Pax* by Aristophanes at Trinity College, Oxford. Dee attributed this invention to his predecessor in the worlds of magic and scholarship, Roger Bacon. Before his death, Faustus is shown the heavenly throne he might have occupied and the stage direction reads, 'Music while the throne descends' (xix.105·1). The music is the celestial equivalent of the diabolic thunder and lightning, its main function being to drown the sound of the ropes and pulleys while 'the creaking throne comes down', as Jonson caustically describes the no doubt laborious process of these primitive devices.[16]

However, all such sequences involve a single character or simple property and it seems very unlikely that such a machine could have borne the weight of all three Weird sisters at once, and a triple lowering and raising of the device would have been extremely protracted. Coghill suggests that the witches might have flown on three independent wires[17] but this is also improbable. It is true that many Elizabethan actors were skilled acrobats and were no doubt capable of flying on wires in this manner, just as their modern-day counterparts were required to be tumblers, jugglers, trapeze artists and walkers on stilts in Peter Brook's 1970 production of *A Midsummer-Night's Dream* for the Royal Shakespeare Company.

Ben Jonson's *An Entertainment of the King and Queen at Theobalds* (1607) has the stage direction:

> Within, as farther off, in Landscape, were seen clouds riding, and in one corner a boy figuring Good Event, attired in white, hovering in the air, with wings displayed, having nothing seen to sustain him by, all the time the Shew lasted. At the other corner, a Mercury descended, in a flying posture, with his Caduceus in his hand . . .     [32–8][18]

Here we have two actors appearing simultaneously, in different areas of the acting space, presumably wearing harnesses attached to wires. However, the approximation to flying seems strictly limited, the impression being more of literally suspended animation than of free flight. Simulated flying effects, as opposed to simple ascents and descents, were no doubt difficult to create with any degree of realism. As late as 1794, Hecate and her companions in Kemble's production of *Macbeth* were forced to fly backwards 'on account of the Machinery being necessary to be kept out of sight of the audience'![19]

The theory that the original *Macbeth* witches flew is also suspect in that although free-flying devices were available in the Banqueting House and other settings for the masques and entertainments, these were almost certainly not installed in any of the public playhouses until after the first performances of *Macbeth*. Indeed, Bernard Beckerman, after a close study of all the plays known to have been performed at the first Globe, where *Macbeth* was probably first presented, concludes that the King's Men did not use any flying machinery until they took over the Blackfriars Theatre in 1608 and that 'for the Globe, at least so far as the plays demonstrate, no machinery for flying existed' (*Shakespeare at the Globe, 1599–1609* (1962), p. 94). Some form of suspension gear must have been available for staging such a scene as that in *Antony and Cleopatra*, produced at the Globe in 1607, where 'they heave Antony aloft to Cleopatra' (IV.xv) but this does not seem to have been capable of being adapted to a free-flying device.

The fact that Davenant's revised *Macbeth*, first produced in 1663/4, boasted among its innovations 'flyings for the witches' also suggests that in the earlier productions no such effects were included. It is very probable that in the First Folio text Hecate enters and departs by means of a flying machine in III.v but this scene is almost certainly an interpolation derived from the similar sequence in *The Witch*, where such a device was clearly employed. Moreover, the mere inclusion of 'hover' in the Sisters' doggerel does not necessitate an actual display of this traditional power. This might have been suggested simply by placing the opening scene on the first upper level above the main stage. The Parcae-like aspect of the Sisters would thus have been stressed, with their beginning the action overlooking the world of men, to which they descend to meet their mortal victim in I.iii. The display of Macbeth's head on this same upper level in the final scene would have brought the play to a visually ironic conclusion.

Alternatively, the first scene might have been played on the main stage and the Sisters could have made their entry through the mechanised trap-door. The trap at the Globe could certainly have accommodated all three

Sisters simultaneously and their entry would have immediately established their demonic natures and hellish origins. A direction in *Tancred and Gismund* (1591) indicates the entry of three Furies in a manner that may well mirror the first appearance of the Sisters:

> *Before the Act Megaera riseth out of hell, with the other Furies, Alecto*
> *and Tysyphone, dancing an hellish round; which done, she saith:*
> Sisters, be gone, bequeath the rest to me,
> That yet belongs unto this Tragedy.                [1855ff]

Such an entrance by the Weird Sisters would have given *Macbeth* an arresting and appropriate opening and Shakespeare certainly seems to have used the trap in previous witchcraft sequences. Joan la Pucelle's familiar spirits are 'culled / Out of the powerful regions under earth' in *Henry VI, Part One* (V.iii) and the Spirit that 'riseth' for Mother Jourdain in *Henry VI, Part Two* (I.iv) is subsequently ordered to 'Descend to darkness and the burning lake'. As the Spirit appears 'it thunders and lightens terribly' and it departs amidst 'thunder and lightning'. This conventional method of masking the noise of the trap's mechanism could give added point to the fact that every entry and departure of the Weird Sisters is similarly accompanied by thunder and lightning.

Shakespeare might also have used for his own particular purposes the traditional emission of sulphurous smoke from the open trap. This established symbol for the entrance to hell could have represented simultaneously the 'fog and filthy air' in which the Sisters depart at the end of I.i. Its use in I.iii would have helped to disguise their descent and enhance their apparently mysterious disappearance implied by Banquo's comment that 'The earth hath bubbles, as the water has, / And these are of them. Whither are they vanish'd?' (ll. 79–80). The amount of smoke or 'fog' that could be created was of quite dense proportions, as an episode in *Arden of Faversham* (1592) indicates. In the fourth Act a thick fog envelops the two murderers, Black Will and Shakbag, as they lie in wait for Arden:

> *Shakbag*: Oh, Will, where are you?
> *Will*: Here, Shakbag, almost in hell's mouth, where I cannot see my
>    way for smoke.
> *Shakbag*: I pray thee speak still, that we may meet by the sound, for I
>    shall fall into some ditch or other, unless my feet see better than
>    my eyes. . . .
>                                        [*Then Shakbag falls into a ditch*]
> *Shakbag*: Help, Will, help! I am almost drowned!        [IV.iii.1–25]

Will's comparison with being in 'hell's mouth' is clearly a reference to the conventional dramatic portrayal of the smoking entrance to Hell. To give a semblance of realism to the action the fog effect must have been quite extensive and it has to be maintained through two scenes and some eighty lines of dialogue. It also has to be controlled because the air has to clear to coincide with Shakbag's comment a little later, 'See how the sun hath cleared the foggy mist; / Now we have mis't the mark of our intent!' (ll. 48–9). The 'fog' was probably produced by burning damp material within a non-inflammable and moveable container positioned under a trap which would be opened at the beginning of the sequence and closed when the effect was no longer required. The scene in *Arden of Faversham* would have needed two open trap-doors because Shakbag's falling into a ditch would presumably have been accomplished by his disappearing through an opening in the stage.

If such a method was used at the end of I.i in *Macbeth* to represent the fog into which the Sisters vanish, the effect could then have merged with the off-stage sounds of battle required by the direction 'Alarum within' at the beginning of I.ii to suggest the smoke-filled battle-field from which emerges the 'bleeding Captain' to meet the ill-fated Duncan.

The Weird Sisters might have used an alternative means of entry at the beginning of I.iii. The impression conveyed by their opening dialogue is that they are meeting for their agreed rendezvous after going their separate ways since I.i. Some Elizabethan theatres—for example the Red Bull—had several non-mechanical traps spaced at intervals on the main stage. The Sisters might have made separate entrances through these, but there is no evidence that the Globe possessed such additional traps. Another possibility is that for this entry the Sisters climbed up stepladders leading from the yard into which the stage projected. The 'groundlings' habitually occupied this area but a space on either side of the stage could have been kept clear. The temporary installation of such steps in Elizabethan playhouses is suggested by Allardyce Nicoll in his article 'Passing over the stage' in *Shakespeare Survey, 12* (1959), where he refers to 'the long-standing tradition in booth stages of ladder-like steps from the ground to the raised acting level, associated with the tradition of steps from stage to floor in Renaissance court theatres' (p. 53).

It is of course very probable that, as in the modern theatre, various production techniques were used in the early years of a play's history. The considerable flexibility of the stage equipment of the period would have permitted—and indeed encouraged—such variations, and moreover the wide range of theatrical facilities available, particularly when a company was on tour, would often have necessitated a range of approaches.

This could well have been the case with IV.i of *Macbeth*, which requires more complex stage business than the earlier witchcraft scenes. It might have opened with the three Sisters ascending through the main trap, grouped around the cauldron and accompanied once more by smoke and perhaps flames—representing both the fires of Hell and the terrestrial blaze over which the cauldron's ingredients are bubbling. No precise locale is given in the Folio directions but an interior setting is implied by the Second Witch's cry at the advent of Macbeth: 'Open locks, who ever knocks!' (l. 46). Macbeth's entry would be through one of the two doors at the rear of the main stage, perhaps the same door through which Macduff and Lennox enter before the discovery of Duncan's murder in II.iii. The knocking which precedes Macbeth's descent into this 'pit of Acheron' is an echo of the insistent knocking required by the stage directions and the dialogue during the earlier episode, prior to the Porter's opening of his metaphorical hell-gate.

The three Apparitions, whose appearances are heralded by the direction 'Thunder', might have used the main trap, apparently emerging from the cauldron by means of a false bottom in the latter. The mechanical trap could accomplish the rapid series of ascents and descents required here, as is demonstrated by the stage directions in the preliminary dumb-show in *The Devil's Charter*, which was first performed at the Globe at about the same time as the early productions of *Macbeth*. The stage direction 'Descends' marking the departures of each Apparition, together with Macbeth's statement that the third figure 'rises like the issue of a king' confirm that a trap was used for these effects.

The Apparitions might have been represented by artificial figures, perhaps equipped with speaking tubes similar to that suggested for Friar Bacon's brazen head. Alternatively, they could have been portrayed by actors, suitably costumed and carrying appropriate properties. The *Macbeth* scene has marked affinities with the conjuration episode in *Henry VI, Part Two* (I.iv) and the nine lines spoken by the Spirit that rises and descends in this scene were probably spoken by an actor directly addressing the audience. In the scene in *Friar Bacon* the head speaks only seven words—'Time is . . . Time was . . . Time is past'—and if the speaking tube had produced a muffled or distorted effect it would not have mattered unduly. In the *Henry VI* and *Macbeth* scenes, on the other hand, it is extremely important for the audience to hear clearly the Spirits' responses.

In *Macbeth* the actors could have appeared either through a trap-door within the main trap or through a smaller opening positioned at the rear of the stage, behind the Sisters and their cauldron. Neither of these traps would have been mechanised and the members of the company producing these effects would have had to mount and descend a ladder placed in the 'hell'. Such a method was probably used in *Richard III*, V.iii, where eleven ghosts 'enter' in succession to threaten Richard and encourage Richmond before the Battle of Bosworth. In *Macbeth* the entrances and exits, marked each time by the direction 'He descends', are carefully placed within the dialogue to allow for the inevitable pauses between each appearance—whichever method was employed. However, one can imagine the hectic scenes off, or rather below stage, as each Apparition made its entry and departure. Booth's theatrical company were later to use the trapdoor and ladder technique for this scene in their 1886/7 production of *Macbeth* and Katherine Goodall (Kitty Molony), who played the Second Apparition, recalled the practical difficulties of performing this sequence:

> The armed head went up first, the 'Child Apparition' followed me. This trap business is a scamper. The first and last apparitions had time for cautious one-way traffic—the first for getting on, the last for getting off—but the middle one to connect with the cues, needs to jump lively both ways.[20]

After the Third Apparition has descended, the cauldron is removed. Macbeth's questions: 'Why sinks that cauldron, and what noise is this?' (l. 106) together with the direction 'Hautboys' are clear indications that the cauldron disappears whence it came, via the mechanised trap, whose noises on this occasion are disguised by music. The stage is thus cleared for the 'Show of eight Kings and Banquo following'. It is possible that these figures also appear in turn by means of the trap-door, and Macbeth's injunction, 'Down', to the spirit of Banquo implies such a method. However, Macbeth's commentary on the line of kings indicates that their entries take place in rapid succession—the last four figures all appear within the space of just over three lines of verse. It is difficult to see how the actors could have mounted the steps to the trap with sufficient speed for their entrances to coincide with Macbeth's words. The below-stage technicians would only just have restored order after the confusion that probably reigned during the Apparitions sequence and they would have been engaged in preparing the trap mechanism for the imminent descent of the Weird Sisters themselves.

An ingenious alternative reconstruction of the staging of this effect is proposed by J. C. Adams in *The Globe Playhouse: its Design and Equipment* (1942), pp. 189–91. He suggests that the line of kings processed in single file at the rear of the main stage, across which a curtain was normally stretched to form a narrow passageway for the actors to move from one side of the stage to the other whilst remaining out of sight of the audience. At the words 'Show ... Show ... Show' (ll. 107–9) the witches would draw the curtains slightly to reveal the line of actors who would appear in turn, timing their entrances to coincide with Macbeth's carefully paced commentary (ll. 112–24). Despite the ingenious suggestion that the eighth king 'who bears a glass' was carrying a mirror whereby King James could see his own image reflected, the object was probably a magic glass of the crystal ball variety.

The final effect in the scene is the apparent vanishing of the Weird Sisters, accomplished once again by means of the main trap. It is little wonder that Macbeth is moved to cry 'But no more sights' (l. 155) for he has witnessed a frightening display of the Sisters' magical powers which at the same time has provided an impressive demonstration of the theatrical effects that were at the disposal of the Jacobean dramatists.[21]

Although it is impossible to be certain about the production of any of the supernatural effects in *Macbeth*, there is no such problem with *The Masque of Queenes*. We know a great deal about the methods of staging masques from the detailed accounts of performances, both in England and on the Continent. The English masque was greatly influenced by the Italian form in particular and the techniques described in such a work as Sabbattini's *Pratica di fabricar scene e machine ne' teatri* can be confidently related to the productions at the Stuart courts.[22] Moreover, the Chatsworth Collection contains a comprehensive assembly of costume and set designs executed by Inigo Jones for masques performed between 1606 and 1640. They include designs made for *The Masque of Queenes* and these, together with Jonson's own account of the staging of the Masque—included in his holograph version—allow us to reconstruct with some certainty the effect the work made in its single performance at the Banqueting House in February 1609.

Jonson tries to recapture something of the air of anticipation that preceded the performance as he describes the opening of the anti-masque:

> First, then, his Ma.<sup>tie</sup> being set, and the whole Company in full expectation, that wch presented it selfe was an ougly Hell; wch, flaming beneath, smoakd unto the top of the Roofe. .. These Witches, wth a kind of hollow and infernall musique, came forth from thence. First one, then two, and three, and more, till theyr number encreasd to Eleven; all differently attir'd; some, wth ratts on theyr heads; some, on theyr shoulders; others wth oyntment-potts at theyr girdles; All wth

165

15  A sketch by Inigo Jones of grotesque heads. The drawing dates from the same period as his designs for *The Masque of Queenes* and may be preliminary drafts for the fantastic head-dresses worn by the witches in the anti-masque.

> spindells, timbrells, rattles, or other veneficall instruments, making a confused noyse, wth strange gestures.                    [23–36][23]

Jonson states that the anti-masque was devised for 'twelve Women, in the habite of Haggs, or Witches', but he presumably means that the actors who performed this sequence, probably members of the King's Men company, portrayed women. He adds that 'the devise of their attire was m^r Jones his'. Although eight of Jones's beautiful designs for the Queens' dresses are preserved in the Chatsworth Collection, there is unfortunately no trace of his designs for the witches' costumes. There is, however, a sketch by Jones dating from about this time, which portrays a series of grotesque heads, with fantastic head-dresses (Chatsworth Collection, design no. 463). These sketches are in the Renaissance tradition of Leonardo and Rosso, but they may possibly be early drafts for the anti-masque, with the head-dresses being stylised representations of the 'ratts on they[r] heads' described by Jonson.

The temporary platform erected in the Banqueting House did not apparently possess mechanical traps and there was no extensive 'hell' area beneath the stage. So it is probable that the hags entered through a curtain painted with a hell-mouth scene. Such a device was frequently used in the masques and it would have divided the front section of the stage, where the anti-masque would be performed, from the main area, where was positioned the spectacular setting for the masque itself. The witches then proceed to dance and utter charms to summon their Dame, who enters: 'Naked arm'd, bare-footed, her frock tuck'd, her hayre knotted, and folded with vipers; In her hand, a Torch made of a dead-Mans arme, lighted; girded with a snake' (95–8). She commands them to create a spell which will destroy the 'soft peace'. The hags contribute a variety of magical objects to the spell-making, which is conducted around a cauldron, and they conclude the ritual by performing their 'praeposterous' dance. Finally:

> in the heate of theyr Daunce, on the sodayne, was heard a sound of loud Musique, as if many Instruments had given one blast. Wth wch, not only the Hagges themselves, but theyr Hell, into wch they ranne, quite vanishd; and the whole face of the Scene alterd; scarse suffring the memory of any such thing: But, in the place of it appear'd a glorious and magnificent Building, figuring the House of Fame, in the upper part of wch were discovered the twelve Masquers sitting upon a Throne triumphall, erected in forme of a Pyramide, and circled wth all store of light. [354–63]

The vanishing of the Hell scene was probably achieved by the rapid drawing or raising of the curtain, with any extraneous sounds being drowned by the blast of 'loud Musique'. Allardyce Nicoll suggests a more complicated arrangement whereby the hell scene was set on a revolving platform which turned to reveal the base of the House of Fame structure.[24] However, if such a method had been used it is likely that Jonson would have noted it in his description of the performance, and it is probable that the more mundane curtain effect was employed. The upper section of the House of Fame was certainly built on some form of turntable for Jonson describes how this massive structure, complete with its twelve masquers, 'being Machina versatilis, sodaynely chang'd; and in the place of it appeard Fama bona'. Jones's design for this 'turning machine' survives in the Chatsworth Collection. He had devised similar structures for *Hymenaei* in 1606 and *The Haddington Masque* in 1608 but neither was as elaborate as that used here. The Accounts of the Audit Office contain a description of the setting up of the structure in the Banqueting House:

> making a greate Throne of cantes borne in the middest by a greate piller with divers wheeles and devices for the moving rounde thereof, framing and setting up of a great stage iiij[or] [four] fote highe whereon the same frame was placed. ... setting up a greate stage ... wth a floore in the midle of the same being made wth sondry devices wth greate gates and turning doores belowe and a globe and sondry seates above for the Quene and Ladies to sitt on and to be turned rounde aboute.[25]

It is hardly surprising, in view of the elaborate nature of the structure, that the Venetian ambassador reported that the Queen 'held daily rehearsals and trials of the machinery'.[26] The reference in the Accounts to the floor in the middle of the lower part of the edifice reinforces the view that the structure as a whole did not revolve.

The splendour of the House of Fame was enhanced oy the 'store of light' which encircled it. Jonson describes how 'the Freezes, both below, and above, were filled wth severall-colour Lights, like Emeralds, Rubies, Saphires, Carbuncles, &c. The Reflexe of wch, wth other lights plac'd in ye concave, upon the Masquers habites, was full of glory' (ll. 695–9). Such effects were used frequently in both England and Italy and were probably obtained by filling glasses with coloured liquids and placing lights—usually candles—behind them.[27]

The masque then proceeded on its stately progress and the hags made a final appearance at its conclusion, when the Queens made a triumphant procession around the stage riding in chariots drawn by heraldic beasts and with 'the Hagges, bound before them' (l. 715).

There are some apparent similarities between the anti-masque and *Macbeth*. The spell-making sequence in Jonson's work is an elaboration of Shakespeare's cauldron scene and the entry of the Hags, erupting on to the stage through the 'ougly' hell-mouth might have been inspired by the appearances of the Weird Sisters from their smoking 'hell'. If *Macbeth* did receive a court performance, either at Greenwich or Hampton Court, where traps would not have been available, the Sisters' entrances could well have been made through a curtain similar to that probably used in the Masque.

Lawrence's theory linking the two works with *The Witch* is strengthened by a comparison of the likely staging methods of the three plays. The first appearance of the witches in Middleton's work—in I.ii—is heralded by the enigmatic stage direction: 'Enter Hecate: and other witches: (with Properties, and Habits fitting)'. This could be theatrical shorthand for the actors' appearance in the appropriate costumes and properties in the possession of the King's Men and which were originally created for their performance of the anti-masque. Similarly, the direction at the end of V.iii—'here they dance the witches' dance and exeunt'—seems to refer to an established piece of stage business. This dance could be one of those originally performed by the Hags in Jonson's Masque. They are described in similar terms. Hecate in *The Witch* commands: 'Round, around, around, about, about' (l. 79), whilst in the Seventh Charm of the Masque, immediately prior to the dance, the Hags go 'About, about, and about . . . Around, around, / Around, around' (ll. 331–9).

The Weird Sisters also process around their cauldron 'in a ring' in IV.1 of *Macbeth*. Eleven hags plus the Dame perform the dances in the masque and the sequence in *The Witch* requires at least six witches. It is therefore significant that immediately prior to the charm in *Macbeth* the Folio stage direction indicates that 'Hecate and the three other witches enter'. The possible connection with *The Witch* could also explain this direction that has puzzled editors and led to such emendations as 'Enter Hecate *to* the other three witches'. As in Middleton's play, Hecate is clearly regarded here as a witch and the direction is similar to that in I.ii of *The Witch*, 'Enter Hecate and other witches.' The First Folio does not indicate any departure for Hecate and the additional witches, so they might have remained on stage to join in the 'antic round' that the Weird Sisters perform to 'cheer' Macbeth later in the scene. John P. Cutts in *Musique de la Troupe de Shakespeare* (Paris, 1959) prints the contemporary music for two witches' dances composed by the court musician, Robert Johnson. He argues that one of these dances was performed in both *The Witch* and *The Masque of Queenes* and that it was then included in the revised version of *Macbeth*. The music is both melodic and measured—even more so than that for the Witches' Dance in Purcell's *Dido and Aeneas*, composed some eighty years later (see Chapter Eleven). There is little indication in the music of the jerky and disjointed rhythm suggested by Jonson's description of the dance as being 'full of praeposterous change, and gesticulation'. Nevertheless, it remains likely that the dance in *Macbeth* originated in the masque and therefore Jonson's account gives us a vivid indication of how the sequences were performed in the interpolated sections of *Macbeth*. Although these dances are usually omitted from modern productions, it is quite possible that Shakespeare sanctioned their inclusion in the revival. A similar process of borrowing from a masque is probably evident in the satyrs' dance in IV.iv of *The Winter's Tale*, which seems to have been taken from the anti-masque of satyrs in Jonson's *Masque of Oberon*, the music for which was also composed by Johnson. This was performed on 1 January 1611 and the *Macbeth* revival could well have been staged at about this time.

Cutts also prints a setting by Johnson of 'Come away, come away', one of the songs performed in *The Witch* and referred to in *Macbeth*. The song occurs in the latter at the end of III.v, a scene that seems to owe a great deal to III.iii of *The Witch*. In the *Macbeth* scene, Hecate clearly departs by means of a flying device; she says she is 'for th' air' (l. 20) and she leaves to join her little spirit who 'Sits in a foggy cloud, and stays for me' (l. 35). Flying machinery was also used in the equivalent scene in *The Witch*. Hecate's exit is signalled by the stage direction 'going up' and she declares 'Now I go, now I fly'. Immediately before this, the machinery must have been used in the reverse direction for Hecate states 'There's one comes down' and the stage direction indicates 'A Spirit like a Cat descends'. It is possible, particularly if the Cat was played by a boy, that the equipment could have borne the weight of both Hecate and the spirit, allowing them to make a spectacular ascent whilst Hecate declaimed her concluding speech, describing the pleasures of flying, from 'above'.

The flight thus seems to have been accomplished on an ascending and descending 'throne' rather than with a free-flying harness. In both scenes the song 'Come away' is performed off-stage by spirits and in each case the singing accompanies the flying, thereby helping to mask the mechanical noises. The singers are clearly positioned at an upper level in *The Witch* for the stage direction reads 'in the air' and in *Macbeth* the spirit summons Hecate from a 'foggy cloud'. This suggests that the flying machinery was concealed in folds of light drapery, a device that was used extensively in the masques to achieve such effects.

The quarto states that *The Witch* was presented at the Blackfriars. Shakespeare's company took over this theatre as their winter quarters in 1608 and it therefore seems highly likely that the Hecate sections in *Macbeth*, including the flying sequence, were inserted for a revival of the play at about this time, to take advantage of their newly acquired machinery. This equipment was also used in the scene in *Cymbeline*, which also dates from the relevant period around 1609, where 'Jupiter descends in thunder and lightning, sitting upon an eagle' (V.iv). This spectacle might provide a further instance of the interchanging of effects between plays and masques for it seems to have been revived for the performance of Townsend's *Tempe Restored* (1632) where, in the midst of 'a new Heaven ... Jove sitting on an Eagle is seen hovering in the air with a glory behind him'.[28]

170

## Notes to Chapter 10

*1*    Quoted in this translation in A. M. Nagler, *A Source Book in Theatrical History* (1959), pp. 46–7.

*2*    For detailed descriptions and realistic reconstructions of the physical features of Elizabethan and Jacobean playhouses see E. K. Chambers, *The Elizabethan Stage* (1923), G. E. Bentley, *The Jacobean and Caroline Stage* (1941–68), C. Walter Hodges, *The Globe Restored: a Study of the Elizabethan Theatre* (1953; revised edn. 1968); Bernard Beckerman, *Shakespeare at the Globe, 1599–1609* (1962), and *The Revels History of Drama in English*, vol. 3 (1975).

*3*    The arguments are summarised in John R. Elliott, Jr., 'Medieval rounds and wooden O's', *Stratford-upon-Avon Studies, 16* (1973), pp. 223–46.

*4*    The description is printed in full in *Stratford-upon-Avon Studies, 16* and also in Chambers, *The Elizabethan Stage*, vol. 3, p. 72.

*5*    Printed in this translation in Bernard Hewitt (ed.), *The Renaissance Stage: Documents of Serlio, Sabbattini, and Furtenbach* (1958).

*6*    Nagler, p. 80.

*7*    Quoted in Chambers, *The Elizabethan Stage*, vol. 3, pp. 423–4.

*8*    Quoted in Jump, *Doctor Faustus* (Revels Plays), p. lix.

*9*    See Leonard H. Miller, *Thrilling Magic* (Colon, Michigan, 1949), p. 11.

*10*    The dual demonic associations of the cat and fiddle, originating in the concepts of the devil taking animal form and accompanying satanic revels on a fiddle, are preserved on numerous public house signs and in the nursery rhyme 'Hey, diddle, diddle!'.

*11*    A detailed discussion of the use of fireworks and other supernatural stage effects is contained in J. Nathan French, *The Staging of Magical Effects in Elizabethan and Jacobean Drama* (unpublished thesis, University of Birmingham, 1964). See also W. J. Lawrence, *Pr-Restoration Stage Studies* (1927).

*12*    Nagler, p. 81.

*13*    Forman's account is printed in the New Arden *Macbeth*, pp. xvi–xvii.

*14*    Nosworthy is on equally unsure ground in arguing that Forman's failure to describe I.i confirms that this scene is a further interpolation. This is surely to ignore the inestimable value of the scene in, as Coleridge puts it, striking 'the keynote . . . of the whole play'.

*15*    Nevill Coghill, *Shakespeare's Professional Skills* (1964), p. 206.

*16*    *Every Man in his Humour* (1598): Prologue.

*17*    '*Macbeth* at the Globe, 1606–1616(?). Three questions' in *The Triple Bond*, edited by J. G. Price (1975).

*18*    Herford and Simpson, *Works*, vol. VIII, p. 155.

*19*    Quoted in A. C. Sprague, *Shakespeare and the Actors* (1945), p. 265.

*20*    Quoted in Sprague, p. 266.

*21*    For a full-length reconstruction of the staging of *Macbeth* see R. Watkins and J. Lemmon, *'Macbeth' in Shakespeare's Playhouse* (1974).

*22*    For a full discussion of the production of masques see Allardyce Nicoll, *Stuart Masques and the Renaissance Stage*.

*23*    Quotations from *The Masque of Queenes* are taken from Herford and Simpson, *Works*, vol. VII.

*24*    Nicoll, *op. cit.*, p. 68.

*25*    Quoted in Herford and Simpson, *Works*, vol. X, p. 494.

26    *Ibid.*
27    See Nicoll, pp. 129–37 and Herford and Simpson, vol. X, pp. 413–20 for detailed discussions of these techniques.
28    Jones's design is preserved in the Chatsworth Collection, No. 162, and is reproduced in Nicoll, p. 94.

# CHAPTER 11

# DIVERTING CONTRIVANCES

## WITCHCRAFT AND MAGIC IN POST-JACOBEAN DRAMA

> *The Lancashire Witches*, **Acted in 1681, made by Mr Shadwell, being a kind of Opera, having several Machines of Flyings for the Witches, and other Diverting Contrivances in 't: All being well perform'd, it prov'd beyond Expectation; very Beneficial to the Poet and Actors.**
>
> [Thomas Downes, *Roscius Anglicanus*]

### I

The surviving court records indicate that the decline in the number of witchcraft trials and executions evident in the later years of James I's reign was maintained under his successors. The Elizabethan/Jacobean pattern continued to some extent, with occasional eruptions of witch-scares in specific areas being followed by periods of comparative quiescence, but the overall impression is of a gradual but definite waning of belief in the efficacy of witchcraft, if not in its existence, through the remainder of the seventeenth century.

This trend was more marked, as might be expected, among the learned than among the uneducated. For example, John Webster in his *The Displaying of Supposed Witchcraft* (1677) reiterated and developed the rational arguments previously put forward by such writers as Scot and Gifford. He did not deny that witches were active and could work evil but he believed that this was achieved by natural means, such as the use of poisons. He rejected all claims for witchcraft that defied reasonable

173

explanation:

> If I deny that a Witch cannot flye in the air, nor be transformed or transsubstantiated into a Cat, a Dog, or an Hare, or that the Witch maketh any visible Covenant with the Devil, or that he sucketh on their bodies, or that the Devil hath carnal copulation with them; I do not thereby deny either the Being of Witches, nor other properties that they may have, for which they may be so called.          [pp. 10–11]

This attitude gained force with the onset of the Age of Reason and in 1711 Joseph Addison expressed the view of most enlightened people of his time in declaring: 'I believe in general that there is, and has been such a thing as Witch-craft; but at the same time can give no Credit to any particular Instance of it.'[1]

However, not all scholars, especially those writing in the earlier part of the seventeenth century, agreed with such views. Sir Thomas Browne stated in *Religio Medici* (1642/3):

> I could believe that Spirits use with man the act of carnality, and that in both sexes . . . For my part, I have ever believed and do now know, that there are Witches: they that doubt of these, do not onely deny them, but Spirits; and are obliquely, and upon consequence a sort not of Infidels, but Atheists.[2]

Browne gave expert evidence for the prosecution at a witchcraft trial at Bury St Edmunds in 1664. The presiding judge, Sir Matthew Hale, agreed with Browne's views and declared, 'That there were such Creatures as Witches he made no doubt at all.'[3] Largely because of his advice to the jury, in the face of clear evidence of fraudulent testimony, the two accused women were found guilty and hanged. In contrast to Hale, Sir John Holt, Chief Justice of the King's Bench from 1682 to 1710, brought an impartial commonsense and open-mindedness to the dozen or more witchcraft cases he heard and in every instance the accused were acquitted. His example did much to hasten the decline of witchcraft prosecutions throughout the country in the latter part of the seventeenth century.

There had been, however, several major witchcraft trials earlier in the post-Jacobean period. During the first seven years of Charles I's reign there was only one recorded execution for witchcraft but in 1633 there occurred the second of the Lancashire witch-scares. This was centred around Pendle Forest and its environs, the same area as in the earlier episode of 1612, and some of the principals had also been involved in the previous events. Janet Device who, as a child, had testified against her own mother, brother and grandmother, was herself accused on the second occasion, with the prosecution largely relying once more on the testimony of a child—that of ten-year-old Edmund Robinson. Amongst his many incredible tales, he claimed that he once beat two greyhounds when they refused to run after a hare, whereupon they turned into human beings, a boy and a woman. The latter unsuccessfully tried to bribe Edmund into silence and then turned the strange boy into a white horse which bore young Robinson to a barn where he saw a group of men and women 'pulling at six severall ropes at which pulling came flesh, smoking, and milke and butter in lumps which fell into basons placed under the ropes'.[4] He also affirmed that on another occasion he was set upon and beaten by a boy with cloven hooves. He finally admitted that all his stories were false but this was not before at least sixty men and women had faced trial and nineteen had been convicted. Fortunately, the presiding judge was not satisfied and at his instigation the King intervened and the verdicts were overturned—but not before three or four of the accused had died in prison.

Another significant episode was the two-year reign of terror conducted by Matthew Hopkins, the self-styled Witch-Finder General. Together with his henchman, John Stearne, he pursued his witch-hunt through seven counties from Essex to Northamptonshire, and was responsible for the execution of over two hundred 'witches' between the years 1655 and 1657.[5] Hopkins was the son of a Puritan minister but he derived many of his ideas about witches and their detection from a close study of *Malleus Maleficarum*. To him, the sabbat, with its sacrificial rituals and devil-worship, was a fact and admissions of involvement in such ceremonies occur in many of the confessions he extorted, by means of various forms of mental and physical torture. Responsible voices were raised against such methods and Hopkins and his associates were finally forced to abandon their abominable activities.

There were other sporadic upsurges of witch-hunts in England during the rest of the century—notably from 1649 to 1650 at Newcastle-upon-Tyne, at Maidstone in 1652, and at Exeter in 1682.[6] The latter case affords a clear indication of the passions which were still aroused by witchcraft amongst the credulous masses. Roger North paints a vivid picture of the emotional scenes that accompanied the hearings:

> The women were very old, decrepit, and impotent, and were brought to the assizes with as much noise and fury of the rabble against them as could be shewed on any occasion. The stories of their acts were in everyone's mouth ... All which the country believed, and accordingly persecuted the wretched old creatures. A less zeal in a city or kingdom hath been the overture of defection and revolution, and if these women

had been acquitted, it was thought that the country people would have committed some disorder.[7]

Exeter was also the scene of the last recorded execution for witchcraft in England—in 1684—but several other cases were heard, with at least one conviction that was later reversed, before the repeal of the 1604 Witchcraft Act in 1736.[8] Whilst provision was retained for the trial of those who pretended to possess or use magical powers, there could no longer be prosecution for witchcraft itself. Whatever practices and beliefs might survive until the present day, as far as the English Statute Book was concerned, withcraft had ceased to exist.


## II

The declining fear of witchcraft (rather than a loss of belief in its existence) is reflected in the drama of the post-1625 period. In contrast to the seriousness with which the subject was treated in nearly all the Jacobean works, it became increasingly a source of humour, particularly in the Restoration theatre. This trend is first evident in Heywood and Broome's *The Late Lancashire Witches*. Printed in 1634, it has many affinities with its Jacobean predecessors, but the treatment is essentially comic. The play was based on the historical case outlined above and was apparently produced whilst the trial was still in progress. The Epilogue begins: 'Now while the witches must expect their due / By lawful justice, we appeal to you / For favourable censure; what their crime / May bring upon 'em, ripeness yet of time / Has not reveal'd.' [9]

To have presented the play at such a time seems highly irresponsible, although a production at London's Globe Theatre would hardly have influenced unduly the deliberations of a jury in far-off Lancaster. Nevertheless, the sceptical attitude to apparently supernatural powers and happenings displayed by Heywood in *The Wise Woman of Hogsdon* is not at all evident in the later play. Patently incredible accusations made at the trial are incorporated into the drama, with no apparent attempt to expose their absurdity, thereby giving a spurious air of verisimilitude to the ridiculous charges. The Epilogue strengthens this impression with the claim: 'We represent as much / As they have done before law's hand did touch / Upon their guilt'. The main elements of Edmund Robinson's fantastic stories are all reproduced in the play.[10] The coven in the barn is portrayed in Act IV, the incident being tenuously linked to other aspects of the play in that the food magically gathered on the ropes has come from

Lawrence and Parnell's wedding-feast. The child's alleged encounter with the cloven-hooved devil/boy is described in V.i in terms very similar to Robinson's actual testimony.

Equally incredible pieces of evidence from other sources are also presented on stage as indisputable fact. Bishop Bridgeman of Chester was asked to examine seven of the prisoners, one of whom, Mary Spencer, was accused of calling 'a collock, or peal [pail] which came running to her of its own accord'. She replied that:

> when she was a young girl and went to the well for water, she used to trundle the collock, or peal, down the hill, and she would run after it to overtake it, and did overye [overtake] it sometimes, and then she might call it to come to her, but utterly denies that she could ever make it come to her by any witchcraft.[11]

This clearly reasonable denial is ignored by the playwrights and the pail-calling is included in a series of minor manifestations of the occult in II.i. Occasionally, the basic evidence given at the trial is elaborated by the dramatists. Margaret Jonson, a sixty-year-old widow, confessed that about six years previously:

> there appeared to her a man in black attire, with black points, who said to her, if she would give him her soul, she should want nothing, but should have power to hurt whom she would ... He called himself Mamilion, and most commonly at his coming had the use of her body.[12]

In the play one of the witches, named Peg, admits to having a demon lover called Mamilion, who appeared to her: 'Gentleman like, but black, black points and all' (V.i.595). She adds that: 'He pleas'd me well, Sir, like a proper man ... / Only his flesh felt cold' (ll. 590–2). The latter detail was not included in Margaret Johnson's testimony but is a recurring element in many similar confessions. Margaret Murray in *The Witch-Cult in Western Europe* suggests that in witchcraft rituals the devil was impersonated by a man and adds:

> The coldness of the devil's entire person, which is vouched for by several witches, suggests that the ritual disguise was not merely a mask over the face, but included a covering, possibly of leather or some other hard and cold substance, over the whole body and even the hands.                                    [p. 63]

The devil's semen was also spoken of as being cold and Miss Murray suggests that in ritual intercourse water or some other liquid might have been used as a substitute by the over-taxed devil-figure.

177

Many other supernatural elements in the play are similarly based on traditional lore and have no apparent connection with the historical events. In this respect, the play, which bears many signs of hasty composition, is comparable with the popular ballads whose appearances coincided with the more sensational cases of the period and which comprised bare outlines of the events of the cases in question, padded out with a rag-bag miscellany of stock folklore material. In their portrayal of the disruption of the Seely household in Act IV the dramatists make use of the traditional tales of families being overthrown by supernatural interference, with children rebelling against their parents and in turn being commanded by the servants. The strange incident in V.i. of the mill being invaded by cats and of the hacked-off paw turning into Mrs Generous's hand is found in various forms in traditional tales,[13] whilst the Skimmington performed in IV.i to ridicule Parnell's quarrels with Lawrence was a custom which survived at least until the last century and is also portrayed, of course, in Hardy's novel *The Mayor of Casterbridge* (1886), chapters 36 and 39.

The lovers have quarrelled over Lawrence's impotence, which has been inflicted by the witches. It will be recalled that the ability to induce this condition is one of the powers claimed by Hecate in *The Witch*.[14] The work has most affinities, however, with *The Witch of Edmonton*. Both plays, based as they are on actual events, interwoven with elements of folklore, give authentic portrayals of essentially English witchcraft beliefs and practices. However, the works differ in one vital respect. Although Mother Sawyer performs deeds of far greater lasting harm—causing insanity and death—she is presented much more sympathetically than are the witches in the latter play, even though their activities are comparatively harmless. Meg demands of her fellow hags:

> What new device, what dainty strain,
> More for our mirth now than our gain
> Shall we in practice put?                    [II.i.2–4]

Nevertheless, they do not engage our emotions in the way that Mother Sawyer does. With one exception, the witches are wholly one-dimensional figures and there is no attempt, for example, to suggest motives for their malicious actions. They are merely malevolent creatures, loving evil for its own sake in the manner of the hags in *Macbeth* and *The Witch*. Once again, the interest lies in the 'maleficia' themselves rather than in the performers of the deeds. The nearest approach to seriousness, or at least pathos, is the confrontation between the trusting Generous and his apparently penitent wife in IV.i, but the dramatists' approach is basically comic. Nobody suffers permanent harm from the witches' activities and the Epilogue, inspired perhaps by the likelihood of a royal pardon, piously expresses the hope that: 'Perhaps great Mercy may / After just condemnation give them day / Of longer life.'

Also dating from about this period is John Kirke's *The Seven Champions of Christendom*, which was first printed in 1638 but was probably performed in about 1634. The work is a curious medley of supernatural lore, bearing many traces of the influence of earlier works. Like *The Birth of Merlin* it is concerned with the adventures of a heroic figure from England's legendary past—in this case, St George, who, together with six of his fellow patron saints, constitutes the play's title figures. He is first seen as a child, the adopted son of Calib, a witch, who has stolen him after poisoning his parents. Calib also has a son, Suckabus, the offspring of her intercourse with the devil Tarpax, 'prince of the grisly north'. Although Tarpax is thus an incubus, he also acts as familiar spirit to Calib, for she suckles him with her witch's teat. Like Marston's Erictho, Calib lives in a cave in a suitably gloomy setting:

> The toad, the bat, the raven and the fell whistling bird
> Are all my anthem singing choristers . . .
> Here is my mansion, within the rugged bowels of this cave,
> This crag, this cliff, this den, which to behold
> Would freeze to ice the hissing trammels of Medusa.  [I.i] [15]

In her cave are imprisoned six Champions who have been 'sent to kill great Calib and confound my charm'. She foolishly gives George a magic wand, with which he summons the ghosts of his parents, who tell him of his origins. He attacks Calib, who is defended by Tarpax and other spirits, and in attempting to escape she climbs on to a rock. This is the signal for the first of the spectacular stage effects that must have enlivened the performances. Calib proclaims: 'Now cleaves the rock, and now I sink to hell; / Roar wind, clap thunder, for great Calib's knell' (I.i). The accompanying stage direction reads: 'Music: the rock opens, she sinks. Thunder and lightning.' Flames also seem to issue from the rock because Tarpax later informs Suckabus that he caused the rock to open and his demons caught her as: 'Those flames ascending up, which put such horror into her, / Were bonfires of their joy and loving hearts' (I.i). This effect is similar to that employed in *The Birth of Merlin* (V.ii) where Merlin rescues his mother by enclosing his devil/father in a rock, from which issue thunder and lightning. Such an incident might have been portrayed by the actor descending through a stage trap from which flames appeared. However, the dialogue makes it clear that in *The Seven Champions* Calib actually climbs on to the rock and so it is likely that for such effects—and they are featured in several other plays of the period—a rock-like structure with a side entrance must actually have been moved onto the stage. Henslowe's inventory for 1598 includes 'Item, j rocke' where it is listed with other items such as 'j cage, j tombe, . . . j bedsteade', which might similarly have been pushed or rolled into position to enhance particular settings. The device might well have originated in the pageant wagons, which were used to transport bulky sets and properties into the acting areas for the mediaeval plays. Rocks equipped with traps or entrances were also recurring features in the settings for the masques, although here they tended to be permanent fixtures in the scenes, rather than being required only for individual sequences.

One unusual feature of Kirke's play is the actual representation of the witch's incubus spirit. Caliban and Firestone are both the children of such spirits but neither seems to have any direct knowledge of his father. Kirke is thus able to develop the complex family relationships of the opening episode. Tarpax tells Suckabus that genuine love had existed between Calib and George—''Twas love, great love, between 'em, boy'—and, jealous of this, he had deliberately engineered the events leading to George's attack on her. There is also quite a touching farewell scene between the devil/father and his son at the conclusion of this scene:

> *Tarpax:*                     So farewell, son.
>     Blessing on thee, boy.
> *Suckabus:* Father, farewell.
>     I were an ungracious boy if I would not obey.      [I.i]

Tarpax gives some superficial unity to the play when he reappears in Act III at the summons of Ormandine, an enchanter in the Prospero mould. He too was formerly a duke, who has been forced into exile by the rulers of his two neighbouring kingdoms and 'to revenge these wrongs I practised on this art'. Tarpax assumes an Ariel-like role and is commanded by Ormandine to:

> Fetch me my characters, my calculation and my glass . . .
> My ever-ready servant, fly to the first aerial degree,
> Snatch thee a cloud and wrap thyself within 't . . .
>                     Bring me my answer swift,
> Whilst I survey my book and magic glass.      [III.i]

He is making these preparations because he fears the arrival of St David, one of the six Champions released by George from Calib's bondage.

Although Tarpax, in the traditional manner, darkens the sun, raises storms and creates earthquakes, the saint's courage is undaunted, so that the demon has to admit: 'There's nought that we can do / Can quell the honour of this Christian knight' (III.i).

Nevertheless, Ormandine is able to put aside David's sword with his wand and the 'spell-bound' saint is borne away by the spirits of Delight, Desire and other excesses to an Acrasian bondage. David has failed in his quest because he was unable to draw a golden sword from a brazen pillar, but St George, in the manner of Arthur, does pull out the sword and thus vanquishes Ormandine.

The hotch-potch continues into Act IV when a second enchanter, Argalio, appears to challenge all seven Champions. He escapes from them in a scene whose only merit would have been its spectacle. He departs, together with his companion Leonides, in a flying throne 'by sable spirits borne'. Other spirits salute their flight from above 'with sweet bays' and St Denis exclaims: 'Oh act of wonder! We in vain pursue. / Look how they raise themselves unto the clouds' (IV.i). The latter, if they were visible to the audience, were probably represented by the billowing materials frequently employed in the masques and other spectacular productions to disguise the flying machinery. The 'foggy cloud' on which Hecate ascends in III.v of *Macbeth* would have been a similar device.

The play ends with George's final triumph over Ormandine, which reaches its climax with a variation on the earlier cleaving rock sequence. The magician mounts steps on to an elevated structure through which he descends to the fiends that await him. The stage direction reads 'Thunder strikes him' which suggests that once again flames are emitted through the opening.

Also dating from 1634 is Milton's *Comus*, which was originally entitled *A Masque presented at Ludlow Castle, 1634*. Although the work is thus designated a masque and clearly owes much to this form, it was also greatly influenced by Classical pastoral dramas and by recent variations within this genre, particularly Fletcher's *The Faithful Shepherdess* (1610). The demonology of the work is also a reflection of ancient rather than contemporary attitudes. Comus is a Classical version of the *homme sauvage*, being the child of the god Bacchus and the enchantress Circe. He combines his father's licentiousness with his mother's powers of sorcery, being 'deep skilled in all his mother's witcheries' (l. 522). In the course of the work he is referred to as a 'damned wizard', 'damned magician', 'foul enchanter', 'juggler' and 'necromancer'. He possesses some of the traditional powers of the magician—much of his magic is wrought by means of his 'charming rod' which can withstand the assaults of swords and with which he can cause paralysis. He can also change his outward form, adopting the personage of a countryman to accost the virtuous Lady. He and his 'monstrous rout' practise 'abhorred rites to Hecate' (l. 534) but in spite of his formidable powers he ultimately fails to seduce the Lady for, as she informs him, despite her physical paralysis:

> Thou canst not touch the freedom of my mind
> With all thy charms, although this corporal rind
> Thou hast immanacled, while heaven sees good.               [662–4][16]

Milton is thus true to the concepts of the inviolability of the human will and the power of virtue to withstand the forces of evil.

Virtue is represented not only by the Lady but by the Attendant Spirit, who is described in the Trinity and Bridgwater manuscripts of the work as a 'guardian spirit or daemon'. His portrayal reflects Plutarch's concept of such demons being the souls of those who have ended their earthly existence and who are now in a situation where they await the separation of soul and mind. In this condition they seek to help those still engaged in the travail of this life and who are striving towards a state of virtue. Like Comus, the Spirit can change his shape and he too takes on the form of a shepherd. He gives the Lady's brothers a magic herb, haemony, which will protect them: ''Gainst all enchantments, mildew blast, or damp / Or ghastly Furies' apparition' (ll. 639–40). Thus armed, the brothers rescue the Lady and disperse Comus and his rout as easily as the forces of virtue overcome the powers of vice in the conventional masques. The lack of dramatic confrontation evident in such works is also a feature of *Comus*. To compensate for his inevitable defeat, Comus is given a powerful speech in praise of licence (ll. 705–54) and because the brothers fail to capture his wand he can live on to resume the practice of his magical art.

Magic in a pastoral setting is also found in Jonson's incomplete *The Sad Shepherd*. The work was included in the 1640 folio edition of Jonson's plays but is difficult to date with any assurance. It might be the lost *The May Lord*, which Jonson was working on in 1618, but the Prologue's reference to the author as one 'that feasted you these forty years' suggests a post-1635 composition date. Whatever its position in the Jonson canon, it is one of his most original compositions. The witchcraft it portrays is, in its way, as sombre as that depicted in *The Masque of Queenes* but it bears no trace of the latter's neo-Classical treatment of the theme. It is indeed an adaptation of the pastoral tragi-comedy but is set, not in Arcadia, but very definitely in the English countryside, in the vale of Belvoir through which flows the River Trent.

The principal characters are Robin Hood and his followers, including Maid Marion, who are opposed by the witch Maudlin, her loutish son Lorrel and daughter Douce, together with the hobgoblin 'Puck-hairy or Robin-Goodfellow'. This latter is much more akin to the demon of English folk-lore than is Puck in *A Midsummer-Night's Dream*. The characters are thus firmly set in English rural traditions. It has been argued that the Robin Hood legends have their origins in the primitive religion that Margaret Murray saw as the source of witchcraft, with Robin and Marion representing the leading figures in the primaeval sabbats or covens.[17] If this is the case, there is a subtle irony in the play's conflict between these characters and Maudlin but such an effect seems too devious to have been intended.

Maudlin's dwelling-place is a Christianised version of the ruined temple that is the haunt of Erictho in *Sophonisba*: It lies:

> Within a gloomy dimble ...
> Down in a pit, o'er-grown with brakes and briars,
> Close by the ruins of a shaken abbey,
> Torn, with an earthquake, down unto the ground,
> 'Mongst graves and grott's, near an old charnel-house.
>
> [II.viii.15–19][18]

As might be expected, there are a few superficial echoes of *The Masque of Queenes*. Puck, like the Dame, can 'sail in an egg-shell ... A cobweb all your cloth' (III.v.10–11), and Alken reports that Maudlin uses similar herbs to those brought to the Dame, including mandrake, nightshade and hemlock. However, the play is much closer in tone to the pastoral *The Entertainment at Althorpe* (1603) and the later masque, *Pan's Entertainment* (1620), than to *The Masque of Queenes*.

The closest parallel between the two works is that in each the witches are engaged in their traditional task of creating discord and destroying the 'Age of Gold' which threatens their powers. Whilst James's court represents this ideal state in the masque, Robin Hood and his fellows fulfil the same role in the play, presenting an idyllic view of the English pastoral scene which, as Jonson suggests, is being threatened not only by the envious Maudlin but by 'the sourer sort of shepherds', who presumably symbolise the growing power of the Puritans of his own time.

In keeping with the pastoral vein, the play is made up of various strands of English folk-lore. Maudlin is a shape-shifter, able to adopt the appearance of other human beings (she even deceives Robin in her guise of

Maid Marion) or of animals, particularly the hare, which was a feat very much in accord with popular superstition.[19] She possesses a talisman in the form of a magic belt, her description of which is paralleled in many folk fairy-tales and is also reminiscent of Othello's handkerchief:

where'er you spy

This broidred belt, with characters, 'tis I.
A gypsy lady, and a right beldame,
Wrought it by moon-shine for me and star-light,
Upo' your gran'ams grave, that very night
We earth'd her, in the shades.                    [II.iii.37–42]

The Sad Shepherd and The Masque of Queenes both concentrate on the evil and sinister aspects of witchcraft but otherwise they have little in common and, indeed, the contrasting treatment of the subject in the two works is a fine instance of the versatile nature of Jonson's literary powers.

## III

The movement away from the more horrific aspects of witchcraft was maintained in the treatment of the subject in the drama that followed the reopening of the theatres in the Restoration period. The operatic spectacles and pantomime-like burlesques so much in vogue lent themselves more readily to a light-hearted approach, and the audience comprised almost exclusively courtiers and their satellites who, in their roles as persons of refined enlightenment, would scorn any suspicion of their taking seriously a matter so irrational as witchcraft. A clear insight into Restoration theatrical tastes is gained from a study of the adaptations made of existing texts, particularly those of Shakespeare.

Davenant's version of Macbeth (1663/4) is a prime example, and the supernatural elements suffer particularly at his hands. Downes's description in Roscius Anglicanus (1709) of a production at the Duke's Theatre in Dorset Garden in 1671 gives an indication of the changes which had been wrought:

> The tragedy of Macbeth, altered by Sir William D'Avenant, being drest in all its finery, as new cloaths, new scenes, machines, as flyings for the witches, with all the singing and dancing in it . . ., it being all excellently performed, being in the nature of an opera, it recompenced double the expence; it proves still a lasting play. [20]

Samuel Pepys, although not the most perceptive of critics, probably reflected popular opinion when he described the revised production as 'a

184

most excellent play in all respects, but especially in "divertissement", though it be a deep tragedy; which is a strange perfection in a tragedy, being most proper here and suitable'.[21]

Most of the 'divertissements' and operatic innovations that Pepys clearly regarded as wholly congruous involve the Weird Sisters. Davenant includes the full versions of the two songs probably interpolated into the original *Macbeth* and referred to only by their introductory lines in the First Folio text. Additions to the original stage directions indicate the inclusion of spectacular effects. At the end of the first scene the witches 'exeunt flying' and when they meet together on the heath in the third scene they 'enter flying'. Hecate's first appearance, in Act III, must have been in some form of flying contrivance for the stage direction requires that the 'Machine descends'. The cauldron scene (IV.i) ends with the direction, 'Music. The witches dance and vanish. The Cave sinks.'[22]

Most of these effects might well have been included in earlier productions. Macbeth's question in Shakespeare's version: 'Why sinks that cauldron? And what noise is this?' (IV.i.106) suggests that the later stage direction merely amplifies existing practice at this point in the play, and other directions not present in the First Folio text may also indicate elements which were in fact present in productions before Davenant's revision. For example, 'A shriek like an owl' in I.i provides a third spirit to augment the cat and toad familiars already referred to in the scene. This addition is wholly acceptable and may well reflect an existing stage tradition. The owl is a recurring motif throughout the play and is consistently associated with supernatural events.

Davenant's other alterations are less appropriate. The potency of the trochaic rhythm of most of the Sisters' utterances is destroyed by their being rendered into a regular and innocuous iambic metre. The cauldron incantation suffers particularly in this repect:

> This toad which, under mossy stone,
> Has days and nights lain thirty-one;
> And swelter'd venom sleeping got
> We'll boil in the inchanted pot.    [IV.i.9–12]

Davenant makes other adjustments to the text, presumably in an attempt either to clarify the language or to correct supposed errors. Such changes are usually unnecessary. For example, the traditional curse spoken by the rump-fed runyon, 'Aroint thee, witch' is amended to 'Anoint thee, witch', and Banquo's reference to the Sisters' beards, fully in keeping with traditional lore, is altered to: 'You should be women, / And yet your looks forbid me to interpret / So well of you' (i.iii.47–9).

One of the most visually striking sequences in the original play is the series of Apparitions conjured up from the cauldron, but this is omitted by Davenant, their prophecies merely being spoken by Hecate. The neglect of this opportunity for spectacle is surprising, although it is possible that Davenant wished to provide a fuller speaking-part for the actress playing Hecate. A similar motive might account for the additional scenes featuring Lady Macduff. Her encounter with the witches in II.v is a complete innovation. More than any other scene, this materially affects the overall impression of the Sisters' natures and demonstrates the disastrous effects of Davenant's 'improvements'. The Sisters perform a pair of dances and songs, which only increase the debasing effect on their portrayal. By indulging in such essentially trivial activities, the Sisters lose much of their aura of mystery, seeming nearer in spirit to Hecate and the hags of *The Witch*. They are much more innocuous than the 'foul anomalies' whom Charles Lamb so much admired when considering the creatures of Shakespeare's play.[23] The debilitating effect of the additional musical material strengthens the view that the songs and dances assigned to the witches in the First Folio text are themselves additions to the original version of the play and Davenant has merely completed the process of debasement.

In their songs in II.v the witches reveal their roles as controllers of fate and of Macbeth's destiny in particular. Speaking of Macbeth's killing of Duncan they declare:

> *Third Witch:* Many more murders must this one ensue,
>     As if in death were propagation too.
> *Second Witch:* He will.
> *First Witch:*          He shall.
> *Third Witch:*                    He must spill much more blood;
>     And become worse, to make his title good.          [II.v.35–8]

As well as removing the original enigma of the Sisters' identities and equating them so firmly with the Goddesses of Destiny, these lines depict Macbeth as a helpless victim of fate. Davenant was presumably attempting thereby to portray him as a more heroic, less culpable figure, in the Classical rather than the Elizabethan mould. However, the impression which Shakespeare's Macbeth creates of his exercising greater control over his actions increases rather than diminishes our sympathetic response to his downfall.

The debasement of the supernatural elements in *Macbeth* was completed by the Epilogue which Thomas Duffett added to his comedy *The Empress of Morocco* (1674). This takes the form of a burlesque, not of Shakespeare's but of Davenant's version, and it ridicules the 'divertissements' that had been introduced into the play. The entertainment begins with the stage direction: 'Thunder and lightning is discovered, not behind painted Tiffany to blind and amuse the senses, but openly, by the most excellent way of Mustard-bowl and Salt-Peter ...' Three Witches fly over the pit, riding upon besoms and then Hecate descends 'in a glorious Chariott adorn'd with pictures of Hells and Devils, and made of a large Wicker Basket'.[24] After a series of farcical exchanges, larded with topical witticisms, the proceedings end with the three witches singing, with fitting incongruity:

> Rosemary's green, Rosemary's green!
> > Derry, derry down.
> When I am King thou shalt be Queen,
> > Derry, derry down.
> If I have gold thou shalt have part,
> > Derry, derry down.
> If I have none thou hast my heart,
> > Derry, derry down.

This travesty at least has the merit of highlighting, in its very absurdity, the trivialising effect of Davenant's innovations. It does seem to have enjoyed some success, for in the following year Duffett produced a parody of *The Enchanted Island*, the revised version of *The Tempest*, which Dryden and Davenant had presented in 1667. Like the latter's *Macbeth*, this work also distorted and trivialised the supernatural elements of Shakespeare's play. This was done partly to satisfy the current demand for symmetry in dramatic structure. Shakespeare's work had been constructed around a complex pattern of balance and antithesis in both plot and characterisation but these are carried to extremes in the later version. The human love matches of Miranda and Ferdinand and of Dorinda and Hippolito are mirrored in the love of Ariel for Milcha. This sub-plot is one of the most absurd of the innovations for this coy romance conflicts with all the conventions of demonology, especially with the tradition that spirits are essentially sexless and incapable of human emotion, a concept which Shakespeare used as the basis of the moving exchange between Ariel and Prospero when the former prompts his master to feelings of pity for his victims.

In the provision of complementary characters, Caliban is not neglected, for he is given a twin sister named—with a singular lack of invention—Sycorax. Until the arrival of Trincalo the two enjoy an incestuous relationship, a traditional element of witchcraft practices that Shakespeare chose to ignore. Throughout the revised text the subtlety of the original portrayal of Caliban is coarsened by a cruder handling of his character. This is seen in the textual presentation of his utterances where, although most of his words are preserved, they are set out in the form of prose rather than blank verse. Some changes are made in his speeches, the most significant being in his final words (in V.i), where his avowal to be 'wise hereafter' is retained but the possibility of his ultimate salvation implied in his desire to 'seek for grace' is omitted.

The original portrayal of Prospero is also seriously distorted in the later play. Presumably in an attempt to increase the existing impression of his human frailty, many of his theurgical qualities are removed. Like Shakespeare's character, the later Prospero acknowledges his dependence on fate. He observes that, 'The planets seem to smile on my designs' (II.ii.73). Shakespeare's Prospero expresses himself in similar terms but in the revision the character is not presented as a personification of destiny in the manner in which he had previously been portrayed. Ariel's identification of himself and his fellows as 'instruments of fate' is omitted. The original Prospero is subject to periods of self doubt but these brief moments of introspection are given much fuller expression in the later play. He ponders:

> Perhaps my Art itself is false:
> On what strange grounds we build our hopes and fears!
> Man's life is all a mist, and in the dark,
> Our fortunes meet us.
> If fate be not, then what can we foresee?
> Or how can we avoid it, if it be? [III.vi.155–60]

The later Prospero considers that he is 'cursed' because of his use of spirits. As was shown in Chapter Nine, this view would accord with the opinions of many theologians of the time, but Shakespeare's character does not make such an explicit admission of his guilt. It is, however, implied in his final abjuration of his magical powers and it is surprising that this episode is not present in the revision. In fact, at the end of the latter, one is left in some doubt as to whether or not Prospero intends to continue with his magical practices on his return to Milan. However, the dangers of his occult powers are stressed by the 'horrid Masque' which he creates in II.iv to afflict Antonio and Alonzo. This is a more fully developed scene than the

188

equivalent attack on the 'men of sin' of the earlier play. The masque is performed by Ariel and his 'meaner fellows' who take the forms of devils and 'dire fiends'. This is a far more explicit demonstration than anything in the original that Prospero's art inevitably involves traffic with hellish spirits.

Moreover, Prospero does not exercise the supreme, godlike power over people and events which Shakespeare's creation usually displays. An essential element in the portrayal of Prospero as a theurgist is his ability both to invoke and command spirits, but the later character does not even have full command over Ariel. The latter informs him, after the event, that, on his own initiative, he: 'Unbidden, this night has flown / O'er almost all the habitable world' (V.i.24–5). He has done this to gather herbs in order to restore to life the apparently dead Hippolito. This power had been claimed by the original Prospero for himself through the exercise of his 'so potent Art'. The dignity of Shakespeare's character and the over-riding impression of the loftiness of his designs are weakened still further in the later play by Prospero's final demonstration of supernatural powers. He creates a sea-masque, for no other purpose than to 'entertain you with my magic Art' (V.ii.236) and this trivial performance forms the climax of the play.

It was perhaps inevitable that the debasement of *The Tempest* should be carried a stage further with the presentation of *The Enchanted Island* in mock-operatic form and Thomas Shadwell obliged in 1673 with a production which seems to have been at least a commercial success.[25] In *Roscius Anglicanus*, Downes notes approvingly that 'all things were performed in it so admirably well, that not any succeeding Opera got more money' (p. 35).

Shadwell followed this adaptation with an original work that combined many of the elements contained in the witchcraft dramas of the seventeenth century. *The Lancashire Witches, and Tegue O Divelly the Irish Priest* was first produced in 1681 (the first quarto edition being dated 1682) and Downes's account indicates that the, by then, almost obligatory spectacular effects figured largely in the performance. He describes the work as 'being a kind of Opera, having several Machines of Flyings for the Witches, and other Diverting Contrivances in 't' (p. 38).

As the title suggests, the play was based in part on the Lancashire witch trials of 1612 and 1633. The setting is 'in Lancashire, near Pendle-Hills' and details are taken from both historical episodes. Amongst the characters portrayed, Mother Demdike was one of the accused in 1612, whilst Goody Dickenson, Mal Spencer and Mother Hargrave had all featured in the second episode. Although he makes no acknowledgment of the fact,

189

Shadwell has clearly drawn on Heywood and Broome's *The Late Lancashire Witches*, for he repeats such incidents as the rustic being bridled and ridden like a horse, the bewitched musicians, and the severed cat's paw—all of which occur in the earlier play. He elaborates on the paw episode by adding a second incident in which a hag is shot in the wing whilst in flight disguised as a bird and who subsequently appears minus a limb.

Shadwell also borrows extensively from Jonson, in particular from *The Masque of Queenes*, and despite his admiration for his predecessor he gives little indication of this indebtedness. On many occasions there are obvious verbal parallels. In Act II the witches recount their exploits to the Devil in a sequence strongly reminiscent of the equivalent scene in *The Masque of Queenes* when the hags report to the Dame. The ingredients of the charms are almost identical, both in content and in the terms in which they are described. For example, the following speech by Mother Demdike is very close to lines 171 to 182 in the Masque:

> To a mother's bed I softly crept,
> And while th' unchristen'd brat yet slept,
> I suc't the breath and blood of that,
> And stole another's flesh and fat . . .
> From a murd'rer that hung in chains
> I bit dried sinews and shrunk veins.[26]

Shadwell also owes far more to Jonson than he acknowledges for the apparently scholarly basis of his witch-lore. He states in his preface 'To The Reader' that whilst Shakespeare derived most of his witchcraft details from his imagination:

> I resolv'd to take mine from Authority. And to that end, there is not one action in the Play, nay scarce a word concerning it, but is borrow'd from some antient, or Modern Witchmonger, Which you will find in the notes, wherein I have presented you a great part of the Doctrine of Witchcraft, believe it who will.

However, just as Jonson's scholarship is not quite so impressive and far-reaching as he would have us believe, so Shadwell has almost certainly used Jonson's annotations for many of his own learned references. This is suggested by the fact that Shadwell uses witchcraft elements that are also to be found in *The Masque of Queenes*, citing identical sources, from both Classical and Renaissance authorities, as those provided by Jonson. It is also probable that Shadwell has made much more extensive use of Scot's *The Discoverie of Witchcraft* than he admits.[27] The Devil's second song at the end of Act II, after extolling the pleasures of flying, ends: 'Then we feast and we revel after long flights, / Or with a lov'd incubus sport all the night'. This is similar to Scot's description of such exploits in *The Discoverie*, whereby 'they seeme to be carried in the aire, to feasting, singing, dancing, kissing, culling, and other acts of venerie, with such youthes as they love and desire most' (book X, chapter viii).

Meda's speech from Ovid's *Metamorphoses*, VII, which Jonson, Middleton and Shakespeare had all incorporated into their dramas, is also used by Shadwell. His version reads:

> At thy command woods from their seats shall rove.
> Stones from their quarries, and fix'd oaks remove.
> Vast standing lakes shall flow, and, at thy will,
> The most impetuous torrents shall stand still:
> Swift rivers shall (while wond'ring banks admire)
> Back to their springs, with violent haste, retire.

These lines are spoken in Act III by the Devil, during an initiation ceremony which includes a five-part song and a dance 'with fantastic unusual postures'. This is one of several instances of Shadwell's adding to the spectacle of the play by portraying grotesque rituals, the details of which he found in his source material. For example, the storm-raising rites performed in Act I, which culminate in a three-part song accompanied by thunder and lightning, include such stage directions as: 'They tear the Black Lamb in pieces, and pour the Blood into the hole' and 'They beat the ground with Vipers, they bark, howl, hiss, cry like Screech Owls, hollo like Owls, and make confused noises'.

Shadwell used the play as a medium for expressing his strongly pro-Whig political views and this led to wholesale deletions by the censor. Shadwell satirises the established Anglican Church through his portrayal of Smerk, who is Sir Edward's chaplain. In the 'dramatis personae' he is described as 'Foolish, Knavish, Popish, Arrogant, Insolent; yet, for his interest, Slavish'. An even fiercer assault is mounted on Roman Catholicism through the depiction of Tegue O Divelly, a fugitive Irish priest. Earlier writers such as Scot, Harsnett and James I had linked the superstitions of witchcraft with the idolatry of Papism, and Shadwell follows in this tradition. The devil-worship rituals he portrays complement the incantations and ineffectual conjurations of Divelly, whose name in itself implies diabolic associations. His seduction by Mother Dickenson in the form of a succubus—a comic parallel of Erictho's deception of Syphax in *Sophonisba*—symbolises the bond between Catholicism and witchcraft.

The arrest of the witches in Act V is followed by the unmasking of the priest and they are carried off to await similar fates. The play was written some three years after the Popish Plot and there is even a possible reminder of the Catholic-inspired Gunpowder Plot of 1605 in that the witches hold their secret covens in the cellars of Sir Edward Hartfort's house.

This detail is a particularly effective irony, for Sir Edward, who embodies reason and common-sense, is the only character in the play to retain his sceptical attitude to witchcraft throughout the course of the drama. Shadwell seems to share this viewpoint, for in his address 'To The Reader' he writes: 'For my part, I am (as it is said of Surly in *The Alchymist*) somewhat costive of belief. The evidences I have represented are natural, viz. slight, and frivolous, such as poor old Women were wont to be hang'd upon.'

This is not entirely borne out in the work itself, for within the confines of the play witches do exist and possess supernatural powers. They create storms and disrupt the household; they turn themselves into birds and hares and transform men into horses; the devil appears to them in both human and animal form. Thus Shadwell is adopting the approach which was to become increasingly common in works of fiction, whereby the supernatural, although disbelieved in by the author, is made true for the purpose of the story. Sir Edward's consistent incredulity is almost literally undermined in the dramatic fiction, and yet it remains, as K. M. Briggs observes in *Pale Hecate's Team*, 'the touchstone of truth outside the play' (p. 105).

Shadwell's preface has made clear his own attitude and it can at least be conjectured that his scepticism was shared by certain of the earlier playwrights who also treated witchcraft as a genuine force within the limits of their works. This might well be the case, for example, with Jonson, who, it will be recalled, uses the hags in *The Masque of Queenes* to symbolise the forces of darkness and ignorance that threaten the world of learning and enlightenment. Shadwell also adopts this approach, with the ordered household of Sir Edward representing the rationalism which is under attack. Shadwell makes effective use of the hackneyed device of the bewitched musicians to underline this theme. Jonson contrasts the discordancy of the hags' music with the harmony of the Masque proper and in the later play Sir Edward's request for music is thwarted when the musicians 'gape and strain, but cannot sing but make an ugly noise' (stage direction, Act IV).

Thus, beneath the farcical trivia and the pantomime-like spectacle there are more serious elements which have not always been recognised. The work is a strange concoction, but it is also an interesting, if not wholly successful, amalgam of the divers approaches to the theme of witchcraft that were adopted by Shadwell's contemporaries and predecessors.

The trend towards the operatic portrayal of magic and witchcraft reached a climax in 1689/90 with Purcell's *Dido and Aeneas*. This work is generally regarded as the first true opera in English, where the librettist is subservient to the composer. The text was the work of Nahum Tate, who is today best remembered for the provision of a happy ending to his version of *King Lear*. In the opera his words effectively complement the varied moods of Purcell's music and in retelling Virgil's familiar narrative he draws on appropriate Classical sources for the supernatural elements, whilst also betraying a clear indebtedness to *Macbeth* and *The Masque of Queenes*.

The principal supernatural figure is the Sorceress, who seeks to destroy the love of Dido and Aeneas. To this end she summons her 'wayward sisters' to raise a storm that will curtail the Trojan prince's hunting. The witches respond with enthusiasm, declaring:

> Harm's our delight,
> And mischief all our skill. . . .
> In our deep vaulted cell
> The charm we'll prepare;
> Too dreadful a practice
> For this open air.          [I]

It is noteworthy that the spell is performed off-stage and the Witches' melodic echo-song at this point is singularly lacking in menace. The Sorceress has an attendant spirit, her 'trusty elf', who assumes the form of Mercury and commands Aeneas to leave Carthage and return to Troy. Aeneas obeys this apparently divine instruction and at his departure the inconsolable Dido prepares for her death, by her own hand. The forces of evil thus triumph and demonic orthodoxy gives way to the demands of art.

However, in the work's original performances the impact made by the powers of witchcraft must have been largely dissipated in that the Sorceress and her followers were played by pupils at the seminary for young ladies in Chelsea for whom the work was composed. The Chorus was probably augmented by a no doubt carefully vetted group of boys from an equivalent establishment in Hatton Garden. The general practice at this time, at least in the continuing revivals of *Macbeth*, was for such parts to be played by men, and the fact that the roles could be assigned to schoolgirls and boys is a further indication of the waning power of witchcraft, in the theatre at least, to inspire either fear or pity. The music of the Witches' Dance in Act III is staccato and disjointed—inasmuch as any score by Purcell can be thus described—and this presumably mirrors the original choreography, but there is a complete absence of any sinister feeling here or elsewhere in the work, and the overall effect, even in modern professional performances, is somewhat less than awesome.

## IV

In addition to the dances, *Dido and Aeneas* also offered spectacular effects such as the climax to the Furies' Dance where 'the Furies sink down in the cave, the rest fly up'. Here again the influence of Davenant's *Macbeth* is evident and it was this version of Shakespeare's play that dominated theatrical production until well into the nineteenth century. In particular, the trivialising of the supernatural elements was retained and extended in a variety of ways. The parts of the Weird Sisters continued to be played by men—usually the comedians of the companies, who would otherwise have been underemployed with the customary omission of the Porter scene. The increasingly sceptical attitude towards the occult generated by the Age of Reason did not diminish interest in the supernatural but in its dramatic portrayal popular taste favoured a comic or melodramatic rather than a sensitive or sombre representation.

The few dissenting voices went unheeded. The *St James Chronicle*, in October 1773, reproved Garrick because his 'comic actors are permitted to turn a solemn incantation into a ridiculous farce for the entertainment of the upper gallery'. It earnestly declared that 'every spectator must join in a wish to see the witches seriously represented' but it was not only the denizens of the upper gallery who approved of such travesties. Fanny Kemble gives an enthusiastic account of similar antics enacted in 1833, at the same time giving some indication of how the performers were costumed: 'We have three jolly-faced fellows, whom we are accustomed to laugh at . . . in every farce . . . with a due proportion of petticoats . . . jocose red faces, peaked hats, and broomsticks.'[28]

The Hecate scenes and 'all the Singing, and Dancing' therein were of course retained and so extensively developed that by the mid nineteenth century groups of a hundred and more performers of both sexes sang and danced to the music composed by Matthew Locke for Davenant's revival.[29] The dialogue would be interrupted by elaborate dances and choral fugues so that all traces of dramatic tension were lost. The occasional gallant attempts to eliminate these smothering accretions were quickly suppressed.

**16** A chorus of witches performing the interpolated song 'Over woods, high rocks and mountains' in Act IV of *Macbeth*. The illustration is taken from the programme of Henry Irving's 1888 production at the Lyceum Theatre, London, with Irving as Macbeth and Ellen Terry as Lady Macbeth.

In 1847 Samuel Phelps staged the play at Sadlers Wells without Davenant's additions but by 1864—at Drury Lane—he had bowed to commercial pressure and presented the work with all its gaudy trivia fully restored. The *Daily Telegraph* commented enigmatically that Locke's music was 'too characteristic to be omitted' whilst the *Daily News* openly regretted the return of the 'modern mixed version' declaring: 'The wild poetic grandeur of the drama is certainly diminished by the introduction of a hundred or more pretty singing wenches, but trading managers are bound to be practical, and Locke's music, with Middleton's words, is found to pay.'

The appearance of the 'singing wenches' is given greater substance by the description of one member of such a chorus who particularly caught the eye of James Boaden in Kemble's production of 1788, in which Sarah Siddons played Lady Macbeth:

> The music of Matthew Locke in this tragedy has crowded the stage with people to sing it; and in the crowd beauty, formerly and since, forced its way into notice. The Witch of the lovely Crouch wore a

195

fancy hat, powdered hair, rough point lace, and fine linen enough to enchant the spectator. . . . Among the mingling black, white, red and grey spirits some may be imagined fantastic enough to assume the garb of beauty, as in all probability many must possess the features.[30]

Locke's was not the only music to be featured in such extravaganzas. A playbill for a production in 1869 at the Prince's Theatre, Manchester, proclaimed that: 'Locke's Celebrated Music will be given, and some Vocal and Instrumental Selections introduced from Verdi's Opera of 'Macbeth', supported by a Powerful and Efficient Chorus under the Direction of Mr Wilson.' In this production the Weird Sisters were played by one male and two females, and from about this time onwards the male monopoly of these roles began to fade, with either a blend of the sexes or actresses in all three roles becoming the norm.

The nineteenth-century theatre-goer's enthusiasm for spectacular sequences and transformation scenes was well catered for by the play's supernatural elements. The witches habitually entered and departed on free-flying wires and their ability to vanish inspired a diversity of ingenious attempts to simulate this power. Phelps in particular experimented with various devices, including gauze screens of varying thicknesses, to convey this illusion. The emphasis on spectacle continued into the twentieth century with the productions of Beerbohm Tree. His *Macbeth* of 1911 at His Majesty's Theatre opened with the flying witches entering to an accompaniment of thunder, lightning, raging winds, falling rocks and the toppling of a blasted oak. In a typical interpolation Duncan was escorted to his last earthly slumber by a hymn-singing chorus, accompanied by a harpist. As the music faded the witches burst on to the empty and darkening stage, cackling over their impending triumph. As the century has progressed there has been an increasing movement towards directorial authority. This has not always been wholly beneficial, with the whims and fancies of actors and actor-managers merely being displaced by those of directors, but the general trend has been towards a rediscovery of the spirit and textual integrity of Shakespeare's works. The diverse efforts of such early champions as Benson, Poel and Granville-Barker have, at least temporarily, won the day and modern productions of *Macbeth* reflect this. They are almost invariably presented without the Hecate scenes and the other Middleton–Davenant 'improvements' and the attempts to reach to the heart of the text with the minimum of 'diverting contrivances' have reached their most impressive level to date in Trevor Nunn's Royal Shakespeare Company studio production in 1976, with Ian McKellen in the title-role.[31]

Although *The Tempest* has never matched the consistent popularity of *Macbeth* in performance, its stage history has followed a similar patttern, with the seventeenth-century operatic version displacing Shakespeare's text for the ensuing two hundred years. Charles Kean's passion for spectacle, meticulously researched and extravagantly presented, led him to stage the hymeneal masque against a backdrop of the Temple of Eleusis. As with nearly all nineteenth-century productions, the play opened with a fully-realised storm, with an authentic galleon foundering on a raging sea, whilst the final scene saw Prospero and his companions sailing homewards in a now restored vessel, propelled by scarlet oars across 'calm seas', its sails billowing in the 'auspicious gales' that Prospero's magic has created. As the ship moved slowly across the stage, Ariel flew from its deck to gain his long-sought liberty.

Fifty years later, in 1904, Beerbohm Tree created a similar climax, with the addition that when the curtain rose, apparently for the curtain-call, the ship was seen on the horizon with Caliban, alone on a rock, stretching out his arms towards it in an attitude of 'mute despair'. He was, as Tree himself noted, 'King once more', and one might therefore question whether this particular 'coup', striking as it must have been, gave an appropriate final impression of Caliban's reaction to the departure of the usurping Prospero.[32]

Of the other works previously discussed, *Doctor Faustus* alone has survived as anything other than a theatrical curiosity. It retained its popularity during the early Stuart period but after a few revivals following the Restoration, in which, inevitably, it was 'now Acted With several New Scenes'[33] it disappeared from the stage until the late nineteenth century. In the intervening period the Faust legend inspired several pantomimes which brought together the magician and Harlequin, and Goethe's version led to a variety of operas and burlesques, including Halford's *Faust and Marguerite*, produced in 1854, with Halford himself playing Mephistopheles and Faust being portrayed by a girl.

Marlowe's work did not resurface until Poel revived it for the Elizabethan Stage Society in St George's Hall in July 1896, on a stage based on the old Fortune playhouse. Since this pioneering venture the play has become a stock alternative to Shakespeare for an increasing number of companies, amateur and professional, and its regained stature reached some kind of peak between 1968 and 1974 when the Royal Shakespeare Company mounted three different productions of the work, with Eric Porter, David Waller and Ian McKellen each playing the title role.

A production of *Doctor Faustus* by the Cambridge University Marlowe

**17** A scene from the Marlowe Society's production of *Friar Bacon and Friar Bungay* in 1953, which was directed by John Barton. Bungay's magical raising of a tree 'with the Dragon shooting fire' is eclipsed by Vandermast's conjuring of the spirit of Hercules 'in his lion's skin'.

Society in 1960 was complemented by performances of *Friar Bacon and Friar Bungay*. Both plays were directed by Michael Bakewell and in addition to presentations at the Arts Theatre, Cambridge, and the Lyceum, London, they were also staged in the open air in the Avonbank Gardens, Stratford-upon-Avon. This interesting venture met with a generally lukewarm response, the *Stratford-upon-Avon Herald* reviewer commenting that, 'Robert Greene's piece is not the greatest of Elizabethan plays, and Michael Bakewell's production did little to improve upon its poverty—yet the shapes of melody and lyricism were occasionally touched, and the production was given a little more vigour than *Faustus*' (8 August 1960). The Marlowe Society also presented Greene's play in 1953 when it was directed by John Barton. It shared a double bill with *Titus Andronicus*—a theatrical experience which must have proved mentally and physically exhausting for both audience and players.

*The Masque of Queenes*, after its single performance before James I, disappeared into the void that awaited nearly all such ephemeral works until it received a unique resuscitation as part of a May-day festival at Bryn

Mawr College, Pennsylvania, in 1906.[34] *Comus* has been more fortunate, at least since the institution of the annual Ludlow Festival, where it has enjoyed several revivals.

In 1936 Michel St Denis chose as his first directorial venture in England to stage *The Witch of Edmonton* at the Old Vic. This seemingly perverse choice presented Marius Goring as Frank and Beatrix Lehmann as Winnifride and, in the title-role, Edith Evans, who gave one of her most memorable performances. Nearly thirty years later Philip Hope-Wallace, writing in *The Guardian* in November 1960, was to recall how, 'in an astonishing assumption [she] gave the Witch her terrible pathos and conjured a Jacobean terror of things unseen which made our hair stand on end'. This memory was evoked by the current production at the Mermaid Theatre, which Bernard Miles had directed as part of the company's Christmas programme. Ruby Head, in the title part, had taken over the role at the last minute when the actress originally cast for the part had unsuccessfully demanded that the devil/dog be played as an imaginary, invisible creature rather than by an actor in costume (Melvyn Hayes). In view of the amount of dialogue assigned to the role, it is difficult to see how such an argument could have been sustained. The critics were generally unimpressed although *The Times* singled out 'a magnificent speech on the humanity of witches which markedly recalls Shylock's defence of the Jews' whilst W. A. Darlington in the *Daily Telegraph* commended its 'bustling action' and concluded that 'its curiosity value is high'—faint praise, perhaps, but a verdict that could well be passed on all the plays considered in this volume.

In addition to such revivals, contemporary dramatists have continued to explore and utilise witchcraft and related supernatural themes. Arthur Miller's *The Crucible* (1952) represents his response to the McCarthy-inspired anti-communist 'witch-hunts' of the early 1950s. However, his portrayal of the Salem witch-scare of 1692 has a more universal significance, in its depiction of public morality posturing before private guilt and its portrayal of group hysteria generated to almost uncontrollable limits within a restrictive, basically insecure community.

David Rudkin in *Afore Night Come* (1962) also portrays the tensions created within a confined group, tensions which culminate in the ritualistic murder of Roche, an Irish itinerant, by his fellow workers on a Worcestershire fruit farm. The climactic beheading sequence is enacted against the thunderous roar of a crop-spraying helicopter as it hovers overhead, but despite the modern setting the victim is in direct line of descent from the seventeenth-century witch figure, the outsider who becomes sacrificial victim, persecuted and destroyed by his companions in their attempts to compensate for their own psychological inadequacies.

Rudkin has further probed the more primaeval aspects of human nature with such works as *The Sons of Light* (1977) and the television play *Penda's Fen* (1974). Interest in the occult shows no sign of diminishing—as witnessed by the vogue in the mid-seventies for films on possession and exorcism themes—and playwrights will doubtless continue to depict its varied manifestations in their explorations of the darker facets of human behaviour.

### Notes to Chapter 11

1    *The Spectator*, 11 July 1711.
2    Everyman edition, edited by C. H. Herford, pp. 34–5.
3    *A Tryal of Witches at the Assizes held at Bury St Edmunds, 1664* (1682), p.55.
4    Quoted in J. Webster, *The Displaying of Supposed Witchcraft* (1677), p. 348.
5    See Stearne's account in his *A Confirmation and Discovery of Witchcraft* (1648), and Hopkins's version in his *The Discovery of Witches* (1647).
6    Kittredge, *Witchcraft in Old and New England*, p. 358.
7    R. North, *Autobiography*, edited by R. Jessop (1887), pp. 131–2.
8    The case of Jane Wenham of Hertfordshire, tried in 1712—see Kittredge, pp. 361–2.
9    The play is included in vol. IV of Heywood's *Dramatic Works*, edited by R. H. Shepherd (1874).
10   In addition to the previously recognised probable sources for the play, particularly the account of the case in BM Additional Ms. 36674, ff. 193–193$^v$, Gareth Roberts, in his previously cited thesis, indicates another description of the trial (Harleian Ms. 6854, ff. 22–29$^v$) which contains details present in the play but not included in the BM text.
11   State Papers Domestic, 1634–5. (Quoted in K. M. Briggs, *Pale Hecate's Team*, pp. 254–5).
12   *Ibid.*
13   See, for example, Kittredge, p. 177.
14   Lawrence's impotence seems to have been caused by the temporary disappearance of his sexual organs, for the lovers have quarrelled over the loss of 'a better implement it seems the bridegroom was unprovided of' (Act IV). In *The Discoverie of Witchcraft* (book IV, chapter iv) Scot cites several tales 'of divers that had their genitals taken away from them by witches'.
15   *The Seven Champions of Christendom* is printed in The Old English Drama series, vol. III (1830).
16   *The Poems of John Milton*, edited by John Carey and Alastair Fowler—Longmans Annotated English Poets (1968).
17   See, for example, Pennethorne Hughes, *Witchcraft*, pp. 67–8.
18   Herford and Simpson, *Works*, vol. VII.
19   There is, for example, Isabel Gowdie's shape-shifting spell:
            I shall go intill a hare,
            With sorrow and sych and meikle care;

And I shall go in the Devil's name,
Ay while I come home again.
(Quoted in Christina Hole, *A Mirror of Witchcraft*, p. 60).

20    Facsimile reprint, edited by J. Knight (1886).

21    *Pepys's Diary*, edited by R. Latham and W. Matthews, vol. 8 (1974).

22    *Five Restoration Adaptations of Shakespeare*, edited by C. Spencer (1965).

23    Lamb's comparison of *The Witch* and *Macbeth*, from which this phrase is taken, is contained in his *Specimens of English Dramatic Poets*, edited by W. Macdonald, pp. 302–3.

24    The text is included in University Microfilm, reel No. 209.

25    There is some disagreement as to whether Shadwell was the author of the opera—or even whether there was such a version, but C. Spencer, after summarising the arguments in the Introduction to *Five Restoration Adaptations of Shakespeare*, comes down in favour of the existence of such a separate work and of Shadwell's authorship (pp. 18–19). Duffet's parody might have been aimed more specifically at this version than at the Dryden–Davenant revision.

26    *The Complete Works of Thomas Shadwell*, edited by Montague Summers, vol. IV (1927).

27    Following its suppression under James I, *The Discoverie* had been reissued in 1651 and again in 1665. The latter edition contained additional material on such topics as 'Divels and Spirits' which would certainly not have met with Scot's approval.

28    Quoted in Marvin Rosenberg, *The Masks of Macbeth* (1978), which provides an exhaustive survey of productions of the play world-wide. Accounts of the varying fashions in theatrical presentations of *Macbeth* can also be found in A. C. Sprague, *Shakespeare and the Actors* (1945), Dennis Bartholomeusz, *Macbeth and the Players* (1969), J. C. Trewin, *Shakespeare on the English Stage: 1900–1964* (1964), and Robert Speaight, *Shakespeare on the Stage* (1973).

29    W. J. Lawrence in *Elizabethan Playhouse and Other Studies* (First series), pp. 209–24, argues that the music used in such revivals was that composed by Purcell for performances in 1688–9. Nevertheless, throughout the nineteenth century the music continued to be assigned invariably to Locke.

30    James Boaden, *Memoirs of the Life of John Philip Kemble*, vol. I (1825), pp. 418–19.

31    An exception was the 1978 production of *Macbeth* at the National Theatre, directed by Peter Hall with John Russell Brown. This followed the First Folio text, virtually uncut, including the Hecate episodes and the interpolated songs. Predictably, the inclusion of these sequences did not, in the main, meet with critical approval.

32    Tree's notes are quoted in Trewin, p. 32.

33    This revised version of the play was printed in 1663. See Allardyce Nicoll, *A History of English Drama 1660–1900* (1952–9), vol. I, p. 348.

34    There is a brief account of the performance in *M.L.N.*, XXI (6 June 1906).

# SELECT BIBLIOGRAPHY

**Plays: editions used for quotation or reference**

Barnes, Barnabe, *The Devil's Charter*, Old English Drama Students' Facsimile Edition, 21 (London, 1913)

Chapman, George, *Bussy D'Ambois*, ed. Nicholas Brooke, The Revels Plays (London, 1964)

Davenant, William, *Macbeth*, and Davenant and Dryden, John, *The Enchanted Island* in *Five Restoration Adaptations of Shakespeare*, ed. Christopher Spencer (Urbana, Ill., 1965)

Dekker, T., Ford, J., and Rowley, W., *The Witch of Edmonton* in *Jacobean and Caroline Comedies*, ed. R. G. Lawrence (London, 1973)

Greene, Robert, *Friar Bacon and Friar Bungay*, ed. J. A. Lavin, The New Mermaids (London, 1969); (attributed) *John of Bordeaux or The Second Part of Friar Bacon*, ed. W. L. Renwick and W. W. Greg, Malone Society Reprint (London, 1935–6)

Heywood, Thomas, *The Wise Woman of Hogsdon* in *Heywood: Dramatic Works*, ed. R. H. Shepherd, 6 vols (London, 1874), vol. V; Heywood and Broome R., *The Late Lancashire Witches* in Shepherd, vol. IV.

Jonson, Ben, *The Alchemist* in *Ben Jonson, Works*, ed. C. H. Herford, Percy and Evelyn Simpson, 11 vols. (Oxford, 1925–52), vol. V (1937); *The Masque of Queenes*, vol.VII (1941); and *The Sad Shepherd*, vol. VII.

Kirke, John, *The Seven Champions of Christendom* in *The Old English Drama*, vol. III (London, 1830)

Lyly, John, *Endimion* and *Mother Bombie* in *Lyly: The Complete Works*, ed. R. W. Bond, 3 vols. (Oxford, 1902), vol. 3

Marlowe, Christopher, *Doctor Faustus*, ed. John D. Jump, The Revels Plays (London, 1962)

Marston, John, *Sophonisba* in *Works*, ed. A. H. Bullen, 3 vols. (London, 1887), vol. 2

Middleton, Thomas, *The Witch* in *The Works of Thomas Middleton*, Mermaid edition, ed. A. H. Bullen, 8 vols. (London, 1885–6), vol. 5

Milton, John, *Comus* in *The Poems of John Milton*, ed. John Carey and Alastair Fowler, Longmans Annotated English Poets (London, 1968)

Rowley, William, *The Birth of Merlin* in *The Shakespeare Apocrypha*, ed., C. F. Tucker Brooke (London, 1908)

Shadwell, Thomas, *The Lancashire Witches, and Tegue O Divelly the Irish Priest* in *The Complete Works*, ed. Montague Summers, 5 vols. (London, 1927), vol. 4

Shakespeare, William, *The Complete Works*, ed. Peter Alexander (London and Glasgow, 1951)

**Sixteenth and seventeenth-century prose works on magic and witchcraft** *(Film numbers refer to reel numbers of the University Microfilm Library Services series—Ann Arbor, Michigan.)*

202

Gifford, George, *A Dialogue Concerning Witches and Witchcraftes* (London, 1593) reprinted in *Shakespeare Association Facsimiles No. 1* (London, 1931)

Goodcole, Henry, *The Wonderfull discoverie of Elizabeth Sawyer a witch, late of Edmonton, her conviction and condemnation and death* . . . (London, 1621). Film No. 838

Harsnett, Samuel, *A Declaration of Egregious Popishe Impostures* (London, 1603/4). Film No. 889.

Hopkins, Matthew, *The Discoverie of Witches* (London, 1647)

James VI and I, *Daemonologie, in forme of a Dialogue* (Edinburgh, 1597). Reprinted in *Bodley Head Quartos No. 9* (London, 1924)

Perkins, William, *A Discourse of the Damned Art of Witchcraft* (Cambridge, 1608). Film No. 725

Potts, Thomas, *The Wonderfull Discoverie of Witches in the Countie of Lancaster* (London, 1613). Edited by G. B. Harrison (London, 1929)

Scot, Reginald, *The Discoverie of Witchcraft* (London, 1584). Edited by Brinsley Nicholson (London, 1886, reprinted 1973)

Stearne, J., *A Confirmation and Discoverie of Witchcraft* (London, 1648). Facsimile reprint (Exeter, 1973)

Webster, John, *The Displaying of Supposed Witchcraft* (London, 1677). Film No. Wing 44

**Literary criticism**

Briggs, K. M., *Pale Hecate's Team* (London, 1962); and *The Anatomy of Puck* (London, 1959)

Curry, W. C., *Shakespeare's Philosophical Patterns* (Baton Rouge, La, 1937)

Farnham, Willard, *Shakespeare's Tragic Frontier* (Berkeley, Calif., 1950); and *The Shakespearean Grotesque* (Oxford, 1971)

Garber, Marjorie B., *Dream in Shakespeare: from Metaphor to Metamorphosis* (New Haven, Conn., 1974)

James, D. G., *The Dream of Prospero* (Oxford, 1967)

Johansson, B., *Religion and Superstition in the Plays of Ben Jonson and Thomas Middleton* (Upsala, 1950)

Jones, Emrys, *The Origins of Shakespeare* (Oxford, 1977)

Lawrence, W. J., *Shakespeare's Workshop* (Oxford, 1928)

Meagher, J. C., *Method and Meaning in Jonson's Masques* (Notre Dame, Ind., 1966)

McElroy, J. F., *Parody and Burlesque in the Tragi-comedies of Thomas Middleton* (Salzburg, 1972)

Orgel, Stephen, *The Jonsonian Masque* (Cambridge, Mass., 1965)

Paul, H. N., *The Royal Play of 'Macbeth'* (New York, 1950)

Price, G. R., *Thomas Dekker* (New York, 1969)

Rosenberg, Marvin, *The Masks of Macbeth* (Berkeley and Los Angeles, 1978)

Stavig, Mark, *John Ford and the Traditional Moral Order* (Madison, Milwaukee, 1968)

Ure, Peter, *Elizabethan and Jacobean Drama*, ed. J. C. Maxwell (Liverpool, 1974)

Welsford, Enid, *The Court Masque* (London, 1927)

West, R. H., *The Invisible World: a Study of Pneumatology in Elizabethan Drama* (Athens, Ga., 1939); and *Shakespeare and the Outer Mystery* (Lexington, Kentucky, 1968)

Yates, Frances A., *Shakespeare's Last Plays: a New Approach* (London, 1975)

## Works on witchcraft and the supernatural

Bloom, J. H., *Folk Lore, Old Customs and Superstitions in Shakespeare's Land* (London, 1929)

Cohn, Norman, *Europe's Inner Demons: an Enquiry Inspired by the Great Witch-Hunt* (London, 1975)

Ewen, C. H. L'Estrange, *Witch Hunting and Witch Trials* (London, 1929)

Frazer, J., *The Golden Bough* (London, 1922)

Hole, Christina, *A Mirror of Witchcraft* (London, 1957); and *Witchcraft in England* (London, 1947)

Hughes, Pennethorne, *Witchcraft* (London, 1952)

Kittredge, G. L., *Witchcraft in Old and New England* (Cambridge, Mass., 1929)

Macfarlane, A. D. J., *Witchcraft in Tudor and Stuart England, a Regional Study* (London, 1970)

Mair, Lucy, *Witchcraft* (London, 1969)

Murray, Margaret A., *The Witch-Cult in Western Europe* (Oxford, 1921)

Notestein, W., *A History of Witchcraft in England from 1558 to 1718* (Oxford, 1911)

Robbins, Rossell Hope, *The Encyclopaedia of Witchcraft and Demonology* (London, 1959)

Spalding, T. A., *Elizabethan Demonology* (London, 1880)

Spence, Leslie, *British Fairy Origins* (London, 1946)

Summers, Montague, *The History of Witchcraft and Demonology* (London, 1926)

Thomas, Keith, *Religion and the Decline of Magic* (London, 1971)

Yates, Frances A., *Giordano Bruno and the Hermetic Tradition* (London, 1964)

## Works on stage conditions and stage history

Bartholomeusz, Dennis, *'Macbeth' and the Players* (Cambridge, 1969)

Beckerman, Bernard, *Shakespeare at the Globe, 1599–1609* (New York, 1962)

Bentley, G. E., *The Jacobean and Caroline Stage* (Oxford, 1941–68)

Chambers, E. K., *The Elizabethan Stage*, 4 vols. (Oxford, 1923); and *The Mediaeval Stage*, 2 vols. (Oxford, 1903)

Hewitt, Bernard (ed.), *The Renaissance Stage: Documents of Serlio, Sabbattini, and Furtenbach* (Coral Gables, Florida, 1958)

Hodges, C. Walter, *The Globe Restored: a Study of the Elizabethan Theatre* (London, 1953; 2nd ed., 1968)

Lawrence, W. J., *Pre-Restoration Stage Studies* Cambridge, Mass., 1927)

Nagler, A. M., *A Source Book in Theatrical History* (New York, 1952). (Originally entitled *Sources of Theatrical History*)

Nicoll, Allardyce, *Stuart Masques and the Renaissance Stage* (London, 1937)

Orgel, Stephen and Strong, Roy, *Inigo Jones: The Theatre of the Stuart Court*, 2 vols. (London, Berkeley and Los Angeles, 1973)

Speaight, Robert, *Shakespeare on the Stage* (London, 1973)

Sprague, A. C., *Shakespeare and the Actors* (Cambridge, Mass., 1945)

Trewin, J. C., *Shakespeare on the English Stage: 1900–1964* (London and New York, 1964)

Watkins, Ronald and Lemmon, Jeremy, *'Macbeth' in Shakespeare's Playhouse* (Newton Abbot, 1974)

Wickham, Glynne, *Early English Stages*, 3 vols. (London, 1959)

# INDEX

(All works, including plays, are listed under authors. For convenience, some titles have been abbreviated.)